Collins
French
Verbs &
Practice

Collins
French
Verbs &
Practice

HarperCollins Publishers
Westerhill Road
Bishopbriggs
Glasgow
G64 2QT
Great Britain

First Edition 2012

Reprint 12 11 10 9 8 7 6 5 4 3 2 1 0

© HarperCollins Publishers 2012

ISBN 978-0-00-745008-4

Collins® is a registered trademark of
HarperCollins Publishers Limited

www.collinslanguage.com

A catalogue record for this book is available
from the British Library

HarperCollins Publishers
10 East 53rd Street
New York, NY 10022

COLLINS BEGINNER'S FRENCH VERBS AND
PRACTICE.
First US Edition 2012

ISBN 978-0-06-219176-2

www.harpercollins.com

HarperCollins books may be purchased for
educational, business, or sales promotional
use. For information, please write to:
Special Markets Department,
HarperCollins Publishers,
10 East 53rd Street,
New York, NY 10022

Typeset by Davidson Publishing Solutions,
Glasgow

Printed in Italy by LEGO Spa, Lavis (Trento)

Acknowledgements
We would like to thank those authors and
publishers who kindly gave permission
for copyright material to be used in the
Collins Word Web. We would also like to
thank Times Newspapers Ltd for providing
valuable data.

SERIES EDITOR
Rob Scriven

PROJECT MANAGEMENT
Patrick Gillard
Susanne Reichert

CONTRIBUTORS
Daphne Day

FOR THE PUBLISHER
Gaëlle Amiot-Cadey
Lucy Cooper
Elaine Higgleton
Lisa Sutherland

Contents

Foreword for language teachers

The *Easy Learning French Verbs & Practice* is designed to be used with both young and adult learners, as a group revision and practice book to complement your course book during classes, or as a recommended text for self-study and homework/coursework.

The text specifically targets learners from *ab initio* to intermediate or GCSE level, and therefore its structural content and vocabulary have been matched to the relevant specifications up to and including Higher GCSE.

The approach aims to develop knowledge and understanding of verbs and to improve the ability of learners to apply it by:

- minimizing the use of grammar terminology and providing clear explanations of terms both within the text and in the **Glossary**

- illustrating all points with examples (and their translations) based on topics and contexts which are relevant to beginner and intermediate course content

The text helps you develop positive attitudes to grammar learning in your classes by:

- giving clear, easy-to-follow explanations

- prioritizing content according to relevant specifications for the levels

- highlighting useful **Tips** to deal with common difficulties

- summarizing **Key points** at the end of sections to consolidate learning

In addition to fostering success and building a thorough foundation in French grammar and verbs, the optional **Grammar Extra** sections will encourage and challenge your learners to further their studies to higher and advanced levels.

Introduction for students

Whether you are starting to learn French for the very first time or revising for your GCSE exams, the *Easy Learning French Verbs & Practice* is here to help. This easy-to-use guide takes you through all the basics you will need to use French verbs correctly and understand modern, everyday French.

Newcomers can sometimes struggle with the technical terms they come across when they start to explore the grammar of a new language. The *Easy Learning French Verbs & Practice* explains how to get to grips with all the verb tenses you will need to know, using simple language and cutting out jargon.

The text is divided into sections, each dealing with a particular area of verbs. Each section can be studied individually, as numerous cross-references in the text point you to relevant points in other sections of the book for further information.

Every major section begins with an explanation of the area of grammar covered on the following pages. For quick reference, these definitions are also collected together on pages x–xii in a glossary of essential grammar terms.

> ### What is a verb?
> A **verb** is a 'doing' word which describes what someone or something does, what someone or something is, or what happens to them, for example, *be, sing, live*.

Each point in the text is followed by simple examples of real French, complete with English translations, to help you understand the rules. Underlining has been used in examples throughout the text to highlight the point being explained.

➤ If you are telling someone <u>NOT TO DO</u> something, you put the object pronouns <u>BEFORE</u> the verb.

Ne <u>me</u> dérange pas.	Don't disturb me.
Ne <u>leur</u> parlons pas.	Let's not speak to them.
Ne <u>le</u> regardez pas.	Don't look at him/it.

In French, as with any foreign language, there are certain pitfalls which have to be avoided. **Tips** and **Information** notes throughout the text are useful reminders of the things that often trip learners up.

> *Tip*
> **je** changes to **j'** in front of a word starting with a vowel, most words starting with **h**, and the French word **y**.

Key points sum up all the important facts about a particular area of grammar, to save you time when you are revising and help you focus on the main grammatical points.

> ### KEY POINTS
> ✔ The imperative has three forms: **tu**, **nous** and **vous**.
> ✔ The forms are the same as the **tu**, **nous** and **vous** forms of the present tense, except that the final **-s** is dropped in the **tu** form of **-er** verbs.
> ✔ Object pronouns go before the verb when you are telling someone not to do something, but after the verb with a hyphen when you are telling someone to do something.
> ✔ **avoir**, **être**, **savoir** and **vouloir** have irregular imperative forms.

After each Key point you can find a number of exercises to help you practise all the important points. You can find the answers to each exercise on pages 152-170.

If you think you would like to continue with your French studies to a higher level, check out the **Grammar Extra** sections. These are intended for advanced students who are interested in knowing a little more about the structures they will come across beyond GCSE.

Grammar Extra!
When a verb takes **avoir**, the past participle usually stays in the masculine singular form, as shown in the table for **donner**, and does not change for the feminine or plural forms.

Il a <u>fini</u> sa dissertation.	He's finished his essay.
Elles ont <u>fini</u> leur dissertation.	They've finished their essay.

Finally, the supplement at the end of the book contains **Verb Tables**, where 115 important French verbs (both regular and irregular) are declined in full. Examples show you how to use these verbs in your own work. If you are unsure of how a verb conjugates in French, you can look up the **Verb Index** on pages 117-130 to find either the conjugation of the verb itself, or a cross-reference to a model verb, which will show you the pattern that verb follows.

We hope that you will enjoy using the *Easy Learning French Verbs & Practice* and find it useful in the course of your studies.

Glossary of Grammar Terms

ADVERB a word usually used with verbs, adjectives or other adverbs that gives more information about when, where, how or in what circumstances something happens, for example, *quickly, happily, now*.

AGREE (to) to change word endings according to whether you are referring to masculine, feminine, singular or plural people or things.

AGREEMENT changing word endings according to whether you are referring to masculine, feminine, singular or plural people or things.

ARTICLE a word like *the, a* and *an*, which is used in front of a noun. See also **definite article** and **indefinite article**.

AUXILIARY VERB a verb such as *be, have* and *do* when it is used with a main verb to form tenses, negatives and questions.

BASE FORM the form of the verb without any endings added to it, for example, *walk, have, be, go*. Compare with **infinitive**.

CLAUSE a group of words containing a verb.

CONDITIONAL a verb form used to talk about things that would happen or would be true under certain conditions, for example, *I would help you if I could*. It is also used to say what you would like or need, for example, *Could you give me the bill?*

CONJUGATE (to) to give a verb different endings according to whether you are referring to *I, you, they* and so on, and according to whether you are referring to past, present or future, for example, *I have, she had, they will have*.

CONJUGATION a group of verbs which have the same endings as each other or change according to the same pattern.

DEFINITE ARTICLE the word *the*. Compare with **indefinite article**.

DEMONSTRATIVE PRONOUN one of the words *this, that, these* and *those* used instead of a noun to point out people or things, for example, *That looks fun.*

DIRECT OBJECT a noun referring to the person or thing affected by the action described by a verb, for example, *She wrote her name.; I shut the window*. Compare with **indirect object**.

DIRECT OBJECT PRONOUN a word such as *me, him, us* and *them* which is used instead of a noun to stand in for the person or thing most directly affected by the action described by the verb. Compare with **indirect object pronoun**.

ENDING a form added to a verb, for example, *go > goes*, and to adjectives and nouns depending on whether they refer to masculine, feminine, singular or plural things.

FEMININE a form of noun, pronoun or adjective that is used to refer to a living being, thing or idea that is not classed as masculine.

FUTURE a verb tense used to talk about something that will happen or will be true.

IMPERATIVE the form of a verb used when giving orders and instructions, for example, *Shut the door!; Sit down!; Don't go!*

IMPERFECT one of the verb tenses used to talk about the past, especially in descriptions, and to say what was happening or used to happen, for example, *I used to walk to school; It was sunny at the weekend*. Compare with **perfect**.

IMPERSONAL VERB one which does not refer to a real person or thing and where the subject is represented by *it*, for example, *It's going to rain; It's 10 o'clock*.

INDEFINITE ARTICLE the words *a* and *an*. Compare with **definite article**.

INDEFINITE PRONOUN a small group of pronouns such as *everything, nobody* and *something*, which are used to refer to people or things in a general way, without saying exactly who or what they are.

INDIRECT OBJECT a noun used with verbs that take two objects. For example, in *I gave the carrot to the rabbit*, *the rabbit* is the indirect object and *carrot* is the direct object. Compare with **direct object**.

INDIRECT OBJECT PRONOUN when a verb has two objects (a direct one and an indirect one), the indirect object pronoun is used instead of a noun to show the person or the thing the action is intended to benefit or harm, for example, *me* in *He gave me a book* and *Can you get me a towel?* Compare with **direct object pronoun**.

INDIRECT QUESTION used to tell someone else about a question and introduced by a verb such as *ask*, *tell* or *wonder*, for example, *He asked me what the time was; I wonder who he is*.

INFINITIVE the form of the verb with *to* in front of it and without any endings added, for example, *to walk, to have, to be, to go*. Compare with **base form**.

IRREGULAR VERB a verb whose forms do not follow a general pattern or the normal rules. Compare with **regular verb**.

MASCULINE a form of noun, pronoun or adjective that is used to refer to a living being, thing or idea that is not classed as feminine.

NEGATIVE a question or statement which contains a word such as *not*, *never* or *nothing*, and is used to say that something is not happening, is not true or is absent, for example, *I never eat meat; Don't you love me?*

NOUN a 'naming' word for a living being, thing or idea, for example, *woman, desk, happiness, Andrew*.

NUMBER used to say how many things you are referring to or where something comes in a sequence.

OBJECT a noun or pronoun which refers to a person or thing that is affected by the action described by the verb. Compare with **direct object**, **indirect object** and **subject**.

OBJECT PRONOUN one of the set of pronouns including *me*, *him* and *them*, which are used instead of the noun as the object of a verb or preposition. Compare with **subject pronoun**.

PART OF SPEECH a word class, for example, *noun, verb, adjective, preposition, pronoun*.

PASSIVE a form of the verb that is used when the subject of the verb is the person or thing that is affected by the action, for example, *we were told*.

PAST HISTORIC one of the verb tenses used to talk about the past when referring to completed actions, whether they happened recently or a long time ago and regardless of how long they lasted.

PAST PARTICIPLE a verb form which is used to form perfect and pluperfect tenses and passives, for example, *watched, swum*. Some past participles are also used as adjectives, for example, *a broken watch*.

PERFECT one of the verb tenses used to talk about the past, especially about actions that took place and were completed in the past. Compare with **imperfect**.

PERSON one of three classes: the first person (*I, we*), the second person (*you* singular and *you* plural), and the third person (*he, she, it* and *they*).

PERSONAL PRONOUN one of the group of words including *I, you* and *they* which are used to refer to yourself, the people you are talking to, or the people or things you are talking about.

PLUPERFECT one of the verb tenses used to describe something that <u>had</u> happened or had been true at a point in the past, for example, *I'd forgotten to finish my homework*.

PLURAL the form of a word which is used to refer to more than one person or thing. Compare with **singular**.

PREPOSITION is a word such as *at, for, with, into* or *from*, which is usually followed by a noun, pronoun or, in English, a word ending in *-ing*. Prepositions show how people and things relate to the rest of the sentence, for example, *She's <u>at</u> home; a tool <u>for</u> cutting grass; It's <u>from</u> David*.

PRESENT a verb form used to talk about what is true at the moment, what happens regularly, and what is happening now, for example, *I'<u>m</u> a student; I <u>travel</u> to college by train; I'<u>m studying</u> languages*.

PRESENT PARTICIPLE a verb form ending in *-ing* which is used in English to form verb tenses, and which may be used as an adjective or a noun, for example, *What are you <u>doing</u>?; the <u>setting</u> sun; <u>Swimming</u> is easy!*

PRONOUN a word which you use instead of a noun, when you do not need or want to name someone or something directly, for example, *it, you, none*.

PROPER NOUN the name of a person, place, organization or thing. Proper nouns are always written with a capital letter, for example, *Kevin, Glasgow, Europe, London Eye*.

REFLEXIVE PRONOUN a word ending in *-self* or *-selves*, such as *myself* or *themselves*, which refers back to the subject, for example, *He hurt <u>himself</u>.; Take care of <u>yourself</u>*.

REFLEXIVE VERB a verb where the subject and object are the same, and where the action 'reflects back' on the subject. A reflexive verb is used with a reflexive pronoun such as *myself, yourself, herself*, for example, *I washed myself.; He shaved himself*.

REGULAR VERB a verb whose forms follow a general pattern or the normal rules. Compare with **irregular verb**.

SINGULAR the form of a word which is used to refer to one person or thing. Compare with **plural**.

STEM the main part of a verb to which endings are added.

SUBJECT the noun in a sentence or phrase that refers to the person or thing that does the action described by the verb or is in the state described by the verb, for example, *<u>My cat</u> doesn't drink milk*. Compare with **object**.

SUBJECT PRONOUN a word such as *I, he, she* and *they* which carries out the action described by the verb. Pronouns stand in for nouns when it is clear who is being talked about, for example, *My brother isn't here at the moment. <u>He</u>'ll be back in an hour*. Compare with **object pronoun**.

SUBJUNCTIVE a verb form used in certain circumstances to express some sort of feeling, or to show doubt about whether something will happen or whether something is true. It is only used occasionally in modern English, for example, *If I <u>were</u> you, I wouldn't bother.; So <u>be</u> it*.

TENSE the form of a verb which shows whether you are referring to the past, present or future.

VERB a 'doing' word which describes what someone or something does, what someone or something is, or what happens to them, for example, *be, sing, live*.

verb reference & exercises

Verbs

The three conjugations

➤ Verbs are usually used with a noun, with a pronoun such as *I*, *you* or *she*, or with somebody's name. They can relate to the present, the past and the future; this is called their <u>tense</u>.

➤ Verbs are either:

- <u>regular</u>; their forms follow the normal rules

- <u>irregular</u>; their forms do not follow the normal rules

➤ Regular English verbs have a <u>base form</u> (the form of the verb without any endings added to it, for example, *walk*). The base form can have *to* in front of it, for example, *to walk*. This is called the <u>infinitive</u>. You will find one of these forms when you look a verb up in your dictionary.

➤ French verbs also have an infinitive, which ends in **-er**, **-ir** or **-re**, for example, **donner** (meaning *to give*), **finir** (meaning *to finish*), **attendre** (meaning *to wait*). <u>Regular</u> French verbs belong to one of these three verb groups, which are called <u>conjugations</u>. We will look at each of these three conjugations in turn on the next few pages.

➤ English verbs have other forms apart from the base form and infinitive: a form ending in *-s* (*walks*), a form ending in *-ing* (*walking*), and a form ending in *-ed* (*walked*).

➤ French verbs have many more forms than this, which are made up of endings added to a <u>stem</u>. The stem of a verb can usually be worked out from the infinitive.

➤ French verb endings change, depending on who you are talking about: **je** (*I*), **tu** (*you*), **il/elle/on** (*he/she/it/one*) in the singular, or **nous** (*we*), **vous** (*you*) and **ils/elles** (*they*) in the plural. French verbs also have different forms depending on whether you are referring to the present, future or past.

➤ Some verbs in French do not follow the normal rules, and are called <u>irregular verbs</u>. These include some very common and important verbs like avoir (meaning *to have*), **être** (meaning *to be*), **faire** (meaning *to do, to make*) and **aller** (meaning *to go*). There is information on many of these irregular verbs in the following sections.

➡ For **Verb tables**, see supplement.

KEY POINTS
✔ French verbs have different forms depending on what noun or pronoun they are used with, and on their tense.
✔ They are made up of a stem and an ending. The stem is usually based on the infinitive.
✔ Regular verbs fit into one of three patterns or conjugations: **-er**, **-ir**, or **-re** verbs.
✔ Irregular verbs do not follow the normal rules.

The present tense

> ### What is the present tense?
> The **present tense** is used to talk about what is true at the moment,
> what happens regularly and what is happening now, for example, I'_m_ a student,
> I _travel_ to college by train, I'_m studying_ languages.

➤ You use a verb in the present tense to talk about:

- things that are happening now
  It'_s_ raining.
  The phone'_s_ ringing.

- things that happen all the time or at certain intervals, or things that you do as a habit
  It always _snows_ in January.
  I _play_ football on Saturdays.

- things that are true at the present time:
  She'_s_ not very well.
  It'_s_ a beautiful house.

➤ There is more than one way to express the present tense in English. For example, you can say either I _give_, I _am giving_, or occasionally I _do give_. In French you use the same form (**je donne**) for all of these!

➤ In English you can also use the present tense to talk about something that is going to happen in the near future. You can do the same in French.

Je _vais_ en France le mois prochain.	I'_m going_ to France next month.
Nous _prenons_ le train de dix heures.	We'_re getting_ the ten o'clock train.

> _Tip_
> Although English sometimes uses parts of the verb _to be_ to form the present tense of other verbs (for example, I _am_ listening, she'_s_ talking), French NEVER uses the verb **être** in this way.

The present tense: regular -er (first conjugation) verbs

➤ If an infinitive in French ends in **-er**, it means the verb belongs to the first conjugation, for example, **donner**, **aimer**, **parler**.

➤ To know which form of the verb to use in French, you need to work out what the stem of the verb is and then add the correct ending. The stem of **-er** verbs in the present tense is formed by taking the infinitive and chopping off **-er**.

Infinitive	Stem (without -er)
donner (to give)	donn-
aimer (to like, to love)	aim-
parler (to speak, to talk)	parl-

For further explanation of grammatical terms, please see pages x-xii.

➤ Now you know how to find the stem of a verb, you can add the correct ending. Which one you choose will depend on whether you are referring to **je**, **tu**, **il**, **elle**, **on**, **nous**, **vous**, **ils** or **elles**.

➤ Here are the present tense endings for **-er** verbs:

Pronoun	Ending	Add to stem, e.g. donn-	Meanings
je (j')	-e	je donn<u>e</u>	I give I am giving
tu	-es	tu donn<u>es</u>	you give you are giving
il elle on	-e	il donn<u>e</u> elle donn<u>e</u> on donn<u>e</u>	he/she/it/ one gives he/she/it/one is giving
nous	-ons	nous donn<u>ons</u>	we give we are giving
vous	-ez	vous donn<u>ez</u>	you give you are giving
ils elles	-ent	ils donn<u>ent</u> elles donn<u>ent</u>	they give they are giving

Marie <u>regarde</u> la télé.   Marie is watching TV.
Le train <u>arrive</u> à deux heures.   The train arrives at 2 o'clock.

> *Tip*
> **je** changes to **j'** in front of a word starting with a vowel (*a, e, i, o* or *u*),
> most words starting with **h**, and the French word **y**.

ⓘ Note that there are a few regular **-er** verbs that are spelled slightly differently from the way you might expect.

⇨ *For more information on **Spelling changes in -er verbs**, see page 28.*

> **KEY POINTS**
> ✔ Verbs ending in **-er** belong to the first conjugation and form their present tense stem by losing the **-er** from the infinitive.
> ✔ The present tense endings for **-er** verbs are:
> **-e, -es, -e, -ons, -ez, -ent**.

Test yourself

1 Fill the gap with the correct form of the present tense.

a Ses enfants lui .... des soucis. **(donner)**

b Vous .... très vite, Madame. **(marcher)**

c Tu .... trop la télé. **(regarder)**

d J'............................ aller au cinéma. **(aimer)**

e Mes amis .... une semaine en Italie. **(passer)**

f Marie .... parce qu'elle est seule. **(pleurer)**

g Tu .... toujours. **(gagner)**

h La dame nous .... **(regarder)**

i Samedi on .... les répétitions. **(commencer)**

j Nous .... une table pour demain. **(réserver)**

2 Match the person to the description.

a C'est un professeur.   Nous n'habitons pas ici.

b Ils sont musulmans.   J'aime beaucoup jouer au tennis.

c Elle est banquière.   Ils ne mangent pas de porc.

d Nous sommes étrangers.   Elle gagne beaucoup d'argent.

e Je suis sportive.   Il enseigne la physique.

Test yourself

3 **Make a sentence using the elements given. Remember that when the object of the verb is a pronoun it usually comes before the verb.**

a nous/visiter/le/dimanche

....

b vous/travailler/dur

....

c ma mère/habiter/là

....

d il/couper/le/en deux

....

e les filles/jouer/dehors

....

f je/parler/lui/souvent

....

g ma femme/détester/la

....

h nous/rester/y/une semaine

....

i vous/arriver/ici/à quelle heure?

....

j nos amis/passer/y/une quinzaine de jours

....

Test yourself

4 **Translate the sentence into French. You can make questions in French simply by adding a question mark.**

a Are you starting straight away? (*Use **tu**.*)

....

b He's talking to the neighbours.

....

c The girls adore our cat.

....

d We like French food.

....

e Are you talking to me? (*Use **tu**.*)

....

f We're spending a week in the Alps with them.

....

g She's arriving at midnight.

....

h Are you watching that? (*Use **tu**.*)

....

i What are you looking for? (*Use **vous**.*)

....

j Why don't you like her? (*Use **tu**.*)

....

5 **Fill the gap with the most likely verb.**

a Il fait froid, je .... la fenêtre.

b C'est une émission très intéressante, nous la .... toutes les semaines.

c C'est son pantalon favori, il le .... presque toujours.

d Ils .... cent personnes au mariage.

e Je .... des tulipes en octobre.

f Les enfants .... à cache-cache.

g Mon chat .... des souris mais il ne les tue pas.

h Je n'ai pas de mémoire, j' .... toujours les noms.

i Il .... d'avis tout le temps.

j Tu .... leur invitation?

Test yourself

6 **Cross out the unlikely items.**

a Nous recyclons — le papier/la monnaie/le plastique/l'essence

b Elle porte toujours — une couronne/des lunettes/un pantalon/
des vêtements de sport

c C'est une proposition intéressante. — On l'accepte./Nous l'acceptons./On la refuse./
Vous l'acceptez?

d Ta chemise n'est pas très propre. — Tu la repasses?/Tu la laves?/
Tu la changes?/Elle est neuve?

e Il regarde — l'écran/le bruit/son ami/son reflet

f Ils louent — des femmes de ménage/des vélos/
un appartement au bord de la mer/une voiture

g Tu es fatiguée. — Je t'aide?/Tu travailles dur./Tu étudies toute la
journée./J'apporte tout de suite l'addition.

h Elle a une bonne nouvelle. — Elle pleure./Elle téléphone à sa mère./Ses amis
la félicitent./Elle l'oublie immédiatement.

i Elles sont sportives. — Elles jouent au tennis./Elles restent assises
toute la journée./Je les rencontre à la salle
de sport./Elles marchent beaucoup.

j Ils donnent de beaux cadeaux — aux enfants/à leurs amies/à n'importe qui/
aux passants

Test yourself

7 **Make a sentence using the elements given. Use the present tense for all verbs and remember that object pronouns usually come before the verb.**

a ma mere/rester/à la maison/aujourd'hui

....

b tu/aimer/cette photo?

....

c si/tu/aimer/les/je/donner/te/les

....

d mes grandparents/habiter/à Lyon,/mon père/habiter/à Marseille

....

e si/tu/tricher/je/ne/jouer/pas/avec toi

....

f vous/apporter/nous/l'addition?

....

g Si/vous/laisser/ouvert/le robinet/vous/gaspiller/de l'eau

....

h vous/rouler/trop vite

....

i la police/chercher/les

....

j elle/commencer/toujours/à pleurer/quand/il/parler/lui/comme ça

....

Test yourself

8 **Translate the questions by making statements and adding question marks to them.**

   a Do they earn a lot of money?

   ....

   b Are you tidying your room? (*Use* **tu**.)

   ....

   c Do the girls like school?

   ....

   d Does she wear those clothes in the office?

   ....

   e Are you working this weekend? (*Use* **vous**.)

   ....

   f Is she looking for somebody?

   ....

   g Are they borrowing money?

   ....

   h Does a ticket really cost 100 euros?

   ....

   i Do you recommend this hotel? (*Use* **vous**.)

   ....

   j Do your parents let you watch that programme? (*Use* **tu**.)

   ....

9 **Fill the gap with the correct form of the present tense.**

   a Nos tantes nous .... de beaux cadeaux. **(donner)**

   b Vous .... bien le français, Madame. **(parler)**

   c Tu .... trop. **(parler)**

   d J' .... jouer au foot. **(aimer)**

   e Mes cousins .... à Paris. **(habiter)**

   f Claire .... parce qu'elle est heureuse. **(chanter)**

   g Tu .... très vite. **(marcher)**

   h Jean .... le match à la télé. **(regarder)**

   i Demain on .... le travail. **(commencer)**

   j Nous l' .... beaucoup. **(admirer)**

The present tense: regular -ir (second conjugation) verbs

➤ If an infinitive ends in **-ir**, it means the verb belongs to the <u>second conjugation</u>, for example, **finir**, **choisir**, **remplir**.

➤ The stem of **-ir** verbs in the present tense is formed by taking the <u>infinitive</u> and chopping off **-ir**.

Infinitive	Stem (without -ir)
finir (to finish)	**fin-**
choisir (to choose)	**chois-**
remplir (to fill, to fill in)	**rempl-**

➤ Now add the correct ending, depending on whether you are referring to **je**, **tu**, **il**, **elle**, **on**, **nous**, **vous**, **ils** or **elles**.

➤ Here are the present tense endings for **-ir** verbs:

Pronoun	Ending	Add to stem, e.g. fin-	Meanings
je (j')	**-is**	je fin<u>is</u>	I finish I am finishing
tu	**-is**	tu fin<u>is</u>	you finish you are finishing
il **elle** **on**	**-it**	il fin<u>it</u> elle fin<u>it</u> on fin<u>it</u>	he/she/it/one finishes he/she/it/one is finishing
nous	**-issons**	nous fin<u>issons</u>	we finish we are finishing
vous	**-issez**	vous fin<u>issez</u>	you finish you are finishing
ils **elles**	**-issent**	ils fin<u>issent</u> elles fin<u>issent</u>	they finish they are finishing

Le cours <u>finit</u> à onze heures. The lesson finishes at eleven o'clock.
Je <u>finis</u> mes devoirs. I'm finishing my homework.

> *Tip*
> **je** changes to **j'** in front of a word starting with a vowel, most words starting with **h**, and the French word **y**.

➤ The **nous** and **vous** forms of **-ir** verbs have an extra syllable.
  tu fi|nis (*two syllables*)
  vous fi|ni|ssez (*three syllables*)

For further explanation of grammatical terms, please see pages x–xii.

KEY POINTS

✔ Verbs ending in **-ir** belong to the second conjugation and form their present tense stem by losing the **-ir** from the infinitive.

✔ The present tense endings for **-ir** verbs are:
-is, **-is**, **-it**, **-issons**, **-issez**, **-issent**.

✔ Remember the extra syllable in the **nous** and **vous** forms.

Test yourself

10 **Fill the gap with the correct form of the present tense.**

a Julien .... toujours la glace au chocolat. **(choisir)**

b Les cerisiers .... en avril. **(fleurir)**

c Vous .... bientôt le travail? **(finir)**

d En ce moment nous .... un nouveau record. **(établir)**

e Le cours .... à midi. **(finir)**

f Je .... une carte? **(choisir)**

g Ils .... le pas, ils sont fatigués. **(ralentir)**

h Il y a de la boue, vous .... vos chaussures. **(salir)**

i Si tu fais ça, l'institutrice te .... **(punir)**

j Nous .... tous ces formulaires? **(remplir)**

11 **Match the related sentences.**

a **Je ne regarde pas la télévision.**   Je remplis sa tasse de thé.

b **Mon amie est au régime.**   Tout le monde maigrit.

c **Ici on mange peu et on marche beaucoup.**   Nous choisissons nos mots avec soin.

d **Elle ne boit pas de café.**   Je finis mes devoirs.

e **C'est délicat de lui dire ça.**   Elle choisit toujours les salades.

Test yourself

12 Make a sentence using the elements given. Remember that when the object of the verb is a pronoun it usually comes before the verb. The first one has been done for you.

a je/finir/ma dissertation/ce soir

Je finis ma dissertation ce soir.

b ils/investir/dans/des actions

c tu/finir/ton déjeuner/avant d'aller jouer

d la piscine est vide,/nous/remplir/la.

e nous/choisir/des rideaux/pour le nouvel appartement

f celui-là coûte moins cher,/vous/choisir/le?

g je/choisir/toujours les moins chers

h en voyant le feu rouge,/elle/ralentir

i ses parents ont de l'argent,/ils/investir/le/dans l'immobilier

j attention,/tu/salir/la nappe!

Test yourself

13 **Translate the sentences into French. You can make questions in French simply by adding a question mark.**

a I'm choosing a new mobile phone.

....

b Why does she always choose that colour?

....

c Does the film finish before eight o'clock?

....

d We're finishing most of it today.

....

e They always choose the most expensive dishes.

....

f You're slowing down, are you tired? (*Use* **vous**.)

....

g What time are you finishing this evening? (*Use* **tu**.)

....

h I'm filling in both the forms.

....

i Why are you punishing them? (*Use* **vous**.)

....

j They're finishing the repairs as quickly as possible.

....

14 **The verbs *ouvrir* and *couvrir* take the same endings as 1st conjugation (-er) verbs in the present tense. Put the correct form of the present tense of one of these verbs in the gap.**

a Les magasins .... à huit heures.

b La neige .... la rue.

c Ils .... les murs de graffiti.

d Cette lettre est pour toi, tu l' .... ?

e Elle .... le robinet pour remplir la bouilloire.

f Cette somme ne .... pas mes frais.

g Il fait chaud, j' .... la fenêtre.

h Vous .... le tapis de sable, les enfants.

i À cause des chiens nous .... le canapé d'un vieux drap.

j Les élèves .... leurs cahiers et commencent à écrire.

15 **In the present tense the verbs *dormir*, *partir* and *sortir* take the same endings as *-er* verbs in the plural, but the singular forms are different. Look at the verb tables and write the correct form in the gap.**

a Les enfants .... sous la tente dans le jardin.

b Nous .... en vacances samedi.

c Il est dix heures mais elle .... encore.

d Si tu n'es pas là, je .... sans toi.

e Elle .... avec moi ce soir.

f Le train .... à onze heures.

g Je .... bien quand je suis en vacances.

h Tu .... de la piscine, Marie?

i Les ouvriers .... de l'usine.

j En juin mes amies .... en Espagne.

Test yourself

16 **Cross out the unlikely options.**

a Mes amies partent   demain./dimanche./hier./avant moi.

b Il ouvre   l'ordinateur./le robinet./son journal./la radio.

c Elle choisit toujours les chaussures   usées./en cuir./basses./à hauts talons.

d Le bébé dort   dans notre chambre./dans la poussette./ sur la table./au jardin.

e Les enfants remplissent leurs sacs à dos   de souvenirs./de vêtements sales./d'outils./ de pierres.

f Il sort   en train./rarement./avec ses copains./seul.

g Les banques ouvrent   le jour de Noël./à neuf heures./le soir./ lundi matin.

h Vous les finissez bientôt, monsieur?   les réparations./les travaux./les graffiti./ les répétitions.

i Vous sortez toujours   à cette heure?/à sept heures?/avec des étrangers?/sans chapeau?

j Le train part   il y a deux heures./de ce quai./avec un peu de retard./maintenant.

17 **Match the question to the answer.**

a Tu ouvres la fenêtre?   Oui, ils y investissent beaucoup d'argent.

b Ils commencent les entretiens la semaine prochaine?   Oui, je choisis un bon bordeaux.

c Vous partez demain?   Non, ils les finissent cette semaine.

d Ils ont une usine en Inde?   Non, je la ferme.

e Tu regardes la liste des vins?   Non, nous restons encore quelques jours.

Test yourself

18 **Translate the sentence into French.**

a I'm choosing a dress for the party.

....

b Usually women choose salads.

....

c I sleep eight hours a night.

....

d The children are already sleeping.

....

e You're finishing early today. (*Use* ***tu***.)

....

f We're finishing the painting tomorrow.

....

g You're covering the kitchen with flour. (*Use* ***tu***.)

....

h We're going out for two hours.

....

i She leaves in a taxi every morning.

....

j She's finishing the report tomorrow.

....

The present tense: regular -re (third conjugation) verbs

➤ If an infinitive ends in **-re**, it means the verb belongs to the <u>third conjugation</u>, for example, **attendre**, **vendre**, **entendre**.

➤ The stem of **-re** verbs in the present tense is formed by taking the <u>infinitive</u> and chopping off **-re**.

Infinitive	Stem (without **-re**)
attendre (*to wait*)	**attend-**
vendre (*to sell*)	**vend-**
entendre (*to hear*)	**entend-**

➤ Now add the correct ending, depending on whether you are referring to **je**, **tu**, **il**, **elle**, **on**, **nous**, **vous**, **ils** or **elles**.

➤ Here are the present tense endings for **-re** verbs:

Pronoun	Ending	Add to stem, e.g. attend-	Meanings
je (j')	**-s**	**j'attend<u>s</u>**	I wait I am waiting
tu	**-s**	**tu attend<u>s</u>**	you wait you are waiting
il **elle** **on**	**-**	**il attend** **elle attend** **on attend**	he/she/it/one waits he/she/it/ one is waiting
nous	**-ons**	**nous attend<u>ons</u>**	we wait we are waiting
vous	**-ez**	**vous attend<u>ez</u>**	you wait you are waiting
ils **elles**	**-ent**	**ils attend<u>ent</u>** **elles attend<u>ent</u>**	they wait they are waiting

J'<u>attends</u> ma sœur.　　　　　　I'm waiting for my sister.
Chaque matin nous <u>attendons</u>　　Every morning we wait for the train
　le train ensemble.　　　　　　　together.

> *Tip*
> **je** changes to **j'** in front of a word starting with a vowel, most words starting with **h**, and the French word **y**.

KEY POINTS

✔ Verbs ending in **-re** belong to the third conjugation and form their present tense stem by losing the **-re** from the infinitive.

✔ The present tense endings for **-re** verbs are: **-s**, **-s**, **-**, **-ons**, **-ez**, **-ent**.

19 **Fill the gap with the correct form of the present tense.**

a J'............................ sa voix. **(entendre)**

b Charles et Paul .... leur appartement. **(vendre)**

c Vous .... les autres? **(attendre)**

d Tu m'............................. ? **(entendre)**

e Il y a trop de bruit, elle ne nous .... pas. **(entendre)**

f Elles .... les vacances avec impatience. **(attendre)**

g Le cygne .... ses petits. **(défendre)**

h Le quatre-quatre n'est pas économique, nous le .... **(vendre)**

i Tu .... le bus pour l'aéroport? **(attendre)**

j Vous .... votre vin à la coopérative? **(vendre)**

20 **Match the related sentences.**

a Le train est en retard.   Ils vendent leurs peintures.

b Ce sont des artistes.   Parle plus fort!

c Vous attendez un enfant?   Je la défends.

d Je ne t'entends pas.   Toutes mes félicitations!

e Elle est ma petite amie.   On attend longtemps.

Test yourself

21 **Make a sentence using the elements given. Remember that when the object of the verb is a pronoun it usually comes before the verb.**

a tu/entendre/me/bien?

....

b je/attendre/vous/depuis longtemps

....

c l'appartement est trop petit,/il/vendre/le

....

d vous/défendre/la violence?

....

e elle/prétendre/être innocente

....

f les mères/défendre/toujours leurs enfants

....

g nos invités sont en retard,/nous/attendre/les

....

h cette poussette,/vous/vendre/la?

....

i ça/dépendre/du prix

....

j on/entendre/à peine/les mots

....

Test yourself

22 Translate the sentences into French. You can make questions in French simply by adding a question mark.

a They're waiting for me at the restaurant.

....

b Why are you selling your flat? (*Use* **vous**.)

....

c We hear the noise.

....

d Perhaps. It depends.

....

e He is defending his boss.

....

f Do you hear the neighbours? (*Use* **tu**.)

....

g The tourists are waiting for the guide.

....

h The women sell their jams at the market.

....

i I hear every word.

....

j Is she expecting a baby?

....

Test yourself

23 The verbs *tendre*, *rendre*, *entendre*, *attendre*, *étendre* and *vendre* all follow the same pattern in the present tense. Fill the gap with the present tense of the most appropriate verb. The first one has been done for you.

a Vous ..*entendez*.... le tonnerre?

b Nous .... son verdict.

c Les mendiants .... la main pour demander de l'argent.

d Elle .... le linge dehors quand il fait beau.

e Il .... des journaux dans la rue.

f Elles parlent très fort, j'........................ chaque mot.

g C'est ici qu'on .... le bus pour le centre commercial.

h Ils .... des milliers de ce modèle.

i Elle est enceinte, elle .... une fille.

j Si tu fermes les yeux et tu .... la main, je te donne un cadeau surprise.

24 Cross out the unlikely options.

a Il défend — le gouvernement./sa décision./ses critiques./son territoire.

b Nous l'entendons tous les soirs. — la chaleur/la télévision de nos voisins/sa voix/des cris dans la rue

c Ça dépend — de la saison./du prix./de son état./s'il nous aide.

d C'est une quincaillerie, ils vendent — des marteaux./des clous./des scies./des timbres.

e C'est son anniversaire, elle attend — le plombier./le facteur./l'arrivée de ses amis./des factures.

f Elle vend ses tableaux — sur Internet./au kilo./dans une petite galerie./au supermarché.

g Ils m'attendent tous les matins — au café./devant la porte./dans le bus./à la gare.

h Je la vends — à un prix raisonnable./comme cadeau./pour cent euros./à mon collègue.

i Elles ne t'entendent pas. — Tu parles trop fort./Tu ne parles pas assez fort./Elles regardent la télé./Elles écoutent une chanson.

j Tu attends — depuis longtemps?/le train de Paris?/quelqu'un?/bientôt?

Test yourself

25 **Match the shop to the goods sold.**

a C'est une boulangerie.	On y vend des timbres et des cigarettes.
b C'est un magasin de produits diététiques.	On y vend des cahiers et des blocs-notes.
c C'est un magasin de brocante.	On y vend toutes sortes de pain.
d C'est un bureau de tabac.	On y vend toute sorte de bric-à-brac.
e C'est une papeterie.	On y vend du pain sans gluten.

26 **The French equivalent for 'I have been waiting for an hour' is *J'attends depuis une heure*. Use the present tense of *attendre* followed by *depuis* to translate the sentences. Form any questions by adding a question mark to a statement. The first one has been done for you.**

a My brothers have been waiting for six months.

Mes frères attendent depuis six mois.

b I've been waiting for half an hour.

....

c You've been waiting for an appointment for a fortnight? (*Use* **vous**.)

....

d We've been waiting for our starters for twenty-five minutes.

....

e You've been waiting for your birthday for months, Max!

....

f We've been waiting for this moment for four years. (*Use* **on**.)

....

g Their mothers have been waiting for them for a long time.

....

h How long have you been waiting, sir? (*Use* **depuis quand**.)

....

i He's angry, he's been waiting for three quarters of an hour.

....

j We've been waiting for a taxi for twenty minutes.

....

Test yourself

27 **Translate the sentences into French. You can make questions in French simply by adding a question mark.**

    a Are you waiting for her? (*Use **vous**.*)

    ....

    b My car's too small, I'm selling it.

    ....

    c We hear their TV.

    ....

    d That depends on the price.

    ....

    e He defends his friends.

    ....

    f Do you hear me? (*Use **tu**.*)

    ....

    g The girls are waiting for the bus.

    ....

    h The computer's useless, they're selling it.

    ....

    i They hear the bells every morning.

    ....

    j She's expecting a baby.

    ....

The present tense: spelling changes in -er verbs

➤ Learning the patterns shown on pages 4–5 means you can now work out the forms of most **-er** verbs. A few verbs, though, involve a small spelling change. This is usually to do with how a word is pronounced. In the tables below the form(s) with the irregular spelling is/are underlined.

Verbs ending in -cer

➤ With verbs such as **lancer** (meaning *to throw*), which end in **-cer**, **c** becomes **ç** before an **a** or an **o**. This is so the letter **c** is still pronounced as in the English word *ice*.

Pronoun	Example verb: lancer
je	lance
tu	lances
il, elle, on	lance
nous	<u>lançons</u>
vous	lancez
ils, elles	lancent

Verbs ending in -ger

➤ With verbs such as **manger** (meaning *to eat*), which end in **-ger**, **g** becomes **ge** before an **a** or an **o**. This is so the letter **g** is still pronounced like the **s** in the English word *leisure*.

Pronoun	Example verb: manger
je	mange
tu	manges
il, elle, on	mange
nous	<u>mangeons</u>
vous	mangez
ils, elles	mangent

Verbs ending in -eler

➤ With verbs such as **appeler** (meaning *to call*), which end in **-eler**, the **l** doubles before **-e**, **-es** and **-ent**. The double consonant (**ll**) affects the pronunciation of the word. In **appeler**, the first **e** sounds like the vowel sound at the end of the English word *teacher*, but in **appelle** the first **e** sounds like the one in the English word *pet*.

Pronoun	Example verb: appeler
j'	<u>appelle</u>
tu	<u>appelles</u>
il, elle, on	<u>appelle</u>
nous	appelons
vous	appelez
ils, elles	<u>appellent</u>

➤ The exceptions to this rule are **geler** (meaning *to freeze*) and **peler** (meaning *to peel*), which change in the same way as **lever** (*see page 30*).

➤ Verbs like this are sometimes called '1, 2, 3, 6 verbs' because they change in the first person singular (**je**), second person singular (**tu**), and third person singular and plural (**il/elle/on** and **ils/elles**).

Verbs ending in -eter

➤ With verbs such as **jeter** (meaning *to throw*), which end in **-eter**, the **t** doubles before **-e**, **-es** and **-ent**. The double consonant (**tt**) affects the pronunciation of the word. In **jeter**, the first **e** sounds like the vowel sound at the end of the English word *teacher*, but in **jette** the first **e** sounds like the one in the English word *pet*.

Pronoun	Example verb: jeter
je	jette
tu	jettes
il, elle, on	jette
nous	jetons
vous	jetez
ils, elles	jettent

➤ The exceptions to this rule include **acheter** (meaning *to buy*), which changes in the same way as **lever** (*see page 30*).

➤ Verbs like this are sometimes called '1, 2, 3, 6 verbs'.

Verbs ending in -yer

➤ With verbs such as **nettoyer** (meaning *to clean*), which end in **-yer**, the **y** changes to **i** before **-e**, **-es** and **-ent**.

Pronoun	Example verb: nettoyer
je	nettoie
tu	nettoies
il, elle, on	nettoie
nous	nettoyons
vous	nettoyez
ils, elles	nettoient

➤ Verbs ending in **-ayer**, such as **payer** (meaning *to pay*) and **essayer** (meaning *to try*), can be spelled with either a **y** or an **i**. So **je paie** and **je paye**, for example, are both correct.

➤ Verbs like this are sometimes called '1, 2, 3, 6 verbs'.

Changes involving accents

➤ With verbs such as **lever** (meaning *to raise*), **peser** (meaning *to weigh*) and **acheter** (meaning *to buy*), **e** changes to **è** before the consonant + **-e**, **-es** and **-ent**. The accent changes the pronunciation too. In **lever** the first **e** sounds like the vowel sound at the end of the English word *teacher*, but in **lève** and so on the first **e** sounds like the one in the English word *pet*.

Pronoun	Example verb: lever
je	lève
tu	lèves
il, elle, on	lève
nous	levons
vous	levez
ils, elles	lèvent

➤ With verbs such as **espérer** (meaning *to hope*), **régler** (meaning *to adjust*) and **préférer** (meaning *to prefer*), **é** changes to **è** before the consonant + **-e**, **-es** and **-ent**.

Pronoun	Example verb: espérer
j'	espère
tu	espères
il, elle, on	espère
nous	espérons
vous	espérez
ils, elles	espèrent

➤ Verbs like this are sometimes called '1, 2, 3, 6 verbs'.

KEY POINTS

✔ In verbs ending in **-cer** and **-ger**:
c → ç and g → ge in the **nous** form.
✔ In verbs ending in **-eler** and **-eter**:
l → ll and t → tt in all but the **nous** and **vous** forms.
✔ In verbs ending in **-yer**:
y → i in all but the **nous** and **vous** forms (optional in **-ayer** verbs).

Test yourself

28 Fill the gap with the correct form of the present tense.

a Tu me .... le ballon? **(lancer)**

b Nous .... une nouvelle gamme. **(lancer)**

c Je .... très peu à midi. **(manger)**

d Nous .... au restaurant demain. **(manger)**

e Vous l'........................... bientôt? **(appeler)**

f Mes parents m'........................... tous les samedis. **(appeler)**

g Si tu ne le veux pas, tu le .... **(jeter)**

h La baignoire n'est pas propre, tu la ....? **(nettoyer)**

i Aujourd'hui, il .... **(geler)**

j On .... avoir de bons résultats. **(espérer)**

29 Cross out the unlikely items.

a Les enfants en mangent au petit déjeuner. — des croissants/de la glace/de la confiture/du beurre

b Je la jette à la corbeille à papier. — de la monnaie/une enveloppe/de l'eau/la facture

c Il gèle souvent en hiver. — en Écosse/en Suisse/à Tahiti/en Suède

d Ma petite amie les préfère. — les chiens méchants/les pains aux raisins/les meubles anciens/les promenades à vélo

e Il s'appelle — Monsieur Aubery./Marie./Nicolas./Docteur LeDuc.

f Nous vous appelons — bientôt./dimanche matin./ce soir./quand il gèle.

g Elle espère — pouvoir vous aider./y aller./se casser la jambe./avoir un bébé.

h Mon oncle pèse 50 kg. — Il mange beaucoup./Il mange peu./Il est gros./Il fume trop.

i La salle de bains n'est pas très propre. — J'ai quatre enfants./Tu la nettoies pour moi?/J'aime beaucoup le ménage./J'en suis contente.

j Le professeur pose une question. — Ils se lèvent./Tous les enfants lèvent le doigt./Même Julien lève le doigt./Nous levons le doigt.

Test yourself

30 **Translate the sentences into French. You can make questions simply by adding a question mark to a statement.**

a Are we eating after the concert?

....

b I'm called Lucie.

....

c Do I throw the bottles in the bin?

....

d Are you throwing the leftovers away? (*Use **vous**.*)

....

e I always peel apples and pears.

....

f Is she sending him a card?

....

g We eat a lot when we're on holiday.

....

h Do you prefer American films? (*Use **tu**.*)

....

i We hope to go there next year.

....

j I'm adjusting the seat.

....

31 **Match the sentences that have a connection.**

a Pauline a de gros problèmes.   Nous mangeons des pâtes.

b Nous lui envoyons la facture à la fin du mois.   Il en achète beaucoup.

c Nos amis sont végétariens.   C'est normal, n'est-ce pas?

d Ces chaussures sont jolies.   J'espère pouvoir l'aider.

e Luc adore les jeux électroniques.   Tu les essaies?

Test yourself

32 **Fill the gap with the correct present tense form of the most appropriate verb.**

   a Les livres sont en désordre, nous les .... ?

   b Ce n'est pas son vrai nom, mais nous l'.................... Skip.

   c Il .... ses vêtements par terre.

   d Elle m'.................... un SMS tous les soirs.

   e Nous .... aller en Chine.

   f Tout va bien, j'.................... .

   g Vous .... la main, les enfants, vous ne criez pas.

   h Depuis sa crise cardiaque, nous .... léger.

   i C'est normal, si nous cassons quelque chose, nous le ....

   j Il est bon, ce plombier, tu l'.................... et il arrive tout de suite.

33 **Replace the highlighted word or words with the correct form of** *préférer.*

   a Souvent elle **aime mieux** aller à pied. ....

   b Tu **choisis toujours** des couleurs sombres. ....

   c Les garçons **aiment mieux** jouer dehors. ....

   d En général nous **choisissons** des places côté fenêtre. ....

   e Vous **aimez mieux** des glaces, les filles? ....

   f Beaucoup de gens **choisissent** les modèles économiques. ....

   g Nous **aimons mieux** faire nos achats en ligne. ....

   h Lesquels **choisissez-vous**? ....

   i Si tu **veux**, on commence demain. ....

   j Nous **aimons mieux** les voitures diesel. ....

34 **Make a sentence with the elements given.**

a pour qui/tu/acheter/ces jolies fleurs?

....

b nous/loger/à l'hôtel

....

c ils/enlever/les ordures/deux fois par semaine

....

d la femme de chambre/nettoyer/la salle de bains

....

e nous/déménager/lundi

....

f on/peler/les concombres pour cette salade

....

g ce livre/révéler/beaucoup de choses intéressantes

....

h nous/lever/nos verres à Alice et Jacques

....

i combien de temps/vous/espérer/rester/y?

....

j le client/régler/la note/en espèces

....

Test yourself

35 **Translate the sentences into French.**

a They're buying a microwave.

    ....

b The lake freezes in winter.

    ....

c I'm taking off my shoes, they're dirty.

    ....

d We buy our bread at the supermarket.

    ....

e We're hoping to have better luck next time.

    ....

f The children call me grandma.

    ....

g Do you call that a luxury hotel? (*Use **vous**.*)

    ....

h You always throw the towels on the floor. (*Use **tu**.*)

    ....

i They pay me at the end of the month.

    ....

j She's trying on the black shoes.

    ....

The present tense: irregular verbs

➤ Some verbs in French do not follow the normal rules. These verbs include some very common and important verbs like **avoir** (meaning *to have*), **être** (meaning *to be*), **faire** (meaning *to do, to make*) and **aller** (meaning *to go*). The present tense of these four verbs is given in full below.

⇨ For **Verb tables**, see supplement.

The present tense of avoir

Pronoun	avoir	Meaning: *to have*
j'	ai	I have
tu	as	you have
il elle on	a	he/she/it/one has
nous	avons	we have
vous	avez	you have
ils elles	ont	they have

J'ai deux sœurs.	I have two sisters.
Il a les yeux bleus.	He has blue eyes.
Elle a trois ans.	She's three.
Qu'est-ce qu'il y a?	What's the matter?

The present tense of être

Pronoun	être	Meaning: *to be*
je	suis	I am
tu	es	you are
il elle on	est	he/she/it/one is
nous	sommes	we are
vous	êtes	you are
ils elles	sont	they are

Je suis heureux.	I'm happy.
Mon père est instituteur.	My father's a primary school teacher.
Il est deux heures.	It's two o'clock.

The present tense of faire

Pronoun	faire	Meaning: *to do, to make*
je	fais	I do/make I am doing/making
tu	fais	you do/make you are doing/making
il elle on	fait	he/she/it/one does/makes he/she/it/one is doing/ making
nous	faisons	we do/make we are doing/making
vous	faites	you do/make you are doing/making
ils elles	font	they do/make they are doing/making

Je <u>fais</u> un gâteau.	I'm making a cake.
Qu'est-ce que tu <u>fais</u>?	What are you doing?
Il <u>fait</u> chaud.	It's hot.
Ça ne <u>fait</u> rien.	It doesn't matter.

The present tense of aller

Pronoun	aller	Meaning: *to go*
je	vais	I go I am going
tu	vas	you go you are going
il elle on	va	he/she/it/one goes he/she/it/one is going
nous	allons	we go we are going
vous	allez	you go you are going
ils elles	vont	they go they are going

Je <u>vais</u> à Londres.	I'm going to London.
'Comment <u>allez</u>-vous?' — 'Je <u>vais</u> bien.'	'How are you?' — 'I'm fine.'
'Comment ça <u>va</u>?' — 'Ça <u>va</u> bien.'	'How are you?' — 'I'm fine.'

Irregular -ir verbs

➤ Many irregular verbs that end in **-ir**, such as **partir** (meaning *to go*) and **tenir** (meaning *to hold*), have a common pattern in the singular. The **je** and **tu** forms often end in **-s**, and the **il/elle/on** form often ends in **-t**.

Pronoun	partir	tenir
je	par**s**	tien**s**
tu	par**s**	tien**s**
il/elle/on	par**t**	tien**t**

Je pars demain. I'm leaving tomorrow.
Elle tient le bébé. She is holding the baby.

⇨ For **Verb tables**, see supplement.

KEY POINTS
✔ Some very important French verbs are irregular, including **avoir**, **être**, **faire** and **aller**. They are worth learning in full.
✔ The **-s**, **-s**, **-t** pattern occurs frequently in irregular **-ir** verbs.

Test yourself

36 **Complete the sentences with the correct form of the present tense.**

    a Nos voisins .... deux chats et un chien. **(avoir)**

    b Nous n'............................ pas d'animaux. **(avoir)**

    c Nous .... à la piscine? **(aller)**

    d Ce pauvre homme .... besoin d'aide. **(avoir)**

    e Qu'est-ce que tu .... ce soir? **(faire)**

    f Il .... midi, on mange bientôt. **(être)**

    g Que .... les enfants pendant les vacances? **(faire)**

    h Ils .... en vacances ensemble. **(partir)**

    i Nous ne .... pas d'ici. **(être)**

    j Tout .... bien, j'espère? **(aller)**

37 **Match the question to the statement.**

    a Tu as l'air triste.   Comment s'appelle-t-elle?

    b J'ai une sœur ainée.   On leur fait une tarte aux pommes?

    c Il fait froid ce matin.   Ils n'ont rien d'intéressant à faire?

    d Ce soir on a des invités.   Qu'est-ce qu'il y a?

    e Élodie et Luc font des bêtises.   On reste à la maison?

38 ***J'ai les yeux bleus*** **is another way of saying** *Mes yeux sont bleus*. **Replace the highlighted words in this way, using** *avoir* + **the definite article.**

    a **Tes mains sont** très grandes. ....

    b **Leurs cheveux sont** blonds. (*Use **elles**.*) ....

    c **Mes hanches sont** plutôt larges. ....

    d **Tes cheveux sont** très secs. ....

    e **Leurs mains sont** gelées. (*Use **elles**.*) ....

    f **Tes mains sont** propres? ....

    g **Sa jambe est** cassée. (*Use **elle**.*) ....

    h **Son cœur est** brisé. (*Use **il**.*) ....

    i **Tes oreilles sont** très petites. ....

    j **Leurs bras sont** bien musclés. (*Use **elles**.*) ....

Test yourself

39 **Translate the sentences into French.**

a What are you doing at the weekend? (*Use **vous**.*)

....

b Everything's fine, thanks. ....

c She doesn't go to school: she's three.

....

d We usually go to France, but this year we're going to Italy.

....

e What is there to see here? – Nothing.

....

f Lisa's a physiotherapist. ....

g It's cold, are you going to put on the heating?

....

h There's no bread, I'm going to the bakery.

....

i I haven't got any change. – It doesn't matter.

....

j The train is leaving in three minutes.

....

40 **Fill the gap with the correct present tense form of the most appropriate verb from the following list:** *avoir/être/faire/aller*.

a Il .... des pieds immenses.

b Mes parents .... à la retraite.

c Il .... du vent.

d Ses jambes lui .... mal.

e J' .... un rhume.

f On .... au supermarché tous les samedi matins.

g Qu'est-ce que vous .... dans la vie?

h Elle .... trente ans.

i Je .... bien, merci.

j Quel âge tu .... ?

Test yourself

41 **A way of saying you play golf/swim etc is** *Je fais du golf/de la natation*. **Replace the highlighted words with the correct form of** *faire du/de la*. **The first one has been done for you.**

a Il **joue au** foot tous les samedis. ..*fait du*...

b En France beaucoup de gens **aiment le** cyclisme. ....

c Tu **aimes l'**équitation? ....

d Vous **jouez au** tennis? ....

e Elle **aime le** piano. ....

f Nous **aimons l'**escalade. ....

g Mes amies **adorent le** yoga. ....

h Mon mari **aime la** marche. ....

i Ici on **joue au** rugby. ....

j Vous **aimez le** jogging? ....

42 **Cross out the wrong answers.**

a **Où allez-vous?** Je vais à Paris./Je vais bien./Nous allons en ville./ On va à la piscine.

b **Qu'est-ce qu'il fait?** Il fait beau./Il regarde ses e-mails./ Il fait le ménage./Il ne fait rien.

c **Ils sont combien?** Six./Ils ont six ans./Moins de dix./Dix au moins.

d **Qu'est-ce qu'elle fait dans la vie?** Elle est professeur./Elle est coiffeuse./ Elle fait du sport./Elle n'a pas de travail.

e **Qu'est-ce que tu as?** J'ai trop chaud./J'ai douze ans./J'ai mal à la tête./ J'ai les yeux verts.

f **Quelle heure est-il?** Il est midi./Il est dix heures./ Il est l'heure du déjeuner./Il est trois heures pile.

g **C'est quoi?** C'est trop./C'est du thé./Je n'ai aucune idée./ C'est un cadeau.

h **Vous avez des enfants, madame?** Non./Oui./Peut-être./Deux.

i **Quand partons-nous?** Bientôt./Avant midi./À onze heures et demie./ Avec eux.

j **Où ça te fait mal?** À l'hôpital./Partout./À la jambe./Au bras.

Test yourself

43 **Match the worker to the activity.**

   a Elle est artisan-bijoutière.   Je fais des robes.

   b Ils sont patissiers.   Nous faisons des poteries.

   c Je suis couturière.   Il fait des fenêtres.

   d Nous sommes potiers.   Elle fait des bagues.

   e Il est menuisier.   Ils font des gâteaux.

44 **Translate the sentences into French.**

   a My grandmother is eighty-five.

   ....

   b She's a bit deaf, but she's fine.

   ....

   c We're having a party for her birthday.

   ....

   d All her grandchildren are going to be there.

   ....

   e She's got four granddaughters and five grandsons.

   ....

   f The youngest of the grandchildren is Luc.

   ....

   g He's five.

   ....

   h The children are getting up to mischief.

   ....

   i I'm making a cake and a pizza.

   ....

   j My sisters are making a photo album.

   ....

The imperative

What is the imperative?

An **imperative** is a form of the verb used when giving orders and instructions, for example, *Shut the door!; Sit down!; Don't go!*

Using the imperative

➤ In French, there are two forms of the imperative that are used to give instructions or orders to someone. These correspond to **tu** and **vous**.

➤ There is also a form of the imperative that corresponds to **nous**. This means the same as *let's* in English. It is not used as often as the **tu** and **vous** forms.

Forming the present tense imperative

➤ For regular verbs, the imperative is the same as the **tu**, **nous** and **vous** forms of the present tense, except that you do not say the pronouns **tu, nous** and **vous**. Also, in the **tu** form of **-er** verbs like **donner**, the final **-s** is dropped.

Pronoun	-er verbs: donner	Meaning	-ir verbs: finir	Meaning	-re verbs: attendre	Meaning
tu	**donne**	give	**finis**	finish	**attends**	wait
nous	**donnons**	let's give	**finissons**	let's finish	**attendons**	let's wait
vous	**donnez**	give	**finissez**	finish	**attendez**	wait

Donne-moi ça!	Give me that!
Finissez vos devoirs et allez vous coucher.	Finish your homework and go to bed.
Attendons le bus.	Let's wait for the bus.

Tip

When a **tu** imperative comes before **en** or **y**, the final **-s** is kept to make the words easier to pronounce. The **s** is pronounced like the *z* in the English word *zip*:

Vas-y!	Go on!
Donnes-en à ton frère.	Give some to your brother.

Where to put the object pronoun

➤ An object pronoun is a word like **la** (meaning *her/it*), **me/moi** (meaning *me*) or **leur** (meaning *to them*) that is used instead of a noun as the object of a sentence. In orders and instructions, the position of these object pronouns in the sentence changes depending on whether you are telling someone TO DO something or NOT TO DO something.

➤ If you are telling someone NOT TO DO something, you put the object pronouns BEFORE the verb.

Ne <u>me</u> dérange pas.	Don't disturb me.
Ne <u>leur</u> parlons pas.	Let's not speak to them.
Ne <u>le</u> regardez pas.	Don't look at him/it.

➤ If you are telling someone TO DO something, you put the object pronouns AFTER the verb and join the two words with a hyphen. The word order is the same as in English.

Excusez-<u>moi</u>.	Excuse me.
Aide-<u>nous</u>.	Help us.
Attendons-<u>la</u>.	Let's wait for her/it.

➤ Orders and instructions telling someone to do something may contain <u>direct object</u> and <u>indirect object pronouns</u>. When this happens, the pronouns go in this order:

DIRECT	BEFORE	INDIRECT	
le		moi	nous
la		toi	vous
les		lui	leur

Prête-<u>les-moi</u>!	Lend them to me! *or* Lend me them!
Donnez-<u>la-nous</u>!	Give it to us! *or* Give us it!

⇨ *For imperatives using **Reflexive verbs**, see page 52.*

Imperative forms of irregular verbs

➤ **avoir** (meaning *to have*), **être** (meaning *to be*), **savoir** (meaning *to know*) and **vouloir** (meaning *to want*) have irregular imperative forms.

Pronoun	avoir	être	savoir	vouloir
tu	aie	sois	sache	veuille
nous	ayons	soyons	sachons	veuillons
vous	ayez	soyez	sachez	veuillez

<u>Sois</u> sage.	Be good.
<u>Veuillez</u> fermer la porte.	Please shut the door.

> ## KEY POINTS
> ✔ The imperative has three forms: **tu**, **nous** and **vous**.
> ✔ The forms are the same as the **tu**, **nous** and **vous** forms of the present tense, except that the final **-s** is dropped in the **tu** form of **-er** verbs.
> ✔ Object pronouns go before the verb when you are telling someone not to do something, but after the verb with a hyphen when you are telling someone to do something.
> ✔ **avoir**, **être**, **savoir** and **vouloir** have irregular imperative forms.

Test yourself

45 *Tu m'apportes un verre?* **is more polite than using the imperative:** *Apporte-moi un verre!* **Change the question into an order, remembering that the pronoun may change. The first one has been done for you.**

a Tu m'écoutes, Marianne?
Écoute-moi, Marianne!

b Vous me suivez, les enfants?

c Tu en parles à ta mère, Pierre?

d Si vous en avez besoin, vous lui demandez?

e Vous me croyez, Monsieur?

f Vous me pardonnez, Madame?

g Tu en prends un peu?

h Tu ranges ta chambre ce matin?

i Vous allez vous coucher?

j Tu nous excuses? ....

46 **Replace the highlighted negative command with a positive one.**

a **Ne partez pas** sans moi! ....

b **N'approche pas**! ....

c **N'y va pas**! ....

d **Ne le faites pas**, je vous en prie! ....

e **Ne la réveillez pas** tôt! ....

f **Ne leur prête pas** ta voiture! ....

g **N'en parlez pas** à vos parents! ....

h J'arrive dans une demi-heure, **ne commencez pas** sans moi! ....

i C'est compliqué: **n'y pense pas**! ....

j Elle marche très lentement, **ne l'attendons pas**! ....

Test yourself

47 **Cross out the items the speaker is not likely to be referring to.**

a Trouvez-les! vos places/vos glaces/vos livres/vos baskets

b Prends-le! le portable/l'argent/ce risque/la gare

c Goûtez-le! le tabac/ce fromage/le poisson/l'engrais

d Donne-le-moi! l'appareil photo/le journal/le rhume/le menu

e Écoutez-la! cette photo/cette musique/la bonne prononciation/ la chanteuse

f Aide-la! la vieille dame/ta tante/la voiture/l'association caritative

g Montrez-les-moi! les cadeaux/les photos/les nouvelles chaussures/les pellicules

h Profitons-en! de la catastrophe/du soleil/de l'occasion/de l'examen

i Envoie-la-moi! l'adresse e-mail/ta sœur/la carte postale/la photocopie

j Demande-la-lui! l'argent/l'addition/la vraie raison/la monnaie

48 **Match the sentences that have a connection.**

a Ferme les yeux! On va les ranger.

b Sois courageux! Il n'est pas capable de faire ça.

c Soyez patient! Ça va faire un peu mal.

d Veuillez les laisser ici. J'ai un cadeau pour toi.

e Soyons réalistes. Tout le monde doit attendre.

49 **Tell someone what do using the form of the imperative indicated by the pronoun in brackets. Remember the rules for the position of the object pronoun with imperatives. The first one has been done for you.**

a (vous)/rester/là/les enfants *Restez là, les enfants!*

b (vous)/choisir/les plus beaux

c (tu)/attendre/les/ici

d (tu)/ne pas/faire/me/rire

e (vous)/ne pas/oublier/les

f (tu)/parler/leur/en

g (vous)/montrer/moi/les

h (tu)/ne pas/être/stupide

i (vous)/ne pas/avoir/peur

j (tu)/ne pas/ toucher/à mes affaires

Test yourself

50 **Replace the highlighted words with the *nous* form of the imperative, and any necessary pronoun. The first one has been done for you.**

a Ils sont vieux. **Il faut les remplacer**. *Remplaçons-les* ....

b C'est notre ami, **il faut l'aider**. ....

c Ce sont les moins chers, **il faut les choisir**. ....

d C'est une nouvelle recette, **il faut la goûter**. ....

e C'est sans doute la meilleure solution, **il faut l'essayer**. ....

f Il reste trois gâteaux, **il faut les finir**. ....

g Elle en a besoin, **il faut les lui prêter**. ....

h **Il ne faut pas avoir** peur. ....

i **Il faut faire preuve** de compréhension. ....

j C'est un bon restaurant, **il faut y aller**. ....

51 **Translate the sentences into French.**

a Take off your coats, children. ....

b Finish your breakfast, Pierre. ....

c Please fill in the form, sir. ....

d Let's call the police. ....

e Listen to me, girls. ....

f Make less noise, boys. ....

g Follow me! (*Use **vous**.*) ....

h Let's be sensible. ....

i Keep the change! (*Use **vous**.*) ....

j Let's change places. ....

Test yourself

52 **Match the object to the verb.**

    a Voilà un autre pantalon.   Attends-le!

    b Voilà son numéro.   Allume-le!

    c Voilà Serge.   Prends-le!

    d Voilà l'ordinateur.   Appelle-le!

    e Voilà un petit cadeau.   Essaye-le!

Reflexive verbs

What is a reflexive verb?
A **reflexive verb** is one where the subject and object are the same, and where the action 'reflects back' on the subject. It is used with a reflexive pronoun such as *myself*, *yourself* and *herself* in English, for example, *I washed myself; He shaved himself.*

Using reflexive verbs

➤ In French, reflexive verbs are much more common than in English, and many are used in everyday French. They are shown in dictionaries as **se** plus the infinitive (**se** means *himself*, *herself*, *itself*, *themselves* or *oneself*). **se** is called a <u>reflexive pronoun</u>.

> *Tip*
> **se** changes to **s'** in front of a word starting with a vowel, most words starting with **h**, and the French word **y**.

➤ Reflexive verbs are often used to describe things you do (to yourself) every day or that involve a change of some sort (going to bed, sitting down, getting angry, going to sleep). Some of the most common French reflexive verbs are listed here:

s'amuser	to play, to enjoy oneself
s'appeler	to be called
s'arrêter	to stop
s'asseoir	to sit down
se baigner	to go swimming
se coucher	to go to bed
se dépêcher	to hurry
s'habiller	to get dressed
s'intéresser à (quelque chose)	to be interested in (something)
se laver	to wash, to have a wash
se lever	to get up, to rise, to stand up
se passer	to take place, to happen, to go
se promener	to go for a walk
se rappeler	to remember
se réveiller	to wake up
se trouver	to be (situated)

Qu'est-ce qui <u>se passe</u>?	What's happening?
Le soleil <u>se lève</u> à cinq heures.	The sun rises at five o'clock.
<u>Asseyez-vous</u>!	Sit down!

⚅ Note that **se** and **s'** are very rarely translated as *himself* and so on in English.

➤ Some French verbs can be used with a reflexive pronoun or without a reflexive pronoun, for example, the verbs **appeler** and **s'appeler**, and **arrêter** and **s'arrêter**. Sometimes, however, their meaning may change.

<u>Appelle</u> le chien.	<u>Call</u> the dog.
Je <u>m'appelle</u> Jacques.	<u>I'm called</u> Jacques.
Il <u>arrête</u> le moteur.	He <u>switches off</u> the engine.
Elle <u>s'arrête</u> devant une vitrine.	She <u>stops</u> in front of a shop window.

Forming the present tense of reflexive verbs

➤ To use a reflexive verb in French, you need to decide which reflexive pronoun to use. The forms shown in brackets in the table are used before a word starting with a vowel, most words starting with **h**, or the French word **y**.

Subject pronoun	Reflexive pronoun	Meaning
je	me (m')	myself
tu	te (t')	yourself
il elle on	se (s')	himself herself itself oneself
nous	nous	ourselves
vous	vous	yourself (*singular*) yourselves (*plural*)
ils elles	se (s')	themselves

Je <u>me lève</u> tôt.	I get up early.
Elle <u>s'habille</u>.	She's getting dressed.
Ils <u>s'intéressent</u> beaucoup aux animaux.	They're very interested in animals.

➤ The present tense forms of a reflexive verb work in just the same way as an ordinary verb, except that the reflexive pronoun is used as well.

Reflexive forms	Meaning
je me lave	I wash (myself)
tu te laves	you wash (yourself)
il se lave elle se lave on se lave	he washes (himself) she washes (herself) it washes (itself) one washes (oneself)
nous nous lavons	we wash (ourselves)
vous vous lavez	you wash (yourself) (*singular*) you wash (yourselves) (*plural*)
ils se lavent elles se lavent	they wash (themselves)

➤ Some reflexive verbs, such as **s'asseoir** (meaning *to sit down*), are irregular. Some of these irregular verbs are shown in the **Verb tables**.

⟹ *For **Verb tables**, see supplement.*

Where to put the reflexive pronoun

➤ In the present tense, the reflexive pronoun almost always comes <u>BEFORE</u> the verb.

Je <u>me</u> couche tôt.	I go to bed early.
Comment <u>t'</u>appelles-tu?	What's your name?

➤ When telling someone <u>NOT TO DO</u> something, you put the reflexive pronoun <u>BEFORE</u> the verb as usual.

Ne <u>te</u> lève pas.	Don't get up.
Ne <u>vous</u> habillez pas.	Don't get dressed.

➤ When telling someone <u>TO DO</u> something, you put the reflexive pronoun <u>AFTER</u> the verb and join the two words with a hyphen.

Lève-<u>toi</u>!	Get up!
Dépêchez-<u>vous</u>!	Hurry up!
Habillons-<u>nous</u>.	Let's get dressed.

Tip

When you are telling someone <u>TO DO</u> something, **te** or **t'** changes to **toi**.

Assieds-<u>toi</u>.   Sit down.

When you are telling someone <u>NOT TO DO</u> something, **te** or **t'** is used, not **toi**.

Ne te lève pas.   Don't get up.

⟹ *For more information on the **Imperative**, see page 43.*

Each other and *one another*

➤ The French reflexive pronouns **nous**, **vous** and **se** can be used to translate the English phrases *each other* and *one another*.

Nous <u>nous</u> parlons tous les jours.	We speak to <u>each other</u> every day.
On <u>se</u> voit demain?	Shall we see <u>each other</u> tomorrow?
Les trois pays <u>se</u> ressemblent beaucoup.	The three countries are really like <u>one another</u>.

KEY POINTS

✔ A reflexive verb is made up of a reflexive pronoun and a verb.
✔ The reflexive pronouns are: **me**, **te**, **se**, **nous**, **vous**, **se** (**m'**, **t'**, **s'**, **nous**, **vous**, **s'** before a vowel, most words beginning with **h** and the French word **y**).
✔ The reflexive pronoun comes before the verb, except when you are telling someone to do something.

Test yourself

53 **Fill the gap with the correct reflexive pronoun. The first one has been done for you.**

a Les petits ....*s'*........ amusent dehors.

b Tu .... laves les cheveux tous les jours?

c Si on .... arrêtait pour manger?

d Les trains ne .... arrêtent pas ici.

e On est en retard, tu .... dépêches?

f Vous .... intéressez à l'art moderne?

g Je ne .... rappelle pas son nom.

h Tu es fatiguée, va .... coucher.

i Qu'est-ce qui .... passe?

j Où .... trouvent les toilettes?

54 **Fill the gap with the correct form of the verb, and a reflexive pronoun if necessary. The first one has been done for you.**

a Le bébé a de la fièvre, tu .....*appelles*......... le docteur? **(appeler)**

b Tu .... Nathalie? **(s'appeler)**

c Julien et moi, nous .... toujours à ce café. **(s'arrêter)**

d Les garçons .... à dix heures du soir. **(se coucher)**

e Tu fais des bêtises: tu ....? **(arrêter)**

f Voulez-vous .... cet après-midi? **(se promener)**

g Nous .... tard dimanche matin. **(se lever)**

h Irène .... son temps à coudre. **(passer)**

i L'histoire .... au moyen âge. **(se passer)**

j Nous avons beaucoup marché, ... ici pour nous reposer. **(s'asseoir)**

Test yourself

55 **Translate the sentences into French.**

a I usually wake up early in summer.

....

b What's happening in the street? ....

c Are the children going to bed soon?

....

d I go swimming every day. ....

e We're here to relax and to enjoy ourselves. (*Use* **on**.)

....

f It's late, are you getting up? (*Use* **tu**.)

....

g The hotel is situated near the beach. ....

h My friends dress very smartly. ....

i So, you're not interested in sport? (*Use* **vous**.)

....

j We're wondering what it is. ....

56 **Tell someone to do something (√) or not to do something (X) using the given elements. The first one has been done for you.**

a s'asseoir √/Monsieur   *Asseyez-vous, Monsieur!* ....

b se baigner X /après le déjeuner, les enfants

....

c s'habiller √/tout de suite/Alain et Michelle

....

d s'amuser √/bien à Paris/chérie ....

e s'inquiéter X /Monsieur/tout va bien

....

f s'asseoir X /à cette table/s'il vous plaît/Mesdames

....

g se détendre √/bien/Laure ....

h se reposer √/au soleil/Mesdames ....

i se lever X /Gaston, reste là ....

j se méfier X /de ce garçon/Florent ....

Test yourself

57 **Fill the gap with the most likely reflexive verb, remembering to add the reflexive pronoun.**

a Il est huit heures, tu .... ?

b Vous n'avez rien à craindre, ne .... pas.

c Tu vas être en retard pour l'école si tu ne .... pas.

d Elle .... Lucie, je pense

e J'écoute de la musique pour ....

f Ils sont fiancés depuis deux ans, je .... quand ils vont se marier.

g Il a perdu la mémoire, il ne .... rien.

h Mes collègues sont tous sympathiques, nous .... très bien.

i Il n'y a rien à faire ici, on ....

j Ils ne s'entendent pas bien. Ils .... souvent.

58 **Fill the gap with a form of *appeler* or *s'appeler*.**

a Comment tu .... ?

b Si tu es en retard, ... -moi sur mon portable.

c C'est notre balcon, mais nous l'..................................... notre jardin.

d Ses fils .... Hugo et Victor.

e S'il y a un problème, ... -moi au bureau, monsieur.

f Ma voiture est en panne, je vais .... le dépanneur.

g Elle s'est mariée. Maintenant elle .... Madame Robert.

h Ils .... par leurs prénoms.

i Elle .... son chien.

j Je ne sais pas comment vous ....

Test yourself

59 **Cross out unlikely options.**

a Elle s'occupe

de leurs enfants./du jardin./du temps./
des réservations.

b Je m'excuse

de mon retard./de mon absence./de ma faute./
de mon manque de tact.

c Il se moque

de toi./du monde./de tout le monde./
des professeurs.

d Tu te sens

bon?/malade?/mieux?/bien?

e Je me méfie

de lui./d'eux./de vous./de nous.

f Ne vous approchez pas!

J'ai la grippe./J'ai chaud./Ce chien est méchant./
J'ai un revolver.

g Peut-être nous nous trompons

de jour./de personne./de place./de date.

h Elle s'habitue

au climat./à temps./à l'école./au mode de vie.

i On se retrouve

au café./au pas./au parking./à la gare.

j Il se porte

à merveille./bien./pire./mieux qu'avant.

60 **Match the activity with its result.**

a Je travaille dur.   Je m'amuse.

b Je suis en train de réparer la voiture.   Je me fatigue.

c Je me renverse de l'eau bouillante sur la main.   Je ne dis rien.

d Je joue aux échecs.   Je me salis.

e Je me contrôle.   Je me brûle.

The imperfect tense

> ## What is the imperfect tense?
> The **imperfect tense** is one of the verb tenses used to talk about the past, especially in descriptions, and to say what used to happen, for example, I _used to walk_ to school; It _was_ sunny at the weekend.

Using the imperfect tense

➤ The imperfect tense is used:

- to describe what things were like and how people felt in the past
  I _was_ very sad when she left.
  It _was pouring_ with rain.

- to say what used to happen or what you used to do regularly in the past
  We _used to get up_ very early in those days.
  I never _used to like_ milk.

- to indicate things that were happening or something that was true when something else took place
  I _was watching_ TV when the phone rang.
  As we _were looking_ out of the window, we saw someone walk across the lawn.

  [_i_] Note that if you want to talk about an event or action that took place and was completed in the past, you use the perfect tense.

  ⇨ _For more information on the **Perfect tense**, see page 86._

➤ You can often recognize an imperfect tense in English because it uses a form like _were looking_ or _was raining_. The words _used to_ also indicate an imperfect tense.

> _Tip_
> Remember that you NEVER use the verb **être** to translate _was_ or _were_ in forms like _was raining_ or _were looking_ and so on. You change the French verb ending instead.

Forming the imperfect tense of -er verbs

➤ To form the imperfect tense of **-er** verbs, you use the same stem of the verb as for the present tense. Then you add the correct ending, depending on whether you are referring to **je**, **tu**, **il**, **elle**, **on**, **nous**, **vous**, **ils** or **elles**.

Pronoun	Ending	Add to stem, e.g. donn-	Meanings
je (j')	-ais	je donn<u>ais</u>	I gave I was giving I used to give
tu	-ais	tu donn<u>ais</u>	you gave you were giving you used to give
il elle on	-ait	il donn<u>ait</u> elle donn<u>ait</u> on donn<u>ait</u>	he/she/it/one gave he/she/it/one was giving he/she/it/one used to give
nous	-ions	nous donn<u>ions</u>	we gave we were giving we used to give
vous	-iez	vous donn<u>iez</u>	you gave you were giving you used to give
ils elles	-aient	ils donn<u>aient</u> elles donn<u>aient</u>	they gave they were giving they used to give

Il <u>portait</u> toujours un grand chapeau noir.	He always wore a big black hat.
Nous <u>habitions</u> à Paris à cette époque.	We were living in Paris at that time.
Pour gagner un peu d'argent, je <u>donnais</u> des cours de français.	To earn a little money I used to give French lessons.

> *Tip*
>
> **je** changes to **j'** in front of a word starting with a vowel, most words starting with **h**, and the French word **y**.

Forming the imperfect tense of -ir verbs

➤ To form the imperfect tense of **-ir** verbs, you use the same stem of the verb as for the present tense. Then you add the correct ending, depending on whether you are referring to **je**, **tu**, **il**, **elle**, **on**, **nous**, **vous**, **ils** or **elles**.

Pronoun	Ending	Add to stem, e.g. fin-	Meanings
je (j')	-issais	je fin<u>issais</u>	I finished I was finishing I used to finish
tu	-issais	tu fin<u>issais</u>	you finished you were finishing you used to finish
il elle on	-issait	il fin<u>issait</u> elle fin<u>issait</u> on fin<u>issait</u>	he/she/it/one finished he/she/it/one was finishing he/she/it/one used to finish
nous	-issions	nous fin<u>issions</u>	we finished we were finishing we used to finish
vous	-issiez	vous fin<u>issiez</u>	you finished you were finishing you used to finish
ils elles	-issaient	ils fin<u>issaient</u> elles fin<u>issaient</u>	they finished they were finishing they used to finish

Il **<u>finissait</u> souvent ses devoirs avant le dîner.**	He often finished his homework before dinner.
Cet après-midi-là ils <u>choisissaient</u> une bague de fiançailles.	That afternoon they were choosing an engagement ring.

Forming the imperfect tense of -re verbs

➤ To form the imperfect tense of **-re** verbs, you use the same stem of the verb as for the present tense. Then you add the correct ending, depending on whether you are referring to **je**, **tu**, **il**, **elle**, **on**, **nous**, **vous**, **ils** or **elles**. These endings are the same as for **-er** verbs.

Pronoun	Ending	Add to stem, e.g. attend-	Meanings
j' (j')	-ais	j'attend<u>ais</u>	I waited I was waiting I used to wait
tu	-ais	tu attend<u>ais</u>	you waited you were waiting you used to wait
il elle on	-ait	il attend<u>ait</u> elle attend<u>ait</u> on attend<u>ait</u>	he/she/it/one waited he/she/it/one was waiting he/she/it/one used to wait
nous	-ions	nous attend<u>ions</u>	we waited we were waiting we used to wait
vous	-iez	vous attend<u>iez</u>	you waited you were waiting you used to wait
ils elles	-aient	ils attend<u>aient</u> elles attend<u>aient</u>	they waited they were waiting they used to wait

Christine m'<u>attendait</u> tous les soirs à la sortie.	Christine used to wait for me every evening at the exit.
Je <u>vivais</u> seule après mon divorce.	I was living alone after my divorce.

Spelling changes in -er verbs

➤ As with the present tense, a few **-er** verbs change their spellings slightly when they are used in the imperfect tense. The forms with spelling changes have been <u>underlined</u> in the tables.

➤ With verbs such as **lancer** (meaning *to throw*), which end in **-cer**, **c** becomes **ç** before an **a** or an **o**. This is so that the letter **c** is still pronounced as in the English word *ice*.

Pronoun	Example verb: lancer
je	<u>lançais</u>
tu	<u>lançais</u>
il, elle, on	<u>lançait</u>
nous	lancions
vous	lanciez
ils, elles	<u>lançaient</u>

➤ With verbs such as **manger** (meaning *to eat*), which end in **-ger**, **g** becomes **ge** before an **a** or an **o**. This is so that the letter **g** is still pronounced like the *s* in the English word *leisure*.

Pronoun	Example verb: manger
je	<u>mangeais</u>
tu	<u>mangeais</u>
il, elle, on	<u>mangeait</u>
nous	mangions
vous	mangiez
ils, elles	<u>mangeaient</u>

➤ These verbs follow the <u>1,2,3,6 pattern</u>. That is, they change in the first, second and third person singular, and in the third person plural.

Reflexive verbs in the imperfect tense

➤ The imperfect tense of reflexive verbs is formed just as for ordinary verbs, except that you add the reflexive pronoun (**me**, **te**, **se**, **nous**, **vous**, **se**).

Subject pronoun	Reflexive pronoun	Example with laver	Meaning
je	me (m')	lavais	I washed I was washing I used to wash
tu	te (t')	lavais	you washed you were washing you used to wash
il elle on	se (s')	lavait	he/she/it/one washed he/she/it/one was washing he/she/it/one used to wash
nous	nous	lavions	we washed we were washing we used to wash
vous	vous	laviez	you washed you were washing you used to wash
ils elles	se (s')	lavaient	they washed they were washing they used to wash

> *Tip*
> **me** changes to **m'**, **te** to **t'** and **se** to **s'** before a vowel, most words starting with **h** and the French word **y**.

Irregular verbs in the imperfect tense

➤ One of the most common verbs that is irregular in the imperfect tense is **être**.

Pronoun	être	Meaning
j'	étais	I was
tu	étais	you were
il, elle, on	était	he/she/it/one was
nous	étions	we were
vous	étiez	you were
ils, elles	étaient	they were

J'<u>étais</u> heureux.   I was happy.
Mon père <u>était</u> instituteur.   My father was a primary school teacher.

> ## KEY POINTS
>
> ✔ The imperfect tense endings for **-er** and **-re** verbs are:
>   **-ais, -ais, -ait, -ions, -iez, -aient**.
> ✔ The imperfect tense endings for **-ir** verbs are:
>   **-issais, -issais, -issait, -issions, -issiez, -issaient**.
> ✔ In verbs ending in **-cer** and **-ger**:
>   **c → ç** and **g → ge** in all but the **nous** and **vous** forms.
> ✔ **être** is irregular in the imperfect tense.

Test yourself

61 **Fill the gap with the correct form of the imperfect. The first one has been done for you.**

a À cette époque les enfants ....*obéissaient*.... sans poser de questions. **(obéir)**

b Vous .... au bord de la mer tous les étés? **(aller)**

c Enfant, il ne .... pas de fromage. **(manger)**

d Quand j'étais étudiante, je .... un appartement avec une Allemande. **(partager)**

e C'était six heures du soir: tout le monde .... son travail. **(finir)**

f Il y a cinquante ans les mines de charbon .... du travail à des milliers de personnes. **(fournir)**

g Nous .... tous les samedis. **(se promener)**

h Quand je t'ai vu, tu .... la rue. **(traverser)**

i Elle .... toujours première: elle courait vite. **(arriver)**

j Mon mari .... à Londres quand nous nous sommes recontrés. **(vivre)**

62 **Match the sentences that are connected.**

a C'était un professeur.   On regardait les vitrines des magasins.

b Ils étaient pauvres.   Il y avait quelqu'un à la porte.

c Elle était au restaurant.   Ils ne partaient jamais en vacances.

d On était en ville.   Elle choisissait son dessert.

e Le chien aboyait.   Elle enseignait l'histoire.

Test yourself

63 **Replace the highlighted present tense with the imperfect. The first one has been done for you.**

a Serge **arrive** souvent avant les autres. ...*arrivait*...

b Je **préfère** me baigner dans la mer. ....

c Ils **choisissent** toujours les vins les plus chers. ....

d Tu **vends** tes tomates au marché? ....

e Nous **lançons** une nouvelle gamme tous les deux ans. ....

f Elle s'**entend** bien avec ses collègues. ....

g Je **commence** mon travail à huit heures. ....

h Vous **avez** peur des cambrioleurs? ....

i Il **cause** avec le voisin. ....

j Il **neige**. ....

64 **Translate the sentences into French.**

a I was watching TV. ....

b Were you feeling ill yesterday? (*Use tu*.)
....

c I looked after him when he was little.
....

d They were finishing when we were starting.
....

e She got on well with the other students.
....

f He was interested in politics. ....

g They were wondering where to go.
....

h The teacher was hopeless: the children didn't listen to him.
....

i It was hot and we were having a swim.
....

j Were you listening to me, girls?
....

Test yourself

65 *J'étais en train de faire* is similar in meaning to *Je faisais*. **Replace the highlighted form of *être en train de* with the correct form of the imperfect. The first one has been done for you.**

a Nous **étions en train de choisir** un DVD. .....*Nous choisissions*.....................

b Elle **était en train de repasser** son chemisier. ....

c Il **était en train d'acheter** une bouteille d'eau. ....

d Ils **étaient en train de manger** leurs sandwichs. ....

e Tu **étais en train d'aller** au lit? ....

f Elle **était en train de finir** le tableau. ....

g Vous **étiez en train de parler** du problème? ....

h Il **était en train de descendre** l'escalier. ....

i Elles **étaient en train de refaire** le travail. ....

j Il **était en train de se raser**. ....

66 **Make a sentence with the elements provided, putting the verb into the imperfect.**

a il y a deux ans/je/faire/une licence de lettres

....

b une fois à la retraite/nous/se lever/plus tard

....

c ils/être/tous les deux professeurs

....

d elle/parler/me/en/souvent

....

e tu/se laver/les cheveux?

....

f ça/sembler/me/bizarre

....

g il/commencer/à faire nuit

....

h je/aller/y/avec eux

....

i la police/chercher/les

....

j à cette époque/je/gagner/beaucoup d'argent

....

Test yourself

67 **Cross out the unlikely options.**

a Elle avait   un rhume./douze ans./déjeuné./raison.

b Nous y passions   les weekends./notre temps libre./nos samedi matins./
les vacances.

c J'écoutais   un SMS./sa réponse./la chanson./le site web.

d Ils ne savaient pas   où aller./quoi dire./cette personne./son nom.

e Vous vous attendiez   au pire?/le train?/à avoir des problèmes?/à de la pluie?

f Il devenait   chauve./célèbre./riche./jeune.

g Nous avions besoin   de toi./d'argent./d'un prêt./d'un plombier.

h Il y avait   beaucoup de monde./les yeux bleus./du choix./des dégâts.

i Vous cherchiez   un parking?/quelque chose?/quelqu'un?/quelque fois?

j J'écrivais   un chèque./un roman./une lettre./une dissertation.

68 **Match the related sentences.**

a Il pleuvait.   Il avait des dettes.

b C'était dimanche après-midi.   Les enfants jouaient dehors.

c Il faisait beau.   Nous étions d'accord avec lui.

d Il était au chômage.   Il n'y avait personne sur la plage.

e Il avait raison.   La boulangerie était fermée.

69 **Translate the sentences into French.**

a I was thinking about you. ....

b What were you doing this afternoon? ....

c I went to the cinema often when I lived in Paris. ....

d We got on well when we were at school. ....

e She felt lonely and cried a lot. ....

f He was always losing his keys. ....

g I was wondering what to do. ....

h The teacher was nice: the children liked him a lot.

....

i It was raining and we were bored. ....

The future tense

What is the future tense?
The **future tense** is a verb tense used to talk about something that will happen or will be true.

Using the future tense

➤ In English the future tense is often shown by *will* or its shortened form *'ll*.
What <u>will</u> you do?
The weather <u>will</u> be warm and dry tomorrow.
He<u>'ll</u> be here soon.
I<u>'ll</u> give you a call.

➤ Just as in English, you can use the present tense in French to refer to something that is going to happen in the future.

Je <u>prends</u> le train de dix heures.	I'm taking the ten o'clock train.
Nous <u>allons</u> à Paris la semaine prochaine.	We're going to Paris next week.

➤ In English we often use *going to* followed by an infinitive to talk about something that will happen in the immediate future. You can use the French verb **aller** (meaning *to go*) followed by an infinitive in the same way.

Tu <u>vas tomber</u> si tu continues.	You're going to fall if you carry on.
Il <u>va manquer</u> le train.	He's going to miss the train.

> *Tip*
> Remember that French has no direct equivalent of the word *will* in verb forms like *will rain* or *will look* and so on. You change the French verb ending instead to form the future tense.

Forming the future tense

➤ To form the future tense in French, you use:

- the <u>infinitive</u> of **-er** and **-ir** verbs, for example, **donner, finir**

- the <u>infinitive without the final **e**</u> of **-re** verbs: for example, **attendr-**

➤ Then add the correct ending to the stem, depending on whether you are talking about **je**, **tu**, **il**, **elle**, **on**, **nous**, **vous**, **ils** or **elles**. The endings are the same for **-er**, **-ir** and **-re** verbs.

> ⓘ Note that apart from the **nous** and **vous** forms, the endings are the same as the present tense of **avoir**.

⇨ *For the present tense of **avoir**, see page 36*.

Pronoun	Ending	Add to stem, e.g. donner-, finir-, attendr-	Meaning
je (j')	-ai	je donner**ai** je finir**ai** j'attendr**ai**	I will give I will finish I will wait
tu	-as	tu donner**as** tu finir**as** tu attendr**as**	you will give you will finish you will wait
il elle on	-a	il/elle/on donner**a** il/elle/on finir**a** il/elle/on attendr**a**	he/she/it/one will give he/she/it/one will finish he/she/it/one will wait
nous	-ons	nous donner**ons** nous finir**ons** nous attendr**ons**	we will give we will finish we will wait
vous	-ez	vous donner**ez** vous finir**ez** vous attendr**ez**	you will give you will finish you will wait
ils elles	-ont	ils/elles donner**ont** ils/elles finir**ont** ils/elles attendr**ont**	they will give they will finish they will wait

Elle te donnera mon adresse. — She'll give you my address.
Le cours finira à onze heures. — The lesson will finish at eleven o'clock.
Nous t'attendrons devant le cinéma. — We'll wait for you in front of the cinema.

Tip
je changes to **j'** in front of a word starting with a vowel, most words starting with **h**, and the French word **y**.

Spelling changes in -er verbs

➤ As with the present and imperfect tenses, a few **-er** verbs change their spellings slightly in the future tense. The forms with spelling changes have been underlined in the tables.

➤ With verbs such as **appeler** (meaning *to call*), which end in **-eler**, the **l** doubles throughout the future tense. The double consonant (**ll**) affects the pronunciation of the word. In **appeler**, the first **e** sounds like the vowel sound at the end of the English word *teacher*, but in **appellerai** the first **e** sounds like the one in the English word *pet*.

Pronoun	Example verb: appeler
j'	appellerai
tu	appelleras
il, elle, on	appellera
nous	appellerons
vous	appellerez
ils, elles	appelleront

For further explanation of grammatical terms, please see pages x-xii.

➤ The exceptions to this rule are **geler** (meaning *to freeze*) and **peler** (meaning *to peel*), which change in the same way as **lever** (*see page 30*).

➤ With verbs such as **jeter** (meaning *to throw*), that end in **-eter**, the **t** doubles throughout the future tense. The double consonant (**tt**) affects the pronunciation of the word. In **jeter**, the first **e** sounds like the vowel sound at the end of the English word *teacher*, but in **jetterai** the first **e** sounds like the one in the English word *pet*.

Pronoun	Example verb: jeter
je	jetterai
tu	jetteras
il, elle, on	jettera
nous	jetterons
vous	jetterez
ils, elles	jetteront

➤ The exceptions to this rule include **acheter** (meaning *to buy*), which changes in the same way as **lever** (*see page 30*).

➤ With verbs such as **nettoyer** (meaning *to clean*), that end in **-yer**, the **y** changes to **i** throughout the future tense.

Pronoun	Example verb: nettoyer
je	nettoierai
tu	nettoieras
il, elle, on	nettoiera
nous	nettoierons
vous	nettoierez
ils, elles	nettoieront

➤ Verbs ending in **-ayer**, such as **payer** (meaning *to pay*) and **essayer** (meaning *to try*), can be spelled with either a **y** or an **i**. So **je paierai** and **je payerai**, for example, are both correct.

➤ With verbs such as **lever** (meaning *to raise*), **peser** (meaning *to weigh*) and **acheter** (meaning *to buy*), **e** changes to **è** throughout the future tense. In **lever** the first **e** sounds like the vowel sound at the end of the English word *teacher*, but in **lèverai** and so on the first **e** sounds like the one in the English word *pet*.

Pronoun	Example verb: lever
je	lèverai
tu	lèveras
il, elle, on	lèvera
nous	lèverons
vous	lèverez
ils, elles	lèveront

Reflexive verbs in the future tense

➤ The future tense of reflexive verbs is formed in just the same way as for ordinary verbs, except that you have to remember to give the reflexive pronoun (**me**, **se**, **nous**, **vous**, **se**).

Subject pronoun	Reflexive pronoun	Example with laver	Meaning
je	me (m')	laverai	I will wash
tu	te (t')	laveras	you will wash
il, elle, on	se (s')	lavera	he/she/it/one will wash
nous	nous	laverons	we will wash
vous	vous	laverez	you will wash
ils, elles	se (s')	laveront	they will wash

> *Tip*
> **me** changes to **m'**, **te** to **t'** and **se** to **s'** before a vowel, most words starting with **h** and the French word **y**.

Irregular verbs in the future tense

➤ There are some verbs that <u>do not</u> use their infinitives as the stem for the future tense, including **avoir**, **être**, **faire** and **aller**, which are shown in full on page 71.

➤ Other irregular verbs include:

Verb	Meaning	je	tu	il/elle/on	nous	vous	ils/elles
devoir	to have to, must	devrai	devras	devra	devrons	devrez	devront
pouvoir	to be able to, can	pourrai	pourras	pourra	pourrons	pourrez	pourront
savoir	to know	saurai	sauras	saura	saurons	saurez	sauront
tenir	to hold	tiendrai	tiendras	tiendra	tiendrons	tiendrez	tiendront
venir	to come	viendrai	viendras	viendra	viendrons	viendrez	viendront
voir	to see	verrai	verras	verra	verrons	verrez	verront
vouloir	to want	voudrai	voudras	voudra	voudrons	voudrez	voudront

➤ **il faut** becomes **il faudra** (meaning *it will be necessary to*).

➤ **il pleut** becomes **il pleuvra** (meaning *it will rain*).

➤ This is the future tense of **avoir**:

Pronoun	avoir	Meaning: *to have*
j'	aurai	I will have
tu	auras	you will have
il, elle, on	aura	he/she/it/one will have
nous	aurons	we will have
vous	aurez	you will have
ils, elles	auront	they will have

➤ This is the future tense of **être**:

Pronoun	être	Meaning: *to be*
je	serai	I will be
tu	seras	you will be
il, elle, on	sera	he/she/it/one will be
nous	serons	we will be
vous	serez	you will be
ils, elles	seront	they will be

➤ This is the future tense of **faire**:

Pronoun	faire	Meaning: *to do, to make*
je	ferai	I will do/make
tu	feras	you will do/make
il, elle, on	fera	he/she/it/one will do/make
nous	ferons	we will do/make
vous	ferez	you will do/make
ils, elles	feront	they will do/make

➤ This is the future tense of **aller**:

Pronoun	aller	Meaning: *to go*
j '	irai	I will go
tu	iras	you will go
il, elle, on	ira	he/she/it/one will go
nous	irons	we will go
vous	irez	you will go
ils, elles	iront	they will go

⇨ For **Verb tables**, *see supplement.*

KEY POINTS

✔ You can use a present tense in French to talk about something that will happen or be true in the future, just as in English.

✔ You can use **aller** with an infinitive to refer to things that will happen in the immediate future.

✔ The stem is the same as the infinitive for **-er**, **-ir** and **-re** verbs, except that the final **-e** of **-re** verbs is lost.

✔ The future tense endings are the same for **-er**, **-ir** and **-re** verbs: **-ai**, **-as**, **-a**, **-ons**, **-ez**, **-ont**.

✔ In verbs ending in **-eler** and **-eter**: l → **ll** and **t** → **tt** throughout the future tense.

✔ In verbs ending in **-yer**: y → **i** throughout the future tense (optional in **-ayer** verbs).

✔ Some verbs are irregular in the future tense. It is worth learning these in full.

For further explanation of grammatical terms, please see pages x-xii.

Test yourself

70 **Replace the highlighted verb with a future tense. The first one has been done for you.**

   a Tu **peux** sortir avec nous? ...*pourras*...

   b Nous **venons** vous voir bientôt. ....

   c Je **nettoie** la cuisine, si tu as autre chose à faire. ....

   d Fin juillet elles **partent** en Floride. ....

   e Ils **déménagent** l'année prochaine. ....

   f Vous les **voyez** souvent? ....

   g Nous **réservons** une table pour demain soir. ....

   h Vous **arrivez** avant nous? ....

   i On **peut** réessayer la semaine prochaine. ....

   j Elle nous **envoie** les billets dans quelques jours. ....

71 **Fill the gap with the correct form of the future tense.**

   a Il n'y .... rien à faire. **(avoir)**

   b Nous .... chez nous à partir de midi. **(être)**

   c Tu penses que tu .... le faire? **(pouvoir)**

   d Ils .... besoin d'une voiture plus économique. **(avoir)**

   e Sa famille .... désolée. **(être)**

   f Je pense que demain il .... **(pleuvoir)**

   g Je crois que ça lui .... bien. **(plaire)**

   h Je te promets, je .... de mon mieux. **(faire)**

   i En hiver, il .... froid ici. **(faire)**

   j Enfin vous .... la vérité. **(savoir)**

72 **Match the consequence to the situation.**

   a Sarah et Paul passent une quinzaine de jours à Genève.   Je devrai travailler dur.

   b Je vais lui dire que tu dois partir.   Tu iras bientôt au lit.

   c Cet hôtel coûte très cher.   Ils y dépenseront beaucoup d'argent.

   d L'examen est très difficile.   Nous irons ailleurs.

   e Tu n'es pas sage.   Elle en sera désolée.

Test yourself

73 **Translate the sentences into French.**

a They'll be able to go swimming.

....

b I'll be able to go out with them on Tuesday.

....

c He'll have to do it again. ....

d The weather will be nice tomorrow.

....

e I'll send her an email. ....

f She'll get a text from her boss.

....

g I think it will hurt. ....

h Will the girls want to come with us?

....

i The doctor will see you this afternoon.

....

j Where will you be next week? (*Use **vous**.*)

....

74 **Fill the gap with the future tense of the most likely verb. The first one has been done for you.**

a Ils vont à Nice, il ....*fera*......... chaud là-bas.

b Si vous me le prêtez, je vous le .... demain.

c Si leur équipe perd le match, les supporters .... très déçus.

d Si je dois acheter tout ça j' .... besoin de plus d'argent.

e Si les filles voient cette grosse araignée, elles .... peur.

f Buvez plus d'eau, ça vous .... du bien.

g Tu as perdu ton chat? J'espère que tu le .... bientôt.

h C'est le meilleur joueur, il .... sûrement.

i Le grenier est en désordre, vous .... le ranger.

j Utilisez des mots plus simples, sinon ils ne vous .... pas.

Test yourself

75 **Fill the gap with the future, present or imperfect tense, as appropriate.**

a Nos amis .... demain matin. **(arriver)**

b Elle .... toujours avant les autres. **(arriver)**

c Si je gagne à la loterie, j'............................. une grande maison. **(acheter)**

d Je suis sûre que ça te .... du bien. **(faire)**

e À cette époque, beaucoup de gens ne .... pas lire. **(savoir)**

f Nous .... depuis une heure. **(attendre)**

g Quelle surprise! Nous ne .... pas à ça. **(s'attendre)**

h Ne vous inquiétez pas, votre voiture .... prête avant midi. **(être)**

i Je dois rentrer, sinon ma mère .... **(s'inquiéter)**

j Il faisait beau, tout le monde .... faire une promenade. **(vouloir)**

76 **Make a sentence with the elements given, putting the main verb into the future tense.**

a vous/avoir/les/demain/sans faute

....

b le voyage/coûter/lui/cher

....

c je ne suis pas sûr que/il/pouvoir/aller/y/l'année prochaine

....

d il y a du vent/le linge/sécher vite

....

e peut-être/vous/avoir besoin/en/demain

....

f sans doute/elle/parler/lui/en

....

g je/envoyer/lui/les/plus tard

....

h cette nouvelle/faire/leur/de la peine

....

i à cette heure/elle/être/déjà au lit

....

j les élèves/connaître/leurs résultats/dans trois semaines

....

Test yourself

77 **Match the person's character and their likely behaviour.**

a Elle est sportive.   Elle tiendra sa promesse.

b Elle est timide.   Elle nous posera beaucoup de questions.

c Elle est dépensière.   Elle participera au marathon.

d Elle est curieuse.   Elle ne dira rien.

e Elle est fiable.   Elle achètera plein de choses.

78 **Replace the highlighted verb with a future tense.**

a Tu **participes** au marathon?...

b Nous **partons** en vacances demain. ....

c Je te le **prête**, si tu veux. ....

d Elles **passent** une semaine chez nous. ....

e Ils se **marient** l'année prochaine..

f Vous m'**offrez** ce cadeau?...

g Nous **nettoyons** la maison avant son arrivée...

h Vous **venez** avec nous? ....

i Peut-être que ce monsieur **peut** vous aider...

j Elle me **rend** l'argent la semaine prochaine. ....

The conditional

What is the conditional?
The **conditional** is a verb form used to talk about things that would happen or that would be true under certain conditions, for example, I _would_ _help_ you if I could.
It is also used to say what you would like or need, for example, _Could_ you _give_ me the bill?

Using the conditional

➤ You can often recognize a conditional in English by the word _would_ or its shortened form _'d_.
  I _would_ be sad if you left.
  If you asked him, he'_d_ help you.

➤ You use the conditional for:

- asking for something formally and politely, especially in shops
  I'_d_ _like_ a kilo of pears, please.

- saying what you would like
  I'_d_ _like_ to go to the United States.

- making a suggestion
  I _could_ _come_ and pick you up.

- giving advice
  You _should_ _say_ you're sorry.

> _Tip_
> There is no direct French translation of _would_ in verb forms like _would be_, _would like_, _would help_ and so on. You change the French verb ending instead.

Forming the conditional

➤ To form the conditional in French, you have to use:

- the infinitive of **-er** and **-ir** verbs, for example, **donner-**, **finir-**

- the infinitive without the final **e** of **-re** verbs, for example, **attendr-**

➤ Then add the correct ending to the stem, depending on whether you are talking about **je**, **tu**, **il**, **elle**, **on**, **nous**, **vous**, **ils** or **elles**. The endings are the same for all verbs. They are the same as the **-er** and **-re** endings for the IMPERFECT TENSE, but the stem is the same as that of the FUTURE TENSE.

➪ _For more information on the **Imperfect tense** and the **Future tense**, see pages 57 and 67._

Pronoun	Ending	Add to stem, e.g. donner-, finir-, attendr-	Meanings
je (j')	-ais	je donner<u>ais</u> je finir<u>ais</u> j'attendr<u>ais</u>	I would give I would finish I would wait
tu	-ais	tu donner<u>ais</u> tu finir<u>ais</u> tu attendr<u>ais</u>	you would give you would finish you would wait
il elle on	-ait	il/elle/on donner<u>ait</u> il/elle/on finir<u>ait</u> il/elle/on attendr<u>ait</u>	he/she/it/one would give he/she/it/one would finish he/she/it/one would wait
nous	-ions	nous donner<u>ions</u> nous finir<u>ions</u> nous attendr<u>ions</u>	we would give we would finish we would wait
vous	-iez	vous donner<u>iez</u> vous finir<u>iez</u> vous attendr<u>iez</u>	you would give you would finish you would wait
ils elles	-aient	ils/elles donner<u>aient</u> ils/elles finir<u>aient</u> ils/elles attendr<u>aient</u>	they would give they would finish they would wait

J'<u>aim</u>erais aller aux États Unis.　　　　I'd like to go to the United States.

> *Tip*
> **je** changes to **j'** in front of a word starting with a vowel, most words starting with **h**, and the French word **y**.

ⓘ Note that you have to be careful not to mix up the future tense and the conditional. They look very similar.

FUTURE
je donnerai
je finirai
j'attendrai
j'aimerai
je voudrai
je viendrai
je serai

CONDITIONAL
je donnerais
je finirais
j'attendrais
j'aimerais
je voudrais
je viendrais
je serais

Spelling changes in -er verbs

➤ As with the future tense, a few **-er** verbs change their spellings slightly in the conditional. The forms with spelling changes have been <u>underlined</u> in the tables below.

➤ With verbs such as **appeler** (meaning *to call*), which end in **-eler**, the **l** doubles throughout the conditional. The double consonant (**ll**) affects the pronunciation of the word. In **appeler**, the first **e** sounds like the vowel sound at the end of the English word *teacher*, but in **appellerais** the first **e** sounds like the one in the English word *pet*.

For further explanation of grammatical terms, please see pages x–xii.

Pronoun	Example verb: appeler
j'	appellerais
tu	appellerais
il, elle, on	appellerait
nous	appellerions
vous	appelleriez
ils, elles	appelleraient

➤ The exceptions to this rule are **geler** (meaning *to freeze*) and **peler** (meaning *to peel*), which change in the same way as **lever** (*see page 30*).

➤ With verbs such as **jeter** (meaning *to throw*), which end in **-eter**, the **t** doubles throughout the conditional. The double consonant (**tt**) affects the pronunciation of the word. In **jeter**, the first **e** sounds like the vowel sound at the end of the English word *teacher*, but in **jetterais** the first **e** sounds like the one in the English word *pet*.

Pronoun	Example verb: jeter
je	jetterais
tu	jetterais
il, elle, on	jetterait
nous	jetterions
vous	jetteriez
ils, elles	jetteraient

➤ The exceptions to this rule include **acheter** (meaning *to buy*), which changes in the same way as **lever** (*see page 30*).

➤ With verbs such as **nettoyer** (meaning *to clean*), that end in **-yer**, the **y** changes to **i** throughout the conditional.

Pronoun	Example verb: nettoyer
je	nettoierais
tu	nettoierais
il, elle, on	nettoierait
nous	nettoierions
vous	nettoieriez
ils, elles	nettoieraient

➤ Verbs ending in **-ayer**, such as **payer** (meaning *to pay*) and **essayer** (meaning *to try*), can be spelled with either a **y** or an **i**. So **je paierais** and **je payerais**, for example, are both correct.

➤ With verbs such as **lever** (meaning *to raise*), **peser** (meaning *to weigh*) and **acheter** (meaning *to buy*), **e** changes to **è** throughout the conditional. In **lever** the first **e** sounds like the vowel sound at the end of the English word *teacher*, but in **lèverais** and so on the first **e** sounds like the one in the English word *pet*.

Pronoun	Example verb: lever
je	lèverais
tu	lèverais
il, elle, on	lèverait
nous	lèverions
vous	lèveriez
ils, elles	lèveraient

Reflexive verbs in the conditional

➤ The conditional of reflexive verbs is formed in just the same way as for ordinary verbs, except that you have to remember to give the reflexive pronoun (**me**, **te**, **se**, **nous**, **vous**, **se**).

Subject pronoun	Reflexive pronoun	Example with laver	Meaning
je	me (m')	laverais	I would wash
tu	te (t')	laverais	you would wash
il, elles, on	se (s')	laverait	he/she/it would wash
nous	nous	laverions	we would wash
vous	vous	laveriez	you would wash
ils, elles	se (s')	laveraient	they would wash

> *Tip*
> **me** changes to **m'**, **te** to **t'** and **se** to **s'** before a vowel, most words starting with **h** and the French word **y**.

Irregular verbs in the conditional

➤ The same verbs that are irregular in the future tense are irregular in the conditional, including: **avoir**, **être**, **faire**, **aller**, **devoir**, **pouvoir**, **savoir**, **tenir**, **venir**, **voir**, **vouloir**.

⇨ *For more information on **Irregular verbs in the future tense**, see page 70.*

➤ To form the conditional of an irregular verb, use the same stem as for the future tense, for example:

> avoir → **aur-**
> être → **ser-**

➤ Then add the usual endings for the conditional.

Infinitive	Future stem	Conditional endings	Conditional form
avoir	aur-	-ais, -ais, -ait, -ions, -iez, -aient	j'aur<u>ais</u>, tu aur<u>ais</u>, il/elle/on aur<u>ait</u>, nous aur<u>ions</u>, vous aur<u>iez</u>, ils/elles aur<u>aient</u>
être	ser-	-ais, -ais, -ait, -ions, -iez, -aient	je ser<u>ais</u>, tu ser<u>ais</u>, il/elle/on ser<u>ait</u>, nous ser<u>ions</u>, vous ser<u>iez</u>, ils/elles ser<u>aient</u>
faire	fer-	-ais, -ais, -ait, -ions, -iez, -aient	je fer<u>ais</u>, tu fer<u>ais</u>, il/elle/on fer<u>ait</u> nous fer<u>ions</u>, vous fer<u>iez</u>, ils/elles fer<u>aient</u>
aller	ir-	-ais, -ais, -ait, -ions, -iez, -aient	j'ir<u>ais</u>, tu ir<u>ais</u>, il/elle/on ir<u>ait</u>, nous ir<u>ions</u>, vous ir<u>iez</u>, ils/elles ir<u>aient</u>

J'<u>irais</u> si j'avais le temps.	I would go if I had time.
Je <u>voudrais</u> un kilo de poires, s'il vous plaît.	I'd like a kilo of pears, please.
Tu <u>devrais</u> t'excuser.	You should say you're sorry.

KEY POINTS

✔ The conditional endings are the same for **-er**, **-ir** and **-re** verbs:
 -ais, **-ais**, **-ait**, **-ions**, **-iez**, **-aient**.

✔ The conditional endings are the same as the endings for the imperfect tense of **-er** and **-re** verbs, but the stem is the same as the stem of the future tense.

✔ In verbs ending in **-eler** and **-eter**:
 l → **ll** and **t** → **tt** throughout the conditional.

✔ In verbs ending in **-yer**:
 y → **i** throughout the conditional (optional in **-ayer** verbs).

✔ The same verbs that are irregular in the future are irregular in the conditional. It is worth learning these in full.

Test yourself

79 **Cross out the unlikely items.**

a **On aurait besoin de ça au bureau:**   un ordinateur/une raquette/un téléphone/
une corbeille à papier

b **Les enfants aimeraient faire ça:**   nettoyer la cuisine/jouer au foot/se baigner/
attendre le bus

c **Mon chef m'offrirait ça:**   un conseil/une augmentation/un café/
de l'après-rasage

d **Ça serait agréable:**   une promenade/un voyage en Espagne/
un enterrement/un bon thé

e **Je voudrais y aller à pied:**   en Chine/au supermarché/à la maison/aux USA

f **Tu serais enchanté de voir ça:**   une aurore boréale/un chaton/un gros rat/
ses blessures

g **Vous trouveriez ça choquant:**   ses remarques racistes/ce musée/
leur pauvreté/la corruption là-bas

h **Nous devrions cesser de faire ça:**   aller en vacances/fumer/gaspiller de l'argent/
se parler

i **Nous devrions en faire des photos:**   de la poubelle/du paysage/de notre petite-fille/
du facteur/

j **Ça ferait mal:**   une piqûre d'abeille/une grosse bise/
une morsure de chien/une fracture

80 **Replace the highlighted verb with a conditional. The first one has been done for you.**

a Je **peux** les accompagner. ...*pourrais*...

b Tu **veux** y aller l'année prochaine? ....

c Mon collègue **doit** avoir le dossier. ....

d Vous **voulez** rester encore deux nuits? ....

e Mes amies en **seront** jalouses. ....

f Mon fils **veut** avoir un chien. ....

g Lequel est-ce que tu **choisis**? ....

h C'est délicat: je ne **sais** pas quoi dire. ....

i Je suis sûre qu'ils **feront** de leur mieux. ....

j Je lui **dirai** que ce n'est pas possible. ....

Test yourself

81 Translate the sentences into French. To translate 'if' use *si*. Use the imperfect for the past tense verb that goes with it. The first one has been done for you.

a If I had the time I'd go to the gym.

Si j'avais le temps, j'irais à la salle de sport.

....

b He'd laugh if you wore those trousers. (*Use* **tu**.)

....

....

c Make an omelette? That wouldn't take long.

....

....

d If they started now they'd finish this afternoon.

....

....

e You could do it if you made an effort. (*Use* **tu**.)

....

....

f We'd like to live here.

....

....

g She'd be astonished if her husband washed up.

....

....

h You ought to stay longer. (*Use* **vous**.)

....

....

i If it hurt she'd cry.

....

....

82 Fill the gap with the conditional of the most likely verb. The first one has been done for you.

a Marie est fatiguée, elle ......*aimerait*...... mieux rester à la maison.

b Si elle me demandait de le faire je le ....

c Je .... aller en Australie, mais le billet coûte trop cher.

d Il a des maux de tête terribles, il .... aller chez le médecin.

e Nous .... contents de vous voir.

f Ils gagnent beaucoup d'argent, ils .... acheter une maison plus grande.

g Si tu mangeais moins de fromage, tu .... du poids.

h Si elles devaient faire ça, elles .... peur.

i S'ils vous offraient cet emploi, vous l' ....?

j Si tu me demandais ça, je ne .... pas quoi dire.

Test yourself

83 **Match the related items.**

a	**Il est tard.**	Il te plairait.
b	**Ces chaussures sont trop petites.**	Tu ferais mieux d'arrêter de fumer.
c	**Tu détestes ton travail?**	Tu pourrais essayer celles-ci.
d	**Tu as mal à la gorge?**	Tu devrais aller au lit.
e	**C'est un bon film.**	À ta place j'en chercherais un autre.

84 **Translate the sentences into French.**

a Perhaps they could try again tomorrow.

....

b It would hurt a lot.

....

c It would be a pity if he couldn't come.

....

d Would you expect that? (*Use **vous**.*)

....

e My parents would worry.

....

f We'd come if we could.

....

g She'd choose the most expensive menu.

....

h If we started today we'd finish on Thursday. (*Use **on**.*)

....

i There'd be more people here if it was fine.

....

j They would find this book boring.

....

Test yourself

85 **Replace the highlighted negative verb with an opposite verb, thus expressing the same meaning. The first one has been done for you.**

a Ils **n'aimeraient pas** ça. ...*détesteraient*...

b Je **n'accepterais pas** une telle proposition. ....

c Elle **ne jetterait pas** cette lettre. ....

d Nous **ne nous amuserions pas** à la campagne. ....

e Tu **ne laisserais pas** le chauffage. ....

f Il **n'augmenterait pas** leurs salaires. ....

g Avec ce régime **vous ne perdriez pas** du poids. ....

h Elles **n'écouteraient pas** vos conseils. ....

i S'ils prenaient ces mesures, les taux d'intérêt **ne monteraient pas**. ....

j Ça **ne renforcerait pas** ses arguments. ....

86 **Replace the highlighted verb with a conditional.**

a Je **veux** venir avec vous. ....

b Tu **dois** le faire tout de suite. ....

c Mon père **peut** nous donner des conseils. ....

d Nous **voulons** aller au cinéma demain soir. ....

e Ma femme **sera** enchantée de faire votre connaissance. ....

f Les employés **veulent** une augmentation de salaire. ....

g Qu'est-ce que vous nous **proposez**? ....

h Ils ne **savent** pas quoi dire. ....

i Ça ne **fait** aucune différence. ....

j Je n'**ose** pas le faire. ....

The perfect tense

> ## What is the perfect tense?
> The **perfect** is one of the verb tenses used in French to talk about the past, especially about actions that took place and were completed in the past.

Using the perfect tense

➤ In English there are two types of past tense: _I gave_, _I finished_, and _I have given_, _I have finished_. Both types are translated by the French perfect.

> _Tip_
> The perfect tense is the tense you will need most to talk about things that have happened or were true in the past. It is used to talk about actions that took place and <u>WERE COMPLETED</u> in the past.
> Use the <u>imperfect tense</u> for regular events and in most descriptions.
>
> ⇨ _For more information on the **Imperfect tense**, see page 57._

Forming the perfect tense

➤ The imperfect, future and conditional tenses in French are made up of just <u>one</u> word, for example, **je donnais**, **tu finira** or **il attendrait**. The perfect tense has <u>TWO</u> parts to it:

- the <u>present</u> tense of the verb **avoir** (meaning _to have_) or **être** (meaning _to be_)

- a part of the main verb called the <u>past participle</u>, such as _given_, _finished_ and _done_ in English

➤ In other words, the perfect tense in French is like the form _I have done_ in English.

⇨ _For more information on forming the present tense of **avoir** and **être**, see page 36._

Forming the past participle

➤ To form the past participle of regular verbs, you use the <u>infinitive</u> of the verb:

- For **-er** verbs, you replace the **-er** at the end of the infinitive with **-é**.

Infinitive	Take off -er	Add -é
donner (_to give_)	donn-	donn<u>é</u>
tomber (_to fall_)	tomb-	tomb<u>é</u>

For further explanation of grammatical terms, please see pages x-xii.

- For **-ir** verbs, you replace the **-ir** at the end of the infinitive with **-i**.

Infinitive	Take off -ir	Add -i
finir (*to finish*)	**fin-**	**fini**
partir (*to leave, to go*)	**part-**	**parti**

- For **-re** verbs, you replace the **-re** at the end of the infinitive with **-u**.

Infinitive	Take off -re	Add -u
attendre (*to wait*)	**attend-**	**attendu**
descendre (*to go down, to come down, to get off*)	**descend-**	**descendu**

Verbs that form their perfect tense with avoir

➤ Most verbs form their perfect tense with **avoir**, for example **donner**:

Pronoun	avoir	Past participle	Meaning
j'	ai	donné	I gave I have given
tu	as	donné	you gave you have given
il, elle, on	a	donné	he/she/it/one gave he/she/it/one has given
nous	avons	donné	we gave we have given
vous	avez	donné	you gave you have given
ils, elles	ont	donné	they gave they have given

Elle <u>a donné</u> son numéro de téléphone à Claude.	She gave Claude her phone number.
Il <u>a acheté</u> un ordinateur.	He's bought a computer.
Je n'<u>ai</u> pas <u>regardé</u> la télé hier.	I didn't watch TV yesterday.

> *Tip*
> **je** changes to **j'** in front of a word starting with a vowel, most words starting with **h**, and the French word **y**.

➤ The perfect tense of **-ir** verbs like **finir** is formed in the same way, except for the different ending of the past participle: **j'ai fini**, **tu as fini** and so on.

➤ The perfect tense of **-re** verbs like **attendre** is formed in the same way, except for the past participle: **j'ai attendu**, **tu as attendu** and so on.

avoir or être?

➤ <u>MOST</u> verbs form their perfect tense with **avoir**; these include **donner** as shown on page 87.

➤ There are two main groups of verbs which form their perfect tense with **être** instead of **avoir**:

- all reflexive verbs

⇨ *For more information on **Reflexive verbs**, see page 50.*

- a group of verbs that are mainly used to talk about movement or a change of some kind, including these ones:

aller	to go
venir	to come
arriver	to arrive, to happen
partir	to leave, to go
descendre	to go down, to come down, to get off
monter	to go up, to come up
entrer	to go in, to come in
sortir	to go out, to come out
mourir	to die
naître	to be born
devenir	to become
rester	to stay
tomber	to fall

Je <u>suis allé</u> au match de football hier.	I went to the football match yesterday.
Il <u>est sorti</u> acheter un journal.	He's gone out to buy a newspaper.
Vous <u>êtes descendu</u> à quelle station?	Which station did you get off at?

Grammar Extra!
Some of the verbs on the previous page take **avoir** when they are used with a direct object, for example:

descendre quelque chose	to get something down, to bring something down, to take something down
monter quelque chose	to go up something, to come up something
sortir quelque chose	to take something out
Est-ce que tu <u>as descendu</u> les bagages?	Did you bring the bags down?
Elle <u>a monté</u> les escaliers.	She went up the stairs.
Elle <u>a sorti</u> son porte-monnaie de son sac.	She took her purse out of her handbag.

Verbs that form their perfect tense with être

➤ When a verb takes **être**, the past participle ALWAYS agrees with the subject of the verb; that is, the endings change in the feminine and plural forms.

	Masculine endings	Examples	Feminine endings	Examples
Singular	-	tombé parti descendu	-e	tombée partie descendue
Plural	-s	tombés partis descendus	-es	tombées parties descendues

Est-ce ton frère est <u>allé</u> à l'étranger?	Did your brother go abroad?
Elle est <u>venue</u> avec nous.	She came with us.
Ils sont <u>partis</u> à six heures.	They left at six o'clock.
Mes cousines sont <u>arrivées</u> hier.	My cousins arrived yesterday. (*The cousins are female.*)

➤ Here are the perfect tense forms of **tomber** in full:

Pronoun	avoir	Past participle	Meaning
je	suis	**tombé** (*masculine*) **tombée** (*feminine*)	I fell/I have fallen
tu	es	**tombé** (*masculine*) **tombée** (*feminine*)	you fell/ you have fallen
il	est	**tombé**	he/it fell, he/it has fallen
elle	est	**tombée**	she/it fell, she/it has fallen
on	est	**tombé** (*singular*) **tombés** (*masculine plural*) **tombées** (*feminine plural*)	one fell/ one has fallen, we fell/ we have fallen
nous	sommes	**tombés** (*masculine*) **tombées** (*feminine*)	we fell/ we have fallen
vous	êtes	**tombé** (*masculine singular*) **tombée** (*feminine singular*) **tombés** (*masculine plural*) **tombées** (*feminine plural*)	you fell/ you have fallen
ils	sont	**tombés**	they fell/ they have fallen
elles	sont	**tombées**	they fell/ they have fallen

Grammar Extra!

When the subject of the sentence is masculine and feminine, such as Marcel et Marie, the past participle has a masculine plural ending.

Marcel et Marie sont <u>tombés</u> amoureux.	Marcel and Marie fell in love.

➤ The perfect tense of **-ir** verbs like **partir** is formed in the same way, except for the past participle: **je suis parti(e)**, **tu es parti(e)** and so on.

➤ The perfect tense of **-re** verbs like **descendre** is formed in the same way, except for the past participle: **je suis descendu(e)**, **tu es descendu(e)** and so on.

Grammar Extra!

When a verb takes **avoir**, the past participle usually stays in the masculine singular form, as shown in the table for **donner**, and does not change for the feminine or plural forms.

Il a <u>fini</u> sa dissertation.	He's finished his essay.
Elles ont <u>fini</u> leur dissertation.	They've finished their essay.

In one particular case, however, the past participle of verbs with **avoir** does change in the feminine and plural forms. In the sentences above, **dissertation** is the direct object of the verb **finir**. When the direct object comes <u>AFTER</u> the verb, as it does in the examples above, then the past participle doesn't change. If the direct object comes <u>BEFORE</u> the verb, however, the past participle has to change to agree with that direct object.

<u>la</u> **dissertation qu'il a fin<u>ie</u> hier**	the essay that he finished yesterday
<u>la</u> **dissertation qu'elles ont fin<u>ie</u> hier**	the essay that they finished yesterday

Since object pronouns usually come BEFORE the verb, the past participle changes to agree with the pronoun.

Il a bu son thé? — Oui, il <u>l'a</u> <u>bu</u>.	Did he drink his tea? — Yes, he's drunk it.
Il a bu sa limonade? — Oui, il <u>l'a</u> <u>bue</u>.	Did he drink his lemonade? — Yes, he's drunk it.

> *Tip*
>
> Remember that with verbs taking **être**, it is the <u>subject</u> of the verb that tells you what ending to add to the past participle. Compare this with the rule for verbs taking **avoir** that have a direct object; in their case, it is the <u>direct object</u> coming before the verb that tells you what ending to add to the past participle.

For further explanation of grammatical terms, please see pages x–xii.

The perfect tense of reflexive verbs

➤ Here is the perfect tense of the reflexive verb **se laver** (meaning *to wash (oneself)*, *to have a wash*, *to get washed*) in full. Remember that all reflexive verbs take **être**, and so the past participle of reflexive verbs usually agrees with the subject of the sentence.

Subject pronoun	Reflexive pronoun	Present tense of être	Past participle	Meaning
je	me	suis	**lavé** (*masculine*) **lavée** (*feminine*)	I washed myself
tu	t'	es	**lavé** (*masculine*) **lavée** (*feminine*)	you washed yourself
il	s'	est	**lavé**	he washed himself
elle	s'	est	**lavée**	she washed herself
on	s'	est	**lavé** (*singular*) **lavés** (*masculine plural*) **lavées** (*feminine plural*)	one washed oneself we washed ourselves
nous	nous	sommes	**lavés** (*masculine*) **lavées** (*feminine*)	we washed ourselves
vous	vous	êtes	**lavé** (*masculine singular*) **lavée** (*feminine singular*) **lavés** (*masculine plural*) **lavées** (*feminine plural*)	you washed yourself (*singular*) you washed yourselves (*plural*)
ils	se	sont	**lavés**	they washed themselves
elles	se	sont	**lavées**	they washed themselves

Tip

When **on** means *we*, and masculine and feminine are involved, the past participle has a masculine ending. You can use either the masculine singular or the masculine plural.

On s'est déjà lavé.
On s'est déjà lavés.　　　We've already washed.

Grammar Extra!
The past participle of reflexive verbs <u>DOES NOT</u> change if the direct object
(**la jambe** in the example below) <u>FOLLOWS</u> the verb.

Elle s'<u>est cassé</u> la jambe.   She's broken her leg.

Irregular verbs in the perfect tense

➤ Some past participles are irregular. There aren't too many, so try to learn them.

avoir (meaning *to have*)	→**eu**
devoir (meaning *to have to, must*)	→**dû**
dire (meaning *to say, to tell*)	→**dit**
être (meaning *to be*)	→**été**
faire (meaning *to do, to make*)	→**fait**
mettre (meaning *to put*)	→**mis**
pouvoir (meaning *to be able to, can*)	→**pu**
prendre (meaning *to take*)	→**pris**
savoir (meaning *to know*)	→**su**
tenir (meaning *to hold*)	→**tenu**
venir (meaning *to come*)	→**venu**
voir (meaning *to see*)	→**vu**
vouloir (meaning *to want*)	→**voulu**

➤ **il pleut** becomes **il a plu** (*it rained*).

➤ **il faut** becomes **il a fallu** (*it was necessary*).

KEY POINTS
✔ The perfect tense describes things that happened and were completed in the past. It is not used for things that happened regularly or in descriptions.
✔ The perfect tense is formed with the present tense of **avoir** or **être** and a past participle.
✔ Most verbs take **avoir** in the perfect tense. All reflexive verbs and a small group of verbs referring to movement or change take **être**.
✔ The past participle ends in **-é** for **-er** verbs, in **-i** for **-ir** verbs, and in **-u** for **-re** verbs.
✔ With verbs that take **avoir**, the past participle does not usually change. With verbs that take **être**, including reflexive verbs, the past participle changes in the feminine and plural.

Test yourself

87 **Fill the gap with the correct form of the past participle of the verb. The first one has been done for you.**

a Mes parents sont ....*allés*........... au concert hier soir. **(aller)**

b Mon grand-père est .... dans l'escalier. **(tomber)**

c Nous avons .... dix kilomètres à pied. **(faire)**

d Paul a .... le chien avant d'aller à l'école. **(sortir)**

e Toutes mes amies sont .... à Paris. **(rentrer)**

f Nous avons .... 4-1. **(gagner)**

g J'ai fait tout ce que j'ai .... **(pouvoir)**

h Notre fille est .... en 2009. **(naître)**

i Alice et Aurélie sont .... ensemble. **(partir)**

j Combien ont-ils .... le travail? **(payer)**

88 **Replace the highlighted present tense with the perfect tense. The first one has been done for you.**

a **Nous rendons** l'argent dès que possible. ..*Nous avons rendu*.....................

b Où est-ce que tu **apprends** le français? ....

c Nos voisins **achètent** une nouvelle voiture. ....

d Ils **prennent** le train de 7h. ....

e Ses cousins **viennent** le voir ce matin. ....

f Tu **t'entends** avec tes collègues, Chantal? ....

g Elle **m'envoie** un SMS de temps en temps. ....

h Alain et Marc **rentrent** ensemble. ....

i Il **faut** faire attention. ....

j Tu lui **écris** une carte? ....

89 **Match the answer to the question.**

a **Tu vas ranger ta chambre?**   Je sais: je lui ai acheté des fleurs.

b **Demain, c'est l'anniversaire de Catherine.**   Oui, j'ai regardé un film à la télévision.

c **Tu t'es couchée tard hier soir, Marie?**   Non, le sol est sec.

d **Il vous a demandé un conseil?**   Non, je l'ai déjà fait.

e **Il a plu pendant la nuit?**   Non, il est très sûr de lui.

Test yourself

90 Translate the sentences into French.

a She gave him her address.

....

b I've had a nice surprise.

....

c We lost 2–1.

....

d We had a walk in the park.

....

e She's gone out with Richard.

....

f He took the bin out last night.

....

g He finished his book before going to bed.

....

h We saw an accident on the motorway.

....

i Claire has lost her mobile phone.

....

j The cost of living has gone up.

....

Test yourself

91 As in English, past participles can be used in French as adjectives. Make an adjective from the verb given, making it agree with its noun in the usual way. The first one has been done for you.

a Les fenêtres sont ......*ouvertes*...... . (**ouvrir**)

b Les travaux seront .... fin juillet. (**finir**)

c La porte est .... (**fermer**)

d Il a le bras .... (**casser**)

e On a retrouvé les clés .... (**perdre**)

f La viande était trop .... (**cuire**)

g C'est un acteur .... (**connaître**)

h Heureusement le revolver n'était pas .... (**charger**)

i Je passerai te prendre à huit heures, c'est .... (**entendre**)

j Elles sont toujours très bien .... (**habiller**)

92 Make the perfect tense by filling the gap with the correct form of *avoir* or *être*.

a Est-ce que je vous .... donné mon adresse?

b Elle .... morte en 2009.

c Ils .... envoyé des e-mails à tous leurs employés.

d Ma mère .... sorti le chien avant d'aller au travail.

e Mon frère .... sorti avec ses copains.

f Je .... déjà allée à Paris.

g Nous .... eu les mains gelées.

h J'aime tous ses romans, je les .... tous lus.

i Vous vous .... levés très tôt ce matin.

j Vous les .... vus hier?

93 Match the two halves of the sentence.

a Il est sorti	le chien.
b Il a sorti	les pires.
c Il nous a promis	ses photos.
d Il nous a donné	de l'hôpital.
e Il nous a montré	de l'aide.

Test yourself

94 **Translate the sentences, using the perfect or the imperfect, as appropriate.**

a I liked her last film.

....

b In those days I liked fast cars.

....

c They often went to this restaurant.

....

d The girls went to the gym this morning.

....

e We ate outside because the weather was nice.

....

f She earned more money when she was in London.

....

g Our team won last night.

....

h You always wore jeans.(*Use tu*.)

....

i I wore this shirt yesterday.

....

j When he said that everyone laughed.

....

95 **Replace the highlighted present tense with the perfect tense.**

a **Je rends** visite à des amis à Perpignan en mai. ....

b Où est-ce que tu **passes** tes vacances? ....

c Nos voisins **déménagent** à la mi-juin. ....

d Ça **prend** cinq minutes à préparer. ....

e Marlène **vient** me voir ce matin. ....

f Vous **vous amusez** au club, les enfants? ....

g Elle **m'écrit** de longs e-mails. ....

h Elles **descendent** au terminus. ....

i Qu'est-ce qui **se passe**? ....

j Tu **mets** le couvert? ....

Grammar Extra!

The pluperfect tense

What is the pluperfect tense?
The **pluperfect** is a verb tense which describes something that <u>had</u> happened or <u>had</u> been true at a point in the past, for example, *I'd forgotten to finish my homework*.

Using the pluperfect tense

➤ Examples of the pluperfect tense in English are *I had arrived*, *you'd fallen*.

Elle <u>avait essayé</u> des douzaines de pulls.	She <u>had tried on</u> dozens of jumpers.
Nous <u>avions</u> déjà <u>commencé</u> à manger quand il est arrivé.	We<u>'d</u> already <u>started</u> eating when he arrived.
J'<u>étais arrivée</u> la première.	I <u>had arrived</u> first.
Mes parents <u>s'étaient couchés</u> tôt.	My parents <u>had gone</u> to bed early.

Forming the pluperfect tense

➤ Like the perfect tense, the pluperfect tense in French has <u>two</u> parts to it:

- the <u>imperfect</u> tense of the verb **avoir** (meaning *to have*) or **être** (meaning *to be*)

- the past participle

➤ If a verb takes **avoir** in the perfect tense, then it will take **avoir** in the pluperfect too. If a verb takes **être** in the perfect, then it will take **être** in the pluperfect too.

⇨ *For more information on the **Imperfect tense** and the **Perfect tense**, see pages 57 and 86.*

Verbs taking avoir

➤ Here are the pluperfect tense forms of **donner** (meaning *to give*) in full.

Pronoun	avoir	Past participle	Meaning
j'	avais	donné	I had given
tu	avais	donné	you had given
il, elle, on	avait	donné	he/she/it/one had given
nous	avions	donné	we had given
vous	aviez	donné	you had given
ils, elles	avaient	donné	they had given

➤ The pluperfect tense of **-ir** verbs like **finir** (meaning *to finish*) is formed in the same way, except for the ending of the past participle: **j'avais fini**, **tu avais fini** and so on.

➤ The pluperfect tense of **-re** verbs like **attendre** (meaning *to wait*) is formed in the same way, except for the past participle: **j'avais attendu**, **tu avais attendu** and so on.

Verbs taking être

➤ Here are the pluperfect tense forms of **tomber** (meaning *to fall*) in full. When a verb takes **être** in the pluperfect tense, the past participle <u>always</u> agrees with the subject of the verb; that is, the endings change in the feminine and plural forms.

Pronoun	être	Past participle	Meaning
j'	étais	**tombé** (*masculine*) **tombée** (*feminine*)	I had fallen
tu	étais	**tombé** (*masculine*) **tombée** (*feminine*)	you had fallen
il	était	**tombé**	he/it had fallen
elle	était	**tombée**	she/it had fallen
on	était	**tombé** (*singular*) **tombés** (*masculine plural*) **tombées** (*feminine plural*)	one had fallen we had fallen
nous	étions	**tombés** (*masculine*) **tombées** (*feminine*)	we had fallen
vous	étiez	**tombé** (*masculine singular*) **tombée** (*feminine singular*) **tombés** (*masculine plural*) **tombées** (*feminine plural*)	you had fallen
ils	étaient	**tombés**	they had fallen
elles	étaient	**tombées**	they had fallen

➤ The pluperfect tense of **-ir** verbs like **partir** (meaning *to leave*, *to go*) is formed in the same way, except for the past participle: **j'étais parti(e)**, **tu étais parti(e)** and so on.

➤ The pluperfect tense of **-re** verbs like **descendre** (meaning *to come down*, *to go down*, *to get off*) is formed in the same way, except for the past participle: **j'étais descendu(e)**, **tu étais descendu(e)** and so on.

> *Tip*
> When **on** means *we*, the past participle can agree with the subject of the sentence, but it is optional.
>
> **On était <u>tombées</u>.**   We had fallen. (*feminine*)

Reflexive verbs in the pluperfect tense

➤ Reflexive verbs in the pluperfect tense are formed in the same way as in the perfect tense, but with the imperfect tense of the verb **être** (*see page* 61).

⇨ *For more information on the **Perfect tense of reflexive verbs,** see page* 91.

Irregular verbs in the pluperfect tense

➤ Irregular past participles are the same as for the perfect tense (*see page* 92).

KEY POINTS

✔ The pluperfect tense describes things that had happened or were true at a point in the past before something else happened.

✔ It is formed with the imperfect tense of **avoir** or **être** and the past participle.

✔ The rules for agreement of the past participle are the same as for the perfect tense.

Test yourself

96 **Match the connected sentences.**

a Il n'y avait plus personne.   J'avais dû longtemps attendre le bus.

b Elle était extrêmement pâle.   Il avait oublié son parapluie.

c Il s'est mouillé.   Leur équipe avait gagné.

d J'étais de mauvaise humeur. Tout le monde était parti.

e Les supporters étaient très contents. Elle avait eu un choc.

97 **Fill the gap with the correct form of the pluperfect. The first one has been done for you.**

a Elle ……*avait retrouvé*…… son portable sous le canapé. **(retrouver)**

b Nous ……………………………… très tard parce que nous avions eu des invités. **(se coucher)**

c Avant cette dispute, nous …………………………… . **(s'entendre)**

d Quand j'ai allumé la télévision, le match …………………………… . **(commencer)**

e Les enfants ……………………………… avant le déjeuner. **(se baigner)**

f Nous ……………………………… avoir un enfant. **(vouloir)**

g Vous ……………………………… sur Internet avant d'acheter les billets? **(regarder)**

h Ils étaient déçus: ils …………………………… à quelque chose de meilleur. **(s'attendre)**

i Si j'…………………………… l'argent, j'y serais allé. **(avoir)**

j On lui …………………………… une augmentation de salaire mais elle est partie quand même . **(donner)**

98 **Fill the gap with a past participle and an appropriate verb. The first one has been done for you.**

a Si tu t'étais ……*couché*…… plus tôt, tu aurais été moins fatigué le lendemain.

b Si vous m'aviez …………………………… au mariage, j'aurais accepté avec plaisir.

c S'il avait …………………………… ce médicament, il serait guéri.

d Si tu étais …………………………… à la maison, ma chérie, tu n'aurais pas dépensé tout ton argent.

e L'accident n'aurait pas eu lieu si le conducteur n'avait pas …………………………… si vite.

f Je n'aurais pas pris l'argent – si je n'en avais pas …………………………… vraiment besoin.

g Je serais venu avec vous, si vous m'aviez …………………………… quelques minutes.

h Si seulement ils m'avaient …………………………… un e-mail, j'aurais été au courant.

i Si elle avait …………………………… le vase, elle en aurait racheté un autre.

j Si j'y étais …………………………… à pied, je serais arrivé trop tard.

Test yourself

99 **Translate the sentences into French. If you use *déjà* put it between the two parts of the verb.**

a They'd quarrelled before the party.

....

b He'd made an effort.

....

c He'd already read a hundred pages.

....

d I'd felt ill the day before.

....

e She had wondered if it was a good idea.

....

f Had you already decided before the meeting?

....

g My boss had already talked to me about it.

....

h I'd seen the film before reading the book.

....

i She'd noticed him at the swimming pool.

....

j They had waited a very long time.

....

Test yourself

100 Make a pluperfect in each sentence by filling the gap with the correct form of *avoir* or *être*.

a Les enfants .... ouvert tous leurs cadeaux de Noël.

b Quand je suis arrivée, elle .... déjà partie.

c On lui .... offert un poste de secrétaire.

d Comme elle était malade je lui .... monté son dîner.

e Il était déjà une heure, et vous n' .... pas encore arrivés.

f Elle était mécontente parce que je n' .... pas répondu à son invitation.

g Je pensais que ces événements s' .... passés en 2010.

h Avant de nous marier nous .... vécu ensemble pendant dix ans.

i Tu pensais que j' .... sortie sans toi?

j Je savais qu'elle .... restée célibataire.

101 Fill the gap with the pluperfect form of the most likely verb. The first one has been done for you.

a C'était mon anniversaire. Il m' *avait acheté* des fleurs.

b Je suis arrivée à l'heure. J' .... un taxi.

c Nous savions que vous .... malade.

d Maintenant elle avait les cheveux blonds. Elle .... chez le coiffeur.

e Le jour du mariage notre voiture était tout propre. Nous l' ....

f Je ne voulais plus être architecte. J' .... d'avis.

g Tu étais très maigre. Tu .... du poids.

h Ils n'étaient pas chez eux. Ils .... en vacances.

i Elle pleurait. Elle .... son vase favori.

j J'étais contente. Le chef m' .... une augmentation de salaire.

102 Match the two parts of the sentence.

a Avant de se faire opérer — il avait sorti les poubelles.

b Avant de participer au marathon — il en avait discuté avec sa copine.

c Avant de donner sa démission — il avait fait son testament.

d Avant d'aller au lit — il avait eu de gros problèmes financiers.

e Avant de gagner à la loterie — il s'était entraîné.

Test yourself

103 **To introduce something you know or are sure of, you can use *savoir que* or *être sûr que*. Use one of these when translating the sentences. The first one has been done for you.**

   a I knew that he had lost his job.

   Je savais qu'il avait perdu son emploi. ....

   b They knew she had stolen the money.

   ....

   c We knew they'd got married.

   ....

   d I was sure the girls had gone out before me.

   ....

   e He knew she had become a Buddhist.

   ....

   f I was sure I'd locked the door.

   ....

   g We knew our neighbours had quarrelled.

   ....

   h I knew she'd fallen down the stairs.

   ....

   i I was sure all this had happened a long time ago.

   ....

   j They were sure we'd gone mad.

   ....

Test yourself

104 Fill the gap with the correct form of the pluperfect.

  a Malheureusement elle .... son appareil photo à la maison. **(oublier)**

  b Nous .... très tôt pour aller à l'aéroport. **(se lever)**

  c Je .... à quelque chose de meilleur. **(s'attendre)**

  d Mes amis .... quand je suis arrivée. **(partir)**

  e Nous les .... avant notre départ. **(appeler)**

  f Enfant, il .... être médecin, comme son père. **(vouloir)**

  g Vous l' .... avant de l'acheter? **(essayer)**

  h Ils sont arrivés avec deux heures de retard: leur voiture .... en panne.
  (tomber)

  i Si j' .... je serais venue te voir. **(savoir)**

  j Elle m' .... la vérité juste avant sa mort. **(dire)**

The passive

What is the passive?
The **passive** is a form of the verb that is used when the subject of the verb is the person or thing that is affected by the action, for example, *I was given, we were told, it had been made.*

Using the passive

➤ In a normal, or *active*, sentence, the 'subject' of the verb is the person or thing that carries out the action described by the verb. The 'object' of the verb is the person or thing that the verb 'happens' to.

  Ryan *(subject)* hit *(active verb)* me *(object).*

➤ In English, as in French, you can turn an <u>active</u> sentence round to make a <u>passive</u> sentence.

  I *(subject)* was hit *(passive verb)* by Ryan *(agent).*

➤ Very often, however, you cannot identify who is carrying out the action indicated by the verb.

  I was hit in the face.
  The trees will be chopped down.
  I've been chosen to represent the school.

> *Tip*
> There is a very important difference between French and English in sentences containing an <u>indirect object</u>. In English we can quite easily turn a normal (active) sentence with an indirect object into a passive sentence.
>
> **Active**
> Someone *(subject)* gave *(active verb)* me *(indirect object)* a book *(direct object).*
>
> **Passive**
> I *(subject)* was given *(passive verb)* a book *(direct object).*
> In French, an indirect object can <u>NEVER</u> become the subject of a passive verb.

Forming the passive

➤ In English we use the verb *to be* with the past participle (*was hit, was given*) to form the passive. In French the passive is formed in exactly the same way, using **être** and the past participle. The past participle agrees with the subject of the passive verb; that is, the endings change in the feminine and plural forms.

Elle <u>est encouragée</u> par ses parents.	She is encouraged by her parents.
Vous <u>êtes</u> tous bien <u>payés</u>.	You are all well paid. (*'you' here is plural and refers to men, or men and women*)
Les portes <u>ont été fermées</u>.	The doors have been closed.

  ⇨ *For more information on the **Past participle**, see pages 86–87.*

➤ Here is the present tense of the **-er** verb **aimer** (meaning *to like, to love*) in its passive form.

Pronoun	Present tense of être	Past participle	Meaning
je	suis	aimé (*masculine*) aimée (*feminine*)	I am loved
tu	es	aimé (*masculine*) aimée (*feminine*)	you are loved
il	est	aimé	he/it is loved
elle	est	aimée	she/it is loved
on	est	aimé (*singular*) aimés (*masculine plural*) aimées (*feminine plural*)	one is loved we are loved
nous	sommes	aimés (*masculine*) aimées (*feminine*)	we are loved
vous	êtes	aimé (*masculine singular*) aimée (*feminine singular*) aimés (*masculine plural*) aimées (*feminine plural*)	you are loved
ils	sont	aimés	they are loved
elles	sont	aimées	they are loved

➤ The passive of **-ir** verbs is formed in the same way, except that the past participle is different. For example, **elle est remplie** (meaning *it is full*).

➤ The passive of **-re** verbs is formed in the same way, except that the past participle is different. For example, **il est défendu** (meaning *it is forbidden*).

Grammar Extra!
When **on** means *we*, the past participle can agree with the subject of the sentence, but it is optional.

On est <u>aimés</u> de tout le monde.　　　We're loved by everyone. (*masculine*)

➤ You can form other tenses of the passive by changing the tense of the verb **être**.
   Imperfect: **j'étais aimé(e)** I was loved
   Future: **tu seras aimé(e)** you will be loved
   Perfect: **il a été aimé** he was loved

   ⇨ *For more information on the **Imperfect**, **future** and **perfect tenses**, see pages 57, 67 and 86.*

➤ Irregular past participles are the same as for the perfect tense (*see page 92*).

Avoiding the passive

➤ Passives are not as common in French as in English. There are <u>two</u> main ways that French speakers express the same idea.

- by using the pronoun **on** (meaning *someone* or *they*) with a normal, active verb

<u>On</u> leur a envoyé une lettre.	They were sent a letter. (*literally: Someone sent them a letter*.)
<u>On</u> m'a dit que tu ne venais pas.	I was told that you weren't coming. (*literally: They told me you weren't coming*.)

- by using a reflexive verb

Les melons <u>se vendent</u> 2 euros la pièce.	Melons are sold for 2 euros each.

⇨ *For more information on* **Reflexive verbs**, *see page* 50.

KEY POINTS

✔ The present tense of the passive is formed by using the present tense of **être** with the past participle.
✔ The past participle always agrees with the subject of the passive verb.
✔ You can sometimes avoid a passive construction by using a reflexive verb or the pronoun **on**.

105 Cross out the unlikely items.

a L'église a été détruite   pendant la guerre./sur ordre du roi./hier soir./ il y a cinquante ans.

b Le nouvel aéroport sera inauguré   en 2009./en 2015./l'année prochaine./ par le président.

c Chantal a été choisie   comme porte-parole./pour l'équipe./ accidentellement./comme chef.

d Les frais seront payés   la semaine dernière./par l'entreprise./ à la fin du mois./par l'employeur.

e Elle était félicitée   par toutes ses amies./sévèrement./ par son professeur./par habitude.

f Ce poème a été écrit   par Victor Hugo./il y a deux cent ans./ quand il avait 18 ans./par hasard.

g Les journaux sont vendus   dans les supermarchés./dans les pharmacies./ dans les offices du tourisme./dans les bibliothèques.

h Les épinards se mangent   avec du sucre./avec du beurre./cuits ou crus./ en dessert.

i On m'a volé mon portefeuille   dans le métro./à Londres./mardi prochain./ la semaine dernière.

j Vous êtes critiquée   par vos admirateurs./par la presse./ pour ces remarques./pour vos bonnes actions.

106 Fill the gap with the correct form of the past participle. The first one has been done for you.

a Cet hôpital a été ....*construit*.......... par les moines. **(construire)**

b Son nouveau roman sera .... par des milliers de personnes. **(lire)**

c Les tapisseries étaient .... à Bruxelles. **(faire)**

d Les contrefaçons sont .... en ligne. **(vendre)**

e Ce sont des émissions .... des enfants. **(adorer)**

f Cet homme est .... par la police. **(rechercher)**

g Le rapport a été .... par ses collaborateurs. **(écrire)**

h Trois soldats ont été .... **(blesser)**

i Ce chanteur est .... dans le monde entier. **(connaître)**

j Le mur de Berlin a été .... en 1989. **(détruire)**

Test yourself

107 Translate the sentences into French.

a They had been warned.

....

b You had been spoiled, my girl. (*Use tu*.)

....

c The work will be redone.

....

d The problem was discovered by an engineer.

....

e The window should be left open.

....

f The house will be repainted in October.

....

g The little boy has been found.

....

h The picture was stolen in 2009.

....

i The back of the seat can be adjusted.

....

j I was promoted in June. (*a woman*)

....

108 Match the active and passive sentences.

a Ils l'ont licenciée.	Ils ont été licenciés.
b Il les a licenciés.	Ils seront envoyés ce matin.
c Il a envoyé cette carte de Malte.	Elle devrait être relue.
d On va envoyer les billets tout de suite.	Elle a été licenciée.
e Tu devrais relire ta dissertation.	Elle a été envoyée de Malte.

Test yourself

109 Replace the highlighted phrase with one that has a passive verb. The object of the active verb will become the subject of the passive verb. Do not say who the action is done by. The first one has been done for you.

a **Nous préparerons tous les plats** la veille de la fête.

Tous les plats seront préparés

b **Ils le payent bien** pour ce travail.

c Avant le commencement du concert **ils baissent les lumières**.

d **Nous avons planté les pommes de terre** trop tard cette année.

e Pour avoir fait ça **on les punira** sévèrement.

f **Nous vous rembourserons** de ce voyage, Madame Faure.

g **Mon grandpère a écrit cette lettre** quand il était en prison.

h **Les archéologues ont découvert plein de choses** sous la mer.

i J'ai entendu dire que **nos voisins vendront leur maison.**

j Ces problèmes veulent dire que **la société retardera le lancement du nouveau modèle.**

Test yourself

110 **Translate the sentences into French, avoiding the passive by using *on*. The first one has been done for you.**

a We were offered another room.

On nous a proposé une autre chambre....

b I was told he was in a meeting.

....

c She was charged two hundred euros.

....

d You'll be given a map and some sandwiches, Marcel.

....

e He'll be sent an email.

....

f They're put to bed at nine.

....

g I was advised to go to the doctor.

....

h They're being told the truth.

....

i They're given food and water.

....

j I was asked to wait.

....

Test yourself

111 **Fill the gap with the past participle of the most suitable verb. The participle should agree with the subject of the sentence.**

    a Les graines sont .... au printemps.

    b Les ordures sont .... une fois par semaine.

    c La piscine sera .... pendant un mois pour cause de travaux.

    d Le biberon doit être .... avant usage.

    e Cette robe a été .... par Marie-Antoinette.

    f À l'époque, tous les vêtements étaient .... à la main.

    g Le tableau est en mauvais état, il va être ....

    h Heureusement personne n'est mort, mais six personnes ont été ....

    i Son autobiographie sera .... par Harper Collins.

    j Il est strictement .... de fumer.

112 **Match cause and effect.**

    a Ils étaient coupables.   On les a fouillés.

    b Ils étaient les meilleurs.   Ils ont été exclus.

    c Ils étaient suspects.   On les a félicités.

    d Ils s'étaient mal comportés. Ils ont été choisis.

    e Ils étaient les gagnants.   Ils ont été condamnés à deux ans de prison.

Grammar Extra!

The present participle

What is a present participle?
The **present participle** is a verb form ending in -*ing* which is used in English to form verb tenses, and which may be used as an adjective or a noun, for example, *What are you <u>doing</u>?; the <u>setting</u> sun; <u>Swimming</u> is easy!*

Using the present participle

➤ Present participles are not as common in French as in English, because they are not used to form tenses. The main uses of the present participle in French are:

● as a verb, on its own, corresponding to the English -*ing* form. It <u>DOES NOT</u> agree with the subject of the verb when it is used in this way.

<u>Habitant</u> près de Paris, je vais assez souvent en ville.	Living close to Paris, I go into town quite often.
Ils m'ont suivi, <u>criant</u> mon nom.	They followed me, shouting my name.

● as a verb, after the preposition **en**. The present participle <u>DOES NOT</u> agree with the subject of the verb when it is used in this way. The subject of the two parts of the sentence is always the same. **en** can be translated in a number of different ways.

<u>En attendant</u> sa sœur, Richard s'est endormi.	While waiting for his sister Richard fell asleep.
Appelle-nous <u>en arrivant</u> chez toi.	Call us when you get home.
<u>En appuyant</u> sur ce bouton, on peut imprimer ses documents.	By pressing this button, you can print your documents.
Il s'est blessé <u>en essayant</u> de sauver un chat.	He hurt himself trying to rescue a cat.

● as an adjective, as in English. As with all adjectives in French, the ending <u>DOES</u> change in the feminine and plural forms.

le soleil <u>couchant</u>	the setting sun
l'année <u>suivante</u>	the following year
Ces enfants sont <u>énervants</u>.	Those children are annoying.
des chaises <u>pliantes</u>	folding chairs

Tip
The French present participle is <u>NEVER</u> used to translate English verb forms like *I was walking, we are leaving*.

⇨ *For more information on the **Imperfect tense** and the **Present tense**, see pages 57 and 4.*

➤ English verbs describing movement that are followed by an adverb such as *out* or *down*, or a preposition such as *across* or *up* are often translated by a verb + **en** + present participle.

Il est sorti en courant.	He ran out. (*literally: He came out running.*)
J'ai traversé la rue en boîtant.	I limped across the street.
	(*literally: I crossed the street limping.*)

Forming the present participle

➤ To form the present participle of regular **-er**, **-ir** and **-re** verbs, you use the **nous** form of the present tense and replace the **-ons** ending with **-ant**.

nous form of present tense	Take off -ons	Add -ant
donnons	donn-	donnant
lançons	lanç-	lançant
mangeons	mange-	mangeant
finissons	finiss-	finissant
partons	part-	partant
attendons	attend-	attendant
descendons	descend-	descendant

Irregular verbs

➤ Three verbs have an irregular present participle:

avoir (meaning *to have*)	→ **ayant**
être (meaning *to be*)	→ **étant**
savoir (meaning *to know*)	→ **sachant**

KEY POINTS

✔ Present participles are never used to form tenses in French, but they can be used as verbs, either on their own or after **en**.

✔ They can also be used as adjectives, in which case they agree with the noun they describe.

✔ They are formed by taking the **nous** form of the present tense and replacing the **-ons** ending with **-ant**. The exceptions are **avoir**, **être** and **savoir**.

---

113 *Ces enfants sont énervants.* is another way of saying *Ces enfants m'énervent.* **Change the sentences to this first pattern, replacing the highlighted verb with the same tense of *être* + a participle adjective. The first one has been done for you.**

a Cette nouvelle **m'inquiète**. *est inquiétante* ....

b Ce genre de bruit **m'agace**. ....

c Leur offre **m'intéresse**. ....

d Son attitude **les déprime**. ....

e Ça **m'étonnerait**. ....

f Ses paroles **l'ont encouragé** . ...

g Ce manque de politesse **me choque**. ....

h Ses résultats **vous ont surpris**? ....

i L'idée **le dégoûtait**. ....

j La tarte aux pommes **me tente**. ....

114 **Using the elements provided make a sentence in the perfect tense, with *en* followed by a participle. The first one has been done for you.**

a les enfants/entrer/en/hurler

Les enfants sont entrés en hurlant. ....

b elle/sourire/en/entendre/sa voix

....

c Nadège/sortir/en/claquer/la porte

....

d il/prendre/un café/en/lire/ses SMS

....

e il/se casser/le bras/en/tomber/du cheval

....

f elle/faire la vaisselle/en/écouter/la radio

....

g Louis/se faire/mal/en/tomber/dans l'escalier

....

h je/se remettre/en forme/en/aller/à la salle de sport tous les jours

....

i il/se guérir/en/prendre/ce médicament

....

j elle/nous/accueillir/en/sourire

....

115 **Fill the gap with the present participle of the verb. The first one has been done for you.**

    a N'...........*étant*............... pas au courant, je n'avais rien à dire. **(être)**

    b Le .... célibataire, elle est sortie avec lui. **(croire)**

    c .... quatre frères, je comprends assez bien les garçons. **(avoir)**

    d .... qu'elle avait peur, j'ai essayé de la calmer. **(savoir)**

    e Elle n'a pas ouvert la lettre, ... que c'était une demande d'argent **(soupçonner)**

    f .... que l'eau était bonne, il a plongé dans la piscine. **(trouvant)**

    g .... tomber sa valise, elle a couru vers eux. **(laisser)**

    h Elle a découpé la pizza, ... trois parts égales. **(faire)**

    i .... dans un petit village, j'aime bien aller à Paris de temps en temps. **(habiter)**

    j .... du bruit, je suis allé à la porte. **(entendre)**

116 **Match the two halves of the sentence**

    a **En attendant le train**   il a compris qu'elle ne disait pas la vérité.

    b **En traversant la rue**   tout le monde est sorti à toute vitesse.

    c **En regardant son visage**   elle a été renversée par une voiture.

    d **En lisant l'e-mail de son petit ami**   j'ai envoyé un SMS.

    e **En entendant la sirène**   elle a fondu en larmes.

Test yourself

117 **Replace the highlighted clause with *en* followed by a present participle. The first one has been done for you.**

a **Pendant qu'il attendait** sa petite amie il a envoyé un SMS.

  En attendant ....

b **Pendant que je préparais** le dîner je discutais avec mes invités.

  ....

c **Pendant qu'elle faisait** la comptabilité elle pensait à son amant.

  ....

d **Pendant que nous cherchions** les clés, nous avons trouvé le porte-monnaie de Lara.

  ....

e **Pendant qu'elle regardait** le film elle tricotait.

  ....

f **Pendant qu'il se rasait** il écoutait la radio.

  ....

g **Pendant qu'elle me racontait** cette histoire, elle guettait ma réaction.

  ....

h **Pendant que je me regardais** dans le miroir, j'ai découvert un bouton sur ma joue gauche.

  ....

i **Pendant que nous rangions** l'appartement nous avons jeté beaucoup de choses.

  ....

j **Pendant qu'elles mangeaient** leurs sandwichs elles regardaient la vue.

  ....

PRACTICE PRACTICE PRACTICE PRACTICE PRACTICE

Test yourself

118 Translate the sentences into French.

a Having six grandchildren, they often go to the toyshop.

....

b Being deaf, she speaks rather loudly.

....

c On opening the curtains he saw that it was raining.

....

d Text me when you leave the house.

....

e Being afraid of flying, I prefer to travel by train.

....

f On reading the e-mail she started to cry.

....

g Alice and Paul met twice the following week.

....

h We heard frightening noises.

....

i Being unemployed, these women are entitled to unemployment benefit.

....

j Not knowing what to do, I called Dad.

....

119 Fill the gap with the participle of the most appropriate verb.

a En .... ce roman il est devenu célèbre.

b En .... ces photos elle se souvient de sa jeunesse.

c Elle espère se mettre en forme en .... souvent à la salle de sport.

d En se .... il s'est coupé le menton.

e .... qu'il n'aimait pas le vin, elle lui a offert une bière.

f .... de la fièvre j'ai pris du paracétamol.

g En .... la vaiselle, j'ai cassé un verre.

h En .... l'aspirateur, j'ai remarqué une grosse tache sur la moquette.

i En .... l'enveloppe, il a trouvé un billet de cent euros.

j .... vétérinaire, elle connaît bien les chiens.

120 Cross out the unlikely options.

a Elle est entrée	en souriant./en pleurant./en écrivant./en courant.
b Ils nous ont appelés	en arrivant en France./en quittant le bureau./ en entendant la nouvelle./en dormant.
c Il s'est fait mal à la jambe	en jouant aux échecs./en se rasant./en jouant au foot./ en tombant.
d J'ai appris le français	en suivant des cours./en habitant en France./ en nageant./en écoutant des chansons françaises.
e Elle est restée eveillée	en buvant du café./en regardant un film./ en se reposant./en écoutant de la musique.
f Ils ont perdu de l'argent	en achetant des actions./en faisant un bénéfice./ en investissant dans cette société./en lançant le nouveau modèle.
g Je reste au courant	en lisant des journaux./en regardant la télévision./ en parlant à mes collègues./en tricotant.
h Elles l'ont énervé	en lui posant des questions./en laissant ouvert le robinet./en l'écoutant avec attention./en disant des bêtises.
i Ils ont économisé sur le chauffage	en restant au lit./en allumant la lumière./en portant des vêtements chauds./en cherchant du bois.
j Tu a gagné	en trichant./en jouant./en courant si vite./en tombant.

Test yourself

121 Fill the gap with the present participle of the verb.

a Ne .... pas quoi dire, je suis resté muet. **(savoir)**

b Le .... tout seul, elle est allée lui parler. **(voir)**

c .... chauffeur de taxi je rencontre beaucoup de personnes. **(être)**

d .... des soucis financiers il m'a demandé de l'argent. **(avoir)**

e Elle est montée dans la voiture .... que c'était un taxi. **(croire)**

f Nous avons invité vingt personnes, la plupart .... des collègues. **(être)**

g En.................... sa voix j'ai raccroché. **(entendre)**

h Ne .... pas venir elle a envoyé des fleurs. **(pouvoir)**

i Ne .... pas de place de stationnement nous sommes partis. **(trouver)**

j .... notre clé, nous avons trouvé une bague. **(chercher)**

Impersonal verbs

What is an impersonal verb?
An **impersonal verb** is one that does not refer to a real person or thing and where the subject is represented by *it*, for example, *It's going to rain; It's ten o'clock.*

➤ <u>Impersonal verbs</u> are only used with **il** (meaning *it*) and in the infinitive. They are called impersonal verbs because **il** does not really refer to a real person, animal or thing, just like *it* and *there* in English in the examples below.

Il pleut.	It's raining.
Il va pleuvoir.	It's going to rain.
Il y a un problème.	There's a problem.
Il pourrait y avoir un problème.	There could be a problem.

➤ There are also some very common verbs that can be used in this way in addition to their normal meanings, for example, **avoir**, **être** and **faire**.

Infinitive	Expression	Meaning
avoir + noun	**il y a**	there is (*singular*) there are (*plural*)
être + time	**il est**	it is
faire + noun	**il fait jour** **il fait nuit**	it's daylight it's dark
falloir + noun	**il faut**	we/you *etc* need it takes
falloir + infinitive	**il faut**	we/you *etc* have to
manquer	**il manque**	there is … missing (*singular*) there are … missing (*plural*)
paraître	**il paraît que**	it appears that it seems that
rester + noun	**il reste**	there is … left (*singular*) there are … left (*plural*)
sembler	**il semble que**	it appears that it seems that
valoir mieux + infinitive	**il vaut mieux**	it would be better to

<u>**Il y a**</u> **quelqu'un à la porte.**	There's somebody at the door.
<u>**Il est**</u> **deux heures.**	It's two o'clock.
<u>**Il faut**</u> **partir.**	I've/We've *etc* got to go.
<u>**Il manque**</u> **cent euros.**	100 euros are missing.
<u>**Il reste**</u> **du pain.**	There's some bread left.
<u>**Il vaut mieux**</u> **ne rien dire.**	It would be better to say nothing.

➤ Several impersonal verbs relate to the weather.

Infinitive	Expression	Meaning
faire + adjective	**il fait beau** **il fait mauvais**	the weather's lovely the weather's bad
faire + noun	**il fait du vent** **il fait du soleil**	it's windy it's sunny
geler	**il gèle**	it's freezing
neiger	**il neige**	it's snowing
pleuvoir	**il pleut**	it's raining

Grammar Extra!
There is another group of useful expressions that start with an impersonal **il.**
These are followed by a form of the verb called the <u>subjunctive</u>.

il faut que
Il faut que je <u>parte</u>.   I've got to go.

il est nécessaire que
Il est nécessaire qu'on le <u>fasse</u>.   We have to do it.

il est possible que
Il est possible qu'il <u>vienne</u>.   He might come.

il est dommage que
Il est dommage que tu ne   It's a shame you didn't see him.
l'<u>aies</u> pas vu.

⇨ *For more information on the **Subjunctive**, see page 127.*

> ### KEY POINTS
> ✔ Impersonal verbs can only be used in the infinitive and the **il** form.
> ✔ **il faut**, **il y a**, **il est** and **il fait** with expressions relating to the weather are very common.

Test yourself

122 **Translate the sentence into French.**

a There are two messages for you.

....

b There is a lot to see in Paris.

....

c There have been demonstrations in several towns.

....

d There was nobody at reception.

....

e There will be a lot of traffic on the motorway.

....

f There are still some problems to sort out.

....

g You've got to set out early. (*Use **il faut**.*)

....

h The instructions are missing.

....

i It would be better to wait a bit.

....

j It seems that they can't help us.

....

123 **Fill the gap with *il* + impersonal verb.**

a Les oiseaux commencent à chanter, ... jour.

b Attention, ... de papier hygiénique dans les toilettes.

c .... bientôt midi, tu restes au lit toute la journée?

d Dans le métro il y a des voleurs, ... faire attention.

e .... un croissant. Quelqu'un le veut?

f Prends tes gants, aujourd'hui .... froid.

g J'ai allumé la lumière parce qu' .... noir.

h .... qu'ils vont divorcer.

i Nous n'étions pas arrivés. .... cinquante kilomètres à faire.

j .... éviter les plages les plus touristiques.

Test yourself

124 Match the related sentences.

   a Je ne veux pas me baigner.   Il y a plein de légumes au frigo.

   b Ce soir je prépare une bonne soupe. Il y a tellement de jolies fleurs.

   c Tout le monde regardait le match   Il fait froid aujourd'hui.
      à la télévision.

   d C'est une personne qui ne
      supporte pas les critiques.   Il n'y avait personne dans les rues.

   e Votre jardin est superbe.   Il vaut mieux ne rien dire.

125 Cross out phrases that could not complete the sentence.

   a Il vaut mieux   réessayer demain./se faire mal./tout laisser tel quel./le refuser.

   b Il ne reste plus de   vin./temps./circulation./fromage.

   c Il y a   la vitesse./quelqu'un avec elle./des moustiques./du vent.

   d Il est   deux heures./midi./jour./dix-huit heures.

   e Il fait   noir/mauvais./du soleil./des nuages.

   f Il faisait déjà   jour./nuit./très chaud./une heure.

   g Il faut que tu   fais attention./fasses attention./travailles mieux./n'oublies pas ça.

   h Il est dommage   puissions pas rester plus longtemps./partions pas en vacances./
      que nous ne   parlons pas l'italien./parlions pas l'italien.

   i Il est possible qu'il   nous attende./nous attend./n'ait pas d'argent./fasse du soleil.

   j Il faut que vous   y aller./y alliez./prenez le train./preniez le métro.

126 Fill the gap with the correct form of the subjunctive of *être*, *avoir* or *faire*.

   a C'est dommage qu'il y .... une décharge près de leur maison.

   b Il faut que tu .... de ton mieux.

   c Il est nécessaire que vous .... à l'heure.

   d Il est possible qu'ils .... déjà arrivés.

   e Il est nécessaire que nous .... les billets avant samedi.

   f Il est possible qu'elle .... malade.

   g Il est dommage que ces chaussures .... un peu justes.

   h Il faut que vous .... vos devoirs.

   i Il est possible que je l' .... oublié à la maison.

   j Il faut que je .... élégante pour leur fête.

Test yourself

127 **Match the question to the answer.**

a Est-ce qu'il faudra réserver?   Oui, il y en a deux.

b Est-ce qu'il reste du riz?   Oui, il n'y a pas de riz.

c Est-ce qu'il vaut mieux se garer ici?   Oui, il y aura beaucoup de monde le 14 février.

d Est-ce qu'il y a des chambres libres?   Oui, il y en a beaucoup.

e Est-ce qu'il manque quelque chose?   Oui, au parking de la gare il faut payer.

128 **Fill the gap with the correct tense of** *il y a*.

a Demain .... une manifestation.

b Actuellement .... beaucoup de personnes qui cherchent du travail.

c Hier .... un accident ici.

d Quand elle était jeune .... moins de possibilités pour les femmes.

e S'il n'y avait pas la limite de vitesse, ... plus d'accidents.

f Regarde, ... deux cartes sous la table.

g Il y a trente ans .... cinq cinémas dans ce quartier.

h Je crains qu' .... encore plus de chômeurs l'année prochaine.

i En 1938, on savait déjà qu' .... une guerre.

j Quel parfum veux-tu? .... vanille, fraise ou cassis.

Test yourself

129 Translate the sentences into French

a There's a button missing.

....

b There's a pancake left.

....

c There's lots to see.

....

d There were three screws missing.

....

e There were mosquitoes in our bedroom.

....

f There were three bottles left.

....

g It seems that some important documents are missing.

....

h It seems there are still some things in their garage. (*Use **il reste**.*)

....

i It seems there are three alternatives.

....

j There was a ping-pong table, but the bats were missing.

....

Grammar Extra!

The subjunctive

> ### What is the subjunctive?
> The **subjunctive** is a verb form that is used in certain circumstances to express some sort of feeling, or to show there is doubt about whether something will happen or whether something is true. It is only used occasionally in modern English, for example, *If I were you, I wouldn't bother.; So be it.*

Using the subjunctive

➤ In French the subjunctive is used after certain verbs and conjunctions when two parts of a sentence have different subjects.
    I'm afraid <u>he</u> won't come back.
    (The subject of the first part of the sentence is 'I'; the subject of the second part of the sentence is 'he'.)

➤ Sometimes, in a sentence like *We want her to be happy*, you use the infinitive of the verb in English (*to be*). This is <u>NOT</u> possible in French when there is a different subject in the two parts of the sentence (*we* and *her*). You have to use a subjunctive for the second verb.
    Nous voulons être heureux. We want to be happy.
    (No change of subject, so you can just use an infinitive – être – in French.)
    Nous voulons qu'elle soit heureuse. We want her to be happy.
    (Subject changes from nous to elle, so you have to use a subjunctive – soit – in French.)

➤ In the case of impersonal verbs, the infinitive can be used instead of the subjunctive.
    Il faut que tu <u>viennes</u> à l'heure.   →   **Il faut <u>venir</u> à l'heure.**
       (using subjunctive)   *(using infinitive)*
    You have to come on time.
    Il vaut mieux que tu <u>restes</u> chez toi.   →   **Il vaut mieux <u>rester</u> chez toi.**
       (using subjunctive)   *(using infinitive)*
    It's better that you stay at home.

Coming across the subjunctive

➤ The subjunctive has several tenses but you are only likely to come across the present subjunctive occasionally in your reading.

➤ You may see a subjunctive after certain verbs when you are:

- wishing something: **vouloir que** and **désirer que** (meaning *to wish that, to want*), **aimer mieux que** and **préférer que** (meaning *to prefer that*)

- fearing something: **avoir peur que** (meaning *to be afraid that*)

- giving your opinion: **croire que** (meaning *to think that*)

- saying how you feel: **regretter que** (meaning *to be sorry that*), **être content que** (meaning *to be pleased that*), **être surpris que** (meaning *to be surprised that*) and so on
  Je suis content que vous les <u>aimiez</u>.   I'm pleased you like them.
  J'ai peur qu'il ne <u>revienne</u> pas.   I'm afraid he won't come back.

➤ You may see a subjunctive after certain verbal expressions starting with **il**, such as **il faut que** (meaning *it is necessary that*) and **il vaut mieux que** (meaning *it is better that*).
  Il faut que je sois <u>prudent</u>.   I need to be careful.

⇨ *For a list of some expressions requiring the subjunctive, see page 122.*

Forming the present subjunctive of -er verbs

➤ To form the stem of the present subjunctive you take the <u>infinitive</u> and chop off **-er**, just as for the present tense. Then you add the correct ending, depending on whether you are referring to **je**, **tu**, **il**, **elle**, **on**, **nous**, **vous**, **ils** or **elles**.

➤ For **-er** verbs the endings are the same as for the ordinary present tense, apart from the **nous** and **vous** forms, which have an extra **i**, as in the imperfect tense.

Pronoun	Ending	Add to stem, e.g. donn-	Meanings
je (j')	-e	je donn<u>e</u>	I give
tu	-es	tu donn<u>es</u>	you give
il elle on	-e	il donn<u>e</u> elle donn<u>e</u> on donn<u>e</u>	he/she/it/ one gives
nous	-ions	nous donn<u>ions</u>	we give
vous	-iez	vous donn<u>iez</u>	you give
ils elles	-ent	ils donn<u>ent</u> elles donn<u>ent</u>	they give

> *Tip*
> **je** changes to **j'** in front of a word starting with a vowel, most words starting with **h**, and the French word **y**.

Forming the present subjunctive of -ir verbs

➤ To form the stem of the present subjunctive you take the <u>infinitive</u> and chop off **-ir**, just as for the present tense. Then you add the correct ending, depending on whether you are referring to to **je**, **tu**, **il**, **elle**, **on**, **nous**, **vous**, **ils** or **elles**.

Pronoun	Ending	Add to stem, e.g. fin-	Meanings
je (j')	-isse	je fin<u>isse</u>	I finish
tu	-isses	tu fin<u>isses</u>	you finish
il elle on	-isse	il fin<u>isse</u> elle fin<u>isse</u> on fin<u>isse</u>	he/she/it/ one finishes
nous	-issions	nous fin<u>issions</u>	we finish
vous	-issiez	vous fin<u>issiez</u>	you finish
ils elles	-issent	ils fin<u>issent</u> elles fin<u>issent</u>	they finish

> *Tip*
> **je** changes to **j'** in front of a word starting with a vowel, most words starting with **h**, and the French word **y**.

Forming the present subjunctive of -re verbs

➤ To form the stem of the present subjunctive you take the <u>infinitive</u> and chop off **-re**, just as for the present tense. Then you add the correct ending, depending on whether you are referring to **je**, **tu**, **il**, **elle**, **on**, **nous**, **vous**, **ils** or **elles**.

Pronoun	Ending	Add to stem, e.g. attend-	Meanings
je (j')	-e	j'attend<u>e</u>	I wait
tu	-es	tu attend<u>es</u>	you wait
il elle on	-e	il attend<u>e</u> elle attend<u>e</u> on attend<u>e</u>	he/she/it/ one waits
nous	-ions	nous attend<u>ions</u>	we wait
vous	-iez	vous attend<u>iez</u>	you wait
ils elles	-ent	ils attend<u>ent</u> elles attend<u>ent</u>	they wait

> *Tip*
> **je** changes to **j'** in front of a word starting with a vowel, most words starting with **h**, and the French word **y**.

Irregular verbs in the subjunctive

➤ Some important verbs have irregular subjunctive forms.

Verb	Meaning	je (j')	tu	il/elle/on	nous	vous	ils/elles
aller	*to go*	aille	ailles	aille	allions	alliez	aillent
avoir	*to have*	aie	aies	ait	ayons	ayez	aient
devoir	*to have to, must*	doive	doives	doive	devions	deviez	doivent
dire	*to say, to tell*	dise	dises	dise	disions	disiez	disent
être	*to be*	sois	sois	soit	soyons	soyez	soient
faire	*to do, to make*	fasse	fasses	fasse	fassions	fassiez	fassent
pouvoir	*to be able to, can*	puisse	puisses	puisse	puissions	puissiez	puissent
prendre	*to take*	prenne	prennes	prenne	prenions	preniez	prennent
(**apprendre** and **comprendre** also behave like this – **j'apprenne**, **tu apprennes** and so on)						
savoir	*to know*	sache	saches	sache	sachions	sachiez	sachent
venir	*to come*	vienne	viennes	vienne	venions	veniez	viennent
vouloir	*to want to*	veuille	veuilles	veuille	voulions	vouliez	veuillent

> ### KEY POINTS
> ✔ After certain verbs you have to use a subjunctive in French when there is a different subject in the two clauses. These verbs mostly relate to wishing, fearing, and saying what you think or what you feel or saying that you are uncertain. A subjunctive is also found after certain verbal expressions that start with **il**.
> ✔ The stem of the present tense subjunctive is the same as the stem used for the ordinary present tense.
> ✔ The present tense subjunctive endings for **-er** and **-re** verbs are: **-e**, **-es**, **-e**, **-ions**, **-iez** and **-ent**.
> ✔ The present tense subjunctive endings for **-ir** verbs are: **-isse**, **-isses**, **-isse**, **-issions**, **-issiez** and **-issent**.

For further explanation of grammatical terms, please see pages x-xii.

Test yourself

130 **Complete the sentence with the correct form of the present subjunctive. The first one has been done for you.**

  a Il faut que vous ....*soyez*........... là avant dix heures. **(être)**

  b Il vaut mieux que tu y .... **(repenser)**

  c Il est nécessaire que vous me .... votre opinion. **(donner)**

  d Il faut qu'elle .... de son mieux. **(faire)**

  e Vous voulez que je .... avec vous? **(venir)**

  f Ils sont ravis que vous .... rester plus longtemps. **(pouvoir)**

  g Il a peur que cent euros ne .... pas. **(suffire)**

  h Tes parents ne veulent pas que tu .... au concert? **(aller)**

  i Je suis déçue qu'il n'y .... pas plus de choix. **(avoir)**

  j Il faut que nous les .... **(prévenir)**

131 **Match the sentences that have the same meaning.**

  a Vous devez partir avant 10h.   C'est normal qu'il y ait beaucoup de monde.

  b Ils doivent prendre le train de 10h.   Je suis surpris que vous parliez le grec.

  c Vous parlez le grec? J'en suis surpris.   Il est possible qu'il ne nous entende pas.

  d Il y a beaucoup de monde? C'est normal.   Il faut que vous partiez avant 10h.

  e Peut-être il ne nous entend pas.   Il faut qu'ils prennent le train de 10h.

Test yourself

132 **Cross out the unlikely options.**

a **Je suis contente que tout soit**   en désordre/réglé/à votre goût/cassé

b **Nous regrettons qu'il ne fasse pas**   un effort/un travail plus intéressant/ du sport/des bêtises

c **Je veux que tu**   prennes cet argent/sois sage/fais tes devoirs/ finisses ta dissertation

d **Ça m'étonne qu'ils veuillent**   plus d'argent/aller en Écosse en novembre/ vendre cette belle maison/s'amuser

e **Nous sommes surpris qu'elles n'aient pas pris**   les plus beaux/les moins difficiles/les plus moches/ les moins confortables

f **J'espère qu'ils sont**   ennuyés/contrariés/blessés/au courant

g **J'ai peur qu'il**   mente/ne veuille plus se marier/soit gentil/ perde son temps

h **Je demande que vous**   arriviez à l'heure/fassiez attention/ ne gaspilliez de l'eau/disiez n'importe quoi

i **Ils préfèrent que nous**   restions ici/choisissions autre chose/venions un autre jour/nous en allions

j **Il est normal qu'il**   ne soit pas content/veuille souffrir/demande les pires/veuille être payé

Test yourself

133 Make a sentence using the elements provided. Put the first verb into the present tense.

a je/espérer/que/vous/avoir/plus de chance cette fois

....

b il faut que/tu/remplir/les deux formulaires

....

c ils/préférer/que/vous/laisser/les clés à la réception

....

d tu/aimer/mieux/que/je/attendre/dehors?

....

e elle/vouloir/que/tu/venir/à sa fête.

....

f vous/croire/que/ce/être/juste?

....

g je/avoir/peur/que/elle/ne/le/rendre/pas

....

h il/vouloir/que/nous/partager/l'appartement avec lui

....

i vous/être/déçus/que/nous/ne/choisir/pas/des meubles modernes?

....

j je/regretter/que/ça/te/faire/tant de peine

....

Test yourself

134 *devoir* is followed by the infinitive while *il faut que* is followed by the subjunctive. Replace the highlighted *devoir* phrase with one containing *il faut que*. The first one has been done for you.

a Je n'ai pas mes lunettes, **tu dois lire** le menu.

il faut que tu lises

b C'est loin, **nous devons prendre** le bus.

c **Vous devez finir** les travaux avant la fin du mois.

d Elle est malade, **elle doit aller** chez le médecin.

e Tu vas marcher beaucoup, **tu dois choisir** des chaussures solides.

f Il n'est pas là, **vous devez revenir** plus tard.

g **Ils doivent nous dire** la vérité.

h **Tu dois l'apprendre** par cœur.

i **Je dois faire** plus attention.

j **Elle doit être** prudente.

Test yourself

135 **Translate the sentences into French. Remember that, to translate expressions such as 'I'm sorry that..', or 'I'm glad that...', *que* must always be used in French, although 'that' can be omitted in English. The first one has been done for you.**

   a She's glad you're coming with us. (*Use* **vous**.)

     Elle est contente que vous veniez avec nous.

   b I'm sorry that you have to leave so early. (*Use* **tu**.)

   c We're surprised he's going out with her.

   d I hope she can come.

   e Her parents are delighted she's got a job.

   f Let's hope the treatment does her good.

   g It's possible that he knows German.

   h Her children want her to retire.

   i They're pleased she wants to be a teacher.

   j I think she's forty.

136 **Match cause and effect.**

a Ma sœur a de la fièvre.	Je crains qu'elle ne soit furieuse contre moi.
b Ma chatte est disparue.	Je crains qu'elle ne meure.
c Ma petite amie est sortie en claquant la porte.	Je crains qu'elle ne soit pas en forme.
d Ma grandmère est gravement malade.	Je crains qu'elle ne revienne plus.
e Élodie joue mal aujourd'hui.	Je crains qu'elle n'ait la grippe.

Test yourself

137 **Fill the gap with the ordinary present tense, or with the present subjunctive, as appropriate.**

a Je sais qu'elle .... beaucoup à faire. **(avoir)**

b C'est dommage qu'elle .... ces idées stupides. **(avoir)**

c Elle croit que je .... les aider. **(devoir)**

d Ils savent que je ne .... pas les comprendre. **(pouvoir)**

e Sans doute il .... ça à tout le monde. **(dire)**

f Il est possible qu'il .... la vérité. **(dire)**

g Tu .... venir ce soir? J'en suis contente. **(pouvoir)**

h Je suis contente que tu .... venir ce soir. **(pouvoir)**

i Il vaut mieux qu'il .... tout de suite. **(venir)**

j Tu es sûre qu'il .... ce soir? **(venir)**

Verbs followed by an infinitive

Linking two verbs together

➤ Many verbs in French can be followed by another verb in the infinitive. The infinitive is the form of the verb that is found in the dictionary, such as **donner** (meaning *to give*), **finir** (meaning *to finish*) and **attendre** (meaning *to wait*).

➤ There are three main ways that verbs can be linked together:

- with no linking word
  Vous voulez attendre?   Would you like to wait?

- with the preposition **à**
  J'apprends <u>à</u> nager.   I'm learning to swim.

- with the preposition **de**
  Essayez <u>de</u> venir.   Try to come.

Verbs followed by an infinitive with no preposition

➤ A number of verbs and groups of verbs can be followed by an infinitive with no preposition. The following important group of verbs are all very irregular, but they crop up so frequently that they are worth learning in full:

- **devoir** (*to have to, must, to be due to*)
  Tu <u>dois être</u> fatiguée.   You must be tired.
  Elle <u>doit partir</u>.   She has to leave.
  **Le nouveau centre commercial   The new shopping centre is due to
  <u>doit ouvrir</u> en mai.**   open in May.

- **pouvoir** (*can, may*)
  Je <u>peux t'aider</u>, si tu veux.   I can help you, if you like.
  <u>Puis-je venir</u> vous voir samedi?   May I come and see you on Saturday?

- **savoir** (*to know how to, can*)
  Tu <u>sais conduire</u>?   Can you drive?
  Je <u>sais faire</u> les omelettes.   I know how to make omelettes.

- **vouloir** (*to want*)
  Élise <u>veut rester</u> un jour de plus.   Élise wants to stay one more day.
  Ma voiture ne <u>veut</u> pas <u>démarrer</u>.   My car won't start.
  <u>Voulez-vous boire</u> quelque chose?   Would you like something to drink?
  Je <u>voudrais acheter</u> un ordinateur.   I'd like to buy a computer.

➤ **falloir** (meaning *to be necessary*) and **valoir mieux** (meaning *to be better*) are only used in the infinitive and with **il**.
  <u>Il faut prendre</u> une décision.   We/you *etc* have to make a decision.
  <u>Il vaut mieux téléphoner</u> avant.   It's better to ring first.

  ⇨ *For more information on **Impersonal verbs**, see page 121.*

➤ The following common verbs can also be followed by an infinitive <u>without</u> a preposition:

adorer	to love
aimer	to like, to love
aimer mieux	to prefer
désirer	to want
détester	to hate
envoyer	to send
espérer	to hope
faire	to make (**faire faire quelque chose** means to have something done)
laisser	to let
préférer	to prefer
sembler	to seem

J'**espère** te <u>voir</u> la semaine prochaine.	I hope to see you next week.
Ne me <u>fais</u> pas <u>rire</u>!	Don't make me laugh!
J'<u>ai fait réparer</u> mes chaussures.	I've had my shoes mended.
Je <u>préfère manger</u> à la cantine.	I prefer to eat in the canteen.

➤ Some of these verbs combine with infinitives to make set phrases with a special meaning.

aller chercher quelque chose	to go and get something
laisser tomber quelque chose	to drop something
vouloir dire quelque chose	to mean something

<u>Va chercher</u> ton papa!	Go and get your dad!
Paul <u>a laissé tomber</u> le vase.	Paul dropped the vase.
Qu'est-ce que ça <u>veut dire</u>?	What does that mean?

➤ Verbs that relate to seeing or hearing, such as **voir** (meaning *to see*), **regarder** (meaning *to watch, to look at*), **écouter** (meaning *to listen to*) and **entendre** (meaning *to hear*) can be followed by an infinitive.

Il nous <u>a vus arriver</u>.	He saw us arrive.
On <u>entend chanter</u> les oiseaux.	You can hear the birds singing.

➤ Verbs that relate to movement of some kind and do not have a direct object, such as **aller** (meaning *to go)* and **venir** (meaning *to come*), can be followed by an infinitive.

Je <u>vais voir</u> Nicolas ce soir.	I'm going to see Nicolas tonight.
<u>Viens voir</u>!	Come and see!

Verbs followed by à + infinitive

➤ There are some common verbs that can be followed by **à** and an infinitive.

s'amuser <u>à</u> faire quelque chose	to have fun doing something
apprendre <u>à</u> faire quelque chose	to learn to do something
commencer <u>à</u> faire quelque chose	to begin to do something
continuer <u>à</u> faire quelque chose	to go on doing something
s'habituer <u>à</u> faire quelque chose	to get used to doing something

J'apprends <u>à</u> skier.	I'm learning to ski.
Il a commencé <u>à</u> pleuvoir.	It began to rain.

➤ Some verbs can be followed by a person's name or by a noun relating to a person, and then by **à** and an infinitive. Sometimes you need to put **à** in front of the person too.

aider quelqu'un <u>à</u> faire quelque chose	to help someone do something
apprendre <u>à</u> quelqu'un <u>à</u> faire quelque chose	to teach someone to do something
inviter quelqu'un <u>à</u> faire quelque chose	to invite someone to do something

Verbs followed by de + infinitive

➤ There are some common verbs that can be followed by **de** and an infinitive.

arrêter <u>de</u> faire quelque chose,	
s'arrêter <u>de</u> faire quelque chose	to stop doing something
commencer <u>de</u> faire quelque chose	to start doing something
continuer <u>de</u> faire quelque chose	to go on doing something
décider <u>de</u> faire quelque chose	to decide to do something
se dépêcher <u>de</u> faire quelque chose	to hurry to do something
essayer <u>de</u> faire quelque chose	to try to do something
s'excuser <u>d'</u>avoir fait quelque chose	to apologize for doing something
finir <u>de</u> faire quelque chose	to finish doing something
oublier <u>de</u> faire quelque chose	to forget to do something
proposer <u>de</u> faire quelque chose	to suggest doing something
refuser <u>de</u> faire quelque chose	to refuse to do something
suggérer <u>de</u> faire quelque chose	to suggest doing something

J'<u>ai décidé de</u> lui écrire.	I decided to write to her.
Je leur <u>ai suggéré de</u> partir de bonne heure.	I suggested that they set off early.

➤ The following verbs meaning asking or telling are also followed by **de** and an infinitive. Sometimes you need to put **à** in front of the person you are asking or telling.

commander <u>à</u> quelqu'un <u>de</u> faire quelque chose	to order someone to do something
demander <u>à</u> quelqu'un <u>de</u> faire quelque chose	to ask someone to do something
dire <u>à</u> quelqu'un <u>de</u> faire quelque chose	to tell someone to do something
empêcher quelqu'un <u>de</u> faire quelque chose	to prevent someone from doing something
remercier quelqu'un <u>de</u> faire quelque chose	to thank someone for doing something

Grammar Extra!
If it is important to emphasize that something is going on at a particular time, you can use the phrase **être en train de faire quelque chose**.

Il <u>est en train de travailler</u>. Est-ce que vous pouvez rappeler plus tard?	He's working. Can you call back later?

If you want to say you have just done something, you can use the phrase **venir de faire quelque chose**. In English you use the <u>PAST</u> tense, but in French you use the <u>PRESENT</u> tense.

Élisabeth <u>vient de partir</u>.	Élisabeth has just left.

KEY POINTS

✔ Many French verbs can be followed by another verb in the infinitive.
✔ The two verbs may be linked by nothing at all, or by the prepositions **à** or **de**.
✔ The construction in French does not always match the English exactly. It's best to learn these constructions when you learn a new verb.

Test yourself

138 **Translate the sentences into French.**

a The players must be very tired.

....

b She hates ironing.

....

c He prefers to go by train.

....

d Do you let him go out alone? (*Use* ***tu***.)

....

e They hope to be able to go on holiday this year.

....

f I heard you coming in last night. (*Use* ***tu***.)

....

g They're going to move house.

....

h What does that mean?

....

i She knows how to make pancakes.

....

j Let him speak! (*Use* ***vous***.)

....

139 **Fill the gap with *à* or *de*.**

a Je me suis dépêchée .... préparer leur chambre.

b Elle s'amuse .... faire les mots croisés.

c Arrête .... plaisanter!

d Il m'a appris .... jouer aux échecs.

e Elle a continué .... parler.

f Ils m'ont suggéré .... aller voir cette exposition.

g Il a refusé .... m'aider.

h Je m'habitue .... vivre seule.

i Nous avons décidé .... accepter leur offre.

j Il a commencé .... neiger.

Test yourself

140 *Il est en train de travailler.* is another way of saying *Il travaille*. Replace the highlighted verb with a phrase containing *en train de*. The first one has been done for you.

a Nous **faisons** nos bagages. *sommes en train de faire* ....

b Ma femme **choisit** une nouvelle voiture. ....

c Ils **repeignent** leur maison. ....

d J'**envoie** un SMS à mon chef. ....

e Elle **couchait** les enfants. ....

f Vous **remplissez** la piscine? ....

g L'usine **licencie** des ouvriers. ....

h Elle **lit** ses e-mails. ....

i Nous **lançons** notre nouvelle gamme. ....

j Il **lavait** la voiture. ....

141 Match the two halves of the sentence.

a Le yoga   m'a demandé de chercher le dossier.

b Le docteur   m'a encouragée à chercher un emploi mieux payé.

c La voisine   m'aide à me détendre.

d Mon collègue   te dira d'arrêter de fumer.

e Mon petit ami   nous a demandé de faire moins de bruit.

142 When talking about the future, both *je ferai* and *je vais faire* can be used. In the sentences, replace the highlighted words with a form of *aller* + the infinitive, putting pronouns before the infinitive. The first one has been done for you.

a Je **les lui enverrai** demain. *vais les lui envoyer* ....

b Il **en parlera** avec ses parents. ....

c Elle a son nouveau roman. Elle **le lira** pendant le weekend. ....

d Vous **devrez** faire attention. ....

e Je **le ferai** quand j'aurai le temps. ....

f On **partira** très tôt demain matin. ....

g Les enfants **auront** une surprise. ....

h Demain nous **saurons** si la banque nous prête l'argent. ....

i Tu **iras** tout seule? ....

j Je me demande si elles **pourront** le faire. ....

Test yourself

143 *il faut que je le fasse* and *je dois le faire* are alternative ways of saying that you have to do something. In the sentences, replace the highlighted words with a form of *devoir* + the infinitive, being careful to put the pronouns in the right place. The first one has been done for you.

a Il est tard. **Il faut que je parte.**

Je dois partir.

b Le chauffage est toujours en panne, **il faut que le plombier revienne.**

....

c Tu avais raison, **il faut que je l'admette.**

....

d Elle a trois chiens. **Il faut qu'elle les sorte** deux fois par jour.

....

e Les voisins sont au lit, **il faut que vous fassiez** moins de bruit.

....

f **Il faut que tu sois** sage, sinon tu n'iras pas à la fête.

....

g **Il faut que je le finisse** avant vendredi.

....

h Ils sont en danger, **il faut qu'on les prévienne.**

....

i **Il faut que j'essaie** cette nouvelle recette.

....

j **Il faut que vous leur écriviez** en français.

....

Test yourself

144 **Cross out the unlikely or grammatically incorrect options.**

a Quand nous sommes arrivés, elle n'avait pas fini   de manger./ses devoirs./faire ses bagages./ de se maquiller.

b Les choses commencent   bien./s'améliorer./à tourner mal./mieux.

c J'essaye   t'aider./ce pantalon./de te l'expliquer/de rester calme.

d Elle leur apprend   nager/l'anglais/des chansons/à lire

e Ils vous invitent   à leur mariage./leur rendre visite./à les retrouver./ au chômage.

f Il a décidé   rien dire./apprendre l'allemand./de se faire tatouer le bras./acheter une nouvelle voiture.

g Je peux vous aider   avec ça?/faire ça?/de faire ça?/à mettre la table?

h Il voudrait   d'acheter un billet./du sucre./y aller./te parler.

i Nous espérons   de pouvoir partir en vacances./vous revoir bientôt./ gagner la prochaine fois./de réussir.

j Malgré les conseils de son médecin il continue   de manger des fruits et des salades./fumer./de boire trop./ à rester toujours assis devant son ordinateur.

145 **Match the two halves of the sentence.**

a Elle s'est excusée   d'être arrivés à l'heure.

b Il y a beaucoup de circulation, elle risque   être en retard.

c Elle a une réunion importante ce matin, elle ne veut pas   d'arriver à l'heure.

d Elle les a remerciés   d'être arrivée en retard.

e Elle leur avait demandé   d'être en retard.

Test yourself

146 Fill the gap with *à* or *de*.

    a Ma mère m'appris .... lire.

    b J'essaye .... l'oublier.

    c Nous nous sommes habitués .... nous lever tôt.

    d Il a continué .... travailler jusqu'à minuit.

    e Nous avons oublié .... payer la facture.

    f Tu peux m'aider .... ranger la cuisine?

    g Ils ont décidé .... vendre leur voiture.

    h J'apprends .... conduire.

    i Alors, vous refusez .... nous aider?

    j Il nous a invités .... nous asseoir à sa table.

Other uses of the infinitive

➤ The infinitive can be used in many other ways:

- after certain adjectives

  content de   happy to
  prêt à   ready to

  Il est toujours <u>prêt à rendre</u> service.   He's always ready to help.

- after certain prepositions

  <u>Pour aller</u> à la gare?   How do you get to the station?
  Il est parti <u>sans dire</u> au revoir.   He left without saying goodbye.

- after certain set phrases involving a verb plus a noun

  avoir envie de <u>faire</u> quelque chose   to feel like doing something
  avoir besoin de <u>faire</u> quelque chose   to need to do something
  avoir peur de <u>faire</u> quelque chose   to be frightened of doing something

  J'ai besoin de <u>changer</u> de l'argent.   I need to change some money.

- in instructions that are aimed at the general public – for example, on signs or in cookery books

  <u>Ajouter</u> le sel et le poivre,   Add the salt and pepper, and mix well.
    et bien <u>mélanger</u>.
  <u>Conserver</u> au frais.   Keep refrigerated.

- as the subject or object of a sentence, when the infinitive corresponds to the -ing form in English used as a noun

  <u>Fumer</u> n'est pas bon pour la santé.   Smoking isn't good for your health.
  J'adore <u>lire</u>.   I love reading.

Tip

You can use the verb **faire** with an infinitive to refer to something you are having done by someone else.

Je dois <u>faire réparer</u> ma voiture.   I have to get my car repaired.

KEY POINTS

✔ Infinitives are found after certain adjectives, prepositions and set phrases, and in instructions to the general public.
✔ They can also function like nouns, as the subject or object of another verb.

Test yourself

147 Translate the sentence into French.

a Our guests feel like having a swim. ....

b I need to get my hair cut. ....

c You mustn't take it without asking, Luc. ....

d They are happy to be able to help. ....

e He did it to please me. ....

f She loves playing football. ....

g I've got to get my car serviced. ....

h Mix the flour with the sugar. (*instruction*) ....

i Pull (*sign on a door*) ....

j Slow down (*road sign*) ....

148 Make a sentence with the elements provided.

a je/être/ravi de/revoir/vous

....

b ils/être/désolé de/ne pas/pouvoir/accepter

....

c la prochaine fois/je/pouvoir/faire/le/sans/demander/te/de l'aide

....

d il/s'en servir/ pour/aller/au travail

....

e tu/être/content de/voir/me?

....

f elle/avoir/peur/de/aller/y/seul

....

g gaspiller/de l'argent/ne/avoir/pas/de sens

....

h il y a deux ans/on/être/censé/changer/le système

....

i je/appelle/te/pour/dire/que/je/ne/avoir/plus/envie/de/aller/y

....

j se laver/les mains/c'est important

....

Test yourself

149 Match the activity to the comment about it.

a	Faire du sport,	coûte cher.
b	Apprendre une langue,	ne me tente pas.
c	Gaspiller l'énergie	ça fait maigrir.
d	Faire ses courses sur Internet,	c'est découvrir une culture.
e	Voyager seule	c'est pratique.

150 Cross out the unlikely options.

a **Nous sommes contents** de pouvoir venir./de devoir attendre./d'avoir réussi./ de le savoir.

b **Tu es sûr** tu peux le faire?/de l'avoir vu?/de savoir le faire?/ d'avoir pris le bon médicament?

c **Je suis ravie** de vous accueillir./de vous revoir./d'avoir mal à la tête./ d'avoir de tes nouvelles.

d **Il est nécessaire** de s'en moquer./de réserver./de payer à l'avance./ d'avoir un mot de passe.

e **Il est important** de se faire vacciner./d'utiliser les bons outils./ de ne rien oublier./de rien voir.

f **Je suis certaine** de l'avoir fait./d'arriver avant eux./de choisir./ de rentrer ce soir.

g **Cette langue est difficile à** prononcer./lire./écrire./oublier.

h **Mon frère est prêt à** faire ce travail./partir avec moi./se réveiller./ rendre service.

i **Je suis triste** de pouvoir le faire./d'apprendre cette nouvelle./ d'avoir de leurs nouvelles./de devoir le dire.

j **Nous avons envie** de nous ennuyer./de nous promener./de jouer au tennis./ de rester ici.

Test yourself

151 Translate the sentences into French.

a We like going to France.

....

b I fancy going to Turkey.

....

c I need to buy some batteries.

....

d They're afraid of getting lost.

....

e Do you need to go to the toilet? (*Use* **tu**.)

....

f Sunbathing isn't good for your skin.

....

g He wants to get his shoes mended.

....

h The children love swimming.

....

i He took the coffee without saying thank you.

....

j We're going to the restaurant to celebrate her birthday.

....

Test yourself

152 Translate the sentences into French.

a I feel like going to the cinema.

....

b I need to buy some stamps.

....

c Don't cross the road without looking, Aurélie.

....

d We are ready to leave.

....

e They did it to help us.

....

f They like playing football.

....

g We've got to get the window mended.

....

h I want to get my hair cut.

....

i Push (*sign on a door*)

....

j Add the milk and the eggs.

....

solutions

Solutions

1
  a donnent
  b marchez
  c regardes
  d aime
  e passent
  f pleure
  g gagnes
  h regarde
  i commence
  j réservons

2
  a C'est un professeur. **Il enseigne la physique.**
  b Ils sont musulmans. **Ils ne mangent pas de porc.**
  c Elle est banquière. **Elle gagne beaucoup d'argent.**
  d Nous sommes étrangers. **Nous n'habitons pas ici.**
  e Je suis sportive. **J'aime beaucoup jouer au tennis.**

3
  a Nous le visitons dimanche.
  b Vous travaillez dur.
  c Ma mère habite là.
  d Il le coupe en deux.
  e Les filles jouent dehors.
  f Je lui parle souvent.
  g Ma femme la déteste.
  h Nous y restons une semaine.
  i Vous arrivez ici à quelle heure?
  j Nos amis y passent une quinzaine de jours.

4
  a Tu commences tout de suite?
  b Il parle aux voisins.
  c Les filles adorent notre chat.
  d Nous aimons la cuisine française.
  e Tu me parles?
  f Nous passons une semaine dans les Alpes avec eux.
  g Elle arrive à minuit.
  h Tu regardes ça?
  i Qu'est-ce que vous cherchez?
  j Pourquoi tu ne l'aimes pas?

5
  a ferme
  b regardons
  c porte
  d invitent
  e plante

f jouent
g attrape
h oublie
i change
j acceptes

6
  a la monnaie/l'essence
  b une couronne
  c On la refuse.
  d Tu la repasses?/Elle est neuve?
  e le bruit
  f des femmes de ménage
  g J'apporte tout de suite l'addition.
  h Elle pleure./Elle l'oublie immédiatement.
  i Elles restent assises toute la journée.
  j à n'importe qui/aux passants

7
  a Ma mère reste à la maison aujourd'hui.
  b Tu aimes cette photo?
  c Si tu les aimes, je te les donne.
  d Mes grandparents habitent à Lyon, mon père habite à Marseille.
  e Si tu triches je ne joue pas avec toi.
  f Vous nous apportez l'addition?
  g Si vous laissez le robinet ouvert vous gaspillez de l'eau.
  h Vous roulez trop vite.
  i La police les cherche.
  j Elle commence toujours à pleurer quand il lui parle comme ça.

8
  a Ils gagnent beaucoup d'argent?
  b Tu ranges ta chambre?
  c Les filles aiment l'école?
  d Elle porte ces vêtements au bureau?
  e Vous travaillez ce weekend?
  f Elle cherche quelqu'un?
  g Ils empruntent de l'argent?
  h Un billet coûte vraiment 100 euros?
  i Vous recommandez cet hôtel?
  j Tes parents te laissent regarder cette émission?

9
  a donnent
  b parlez
  c parles
  d aime
  e habitent
  f chante

Solutions

g marches
h regarde
i commence
j admirons

10 a choisit
b fleurissent
c finissez
d établissons
e finit
f choisis
g ralentissent
h salissez
i punit
j remplissons

11 a Je ne regarde pas la télévision. **Je finis mes devoirs.**
b Mon amie est au régime. **Elle choisit toujours les salades.**
c Ici on mange peu et on marche beaucoup. **Tout le monde maigrit.**
d Elle ne boit pas de café. **Je remplis sa tasse de thé.**
e C'est délicat de lui dire ça. **Nous choisissons nos mots avec soin.**

12 a Je finis ma dissertation ce soir.
b Ils investissent dans des actions.
c Tu finis ton déjeuner avant d'aller jouer.
d La piscine est vide, nous la remplissons.
e Nous choisissons des rideaux pour le nouvel appartement.
f Celui-là coûte moins cher, vous le choisissez?
g Je choisis toujours les moins chers.
h En voyant le feu rouge, elle ralentit.
i Ses parents ont de l'argent, ils l'investissent dans l'immobilier.
j Attention, tu salis la nappe!

13 a Je choisis un nouveau portable.
b Pourquoi elle choisit toujours cette couleur?
c Le film finit avant vingt heures?
d Nous finissons la plus grande partie aujourd'hui.
e Ils choisissent toujours les plats les plus chers.

f Vous ralentissez, vous êtes fatigué?
g Tu finis à quelle heure ce soir?
h Je remplis les deux formulaires.
i Pourquoi vous les punissez?
j Ils finissent les réparations aussi vite que possible.

14 a ouvrent
b couvre
c couvrent
d ouvres
e ouvre
f couvre
g ouvre
h couvrez
i couvrons
j ouvrent

15 a dorment
b partons
c dort
d pars
e sort
f part
g dors
h sors
i sortent
j partent

16 a hier.
b l'ordinateur./la radio.
c usées.
d sur la table.
e d'outils./de pierres.
f en train.
g le jour de Noël./le soir.
h les graffiti.
i avec des étrangers?
j il y a deux heures.

17 a Tu ouvres la fenêtre? **Non, je la ferme.**
b Ils commencent les entretiens la semaine prochaine? **Non, ils les finissent cette semaine.**
c Vous partez demain? **Non, nous restons encore quelques jours.**
d Ils ont une usine en Inde? **Oui, ils y investissent beaucoup d'argent.**
e Tu regardes la liste des vins? **Oui, je choisis un bon bordeaux.**

Solutions

18
a Je choisis une robe pour la fête.
b D'habitude les femmes choisissent des salades.
c Je dors huit heures par nuit.
d Les enfants dorment déjà.
e Tu finis tôt aujourd'hui.
f Nous finissons la peinture demain.
g Tu couvres la cuisine de farine.
h Nous sortons pour deux heures.
i Elle part dans un taxi tous les matins.
j Elle finit le compte rendu demain.

19
a entends
b vendent
c attendez
d entends
e entend
f attendent
g défend
h vendons
i attends
j vendez

20
a Le train est en retard. **On attend longtemps.**
b Ce sont des artistes. **Ils vendent leurs peintures.**
c Vous attendez un enfant? **Toutes mes félicitations!**
d Je ne t'entends pas. **Parle plus fort!**
e Elle est ma petite amie. **Je la défends.**

21
a Tu m'entends bien?
b Je vous attends depuis longtemps.
c L'appartement est trop petit, il le vend.
d Vous défendez la violence?
e Elle prétend être innocente.
f Les mères défendent toujours leurs enfants.
g Nos invités sont en retard, nous les attendons.
h Cette poussette, vous la vendez?
i Ça dépend du prix.
j On entend à peine les mots.

22
a Ils m'attendent au restaurant.
b Pourquoi vous vendez votre appartement?
c Nous entendons le bruit.

d Peut-être. Ça dépend.
e Il défend son chef.
f Tu entends les voisins?
g Les touristes attendent le guide.
h Les femmes vendent leurs confitures au marché.
i J'entends chaque mot.
j Elle attend un enfant?

23
a entendez
b attendons
c tendent
d étend
e vend
f entends
g attend
h vendent
i attend
j tends

24
a ses critiques.
b la chaleur/des cris dans la rue
c s'il nous aide.
d des timbres.
e le plombier./des factures.
f au kilo./au supermarché.
g dans le bus.
h comme cadeau.
i Tu parles trop fort.
j bientôt?

25
a C'est une boulangerie. **On y vend toutes sortes de pain.**
b C'est un magasin de produits diététiques. **On y vend du pain sans gluten.**
c C'est un magasin de brocante. **On y vend toute sorte de bric-à-brac.**
d C'est un bureau de tabac. **On y vend des timbres et des cigarettes.**
e C'est une papeterie. **On y vend des cahiers et des blocs-notes.**

26
a Mes frères attendent depuis six mois.
b J'attends depuis une demi-heure.
c Vous attendez un rendez-vous depuis quinze jours?
d Nous attendons nos hors-d'œuvre depuis vingt-cinq minutes.
e Tu attends ton anniversaire depuis des mois, Max!

Solutions

f On attend ce moment depuis quatre ans.

g Leurs mères les attendent depuis longtemps.

h Depuis quand vous attendez, monsieur?

i Il est fâché, il attend depuis trois quarts d'heure.

j Nous attendons un taxi depuis vingt minutes.

27
a Vous l'attendez?
b Ma voiture est trop petite, je la vends.
c Nous entendons leur télé.
d Ça dépend du prix.
e Il défend ses amis.
f Tu m'entends?
g Les filles attendent le bus.
h L'ordinateur est nul, ils le vendent.
i Ils entendent les cloches tous les matins.
j Elle attend un enfant.

28
a lances
b lançons
c mange
d mangeons
e appelez
f appellent
g jettes
h nettoies
i gèle
j espère

29
a de la glace
b de la monnaie/de l'eau
c à Tahiti
d les chiens méchants
e Marie.
f quand il gèle.
g se casser la jambe.
h Il mange beaucoup./Il est gros.
i J'aime beaucoup le ménage./J'en suis contente.
j Ils se lèvent.

30
a Nous mangeons après le concert?
b Je m'appelle Lucie.
c Je jette les bouteilles à la poubelle?
d Vous jetez les restes?

e Je pèle toujours les pommes et les poires.
f Elle lui envoie une carte?
g Nous mangeons beaucoup quand nous sommes en vacances.
h Tu préfères les films américains?
i Nous espérons y aller l'année prochaine.
j Je règle le siège.

31
a Pauline a de gros problèmes. **J'espère pouvoir l'aider.**
b Nous lui envoyons la facture à la fin du mois. **C'est normal, n'est-ce pas?**
c Nos amis sont végétariens. **Nous mangeons des pâtes.**
d Ces chaussures sont jolies. **Tu les essaies?**
e Luc adore les jeux électroniques. **Il en achète beaucoup.**

32
a rangeons
b appelons
c jette
d envoie
e espérons
f espère
g levez
h mangeons
i remplaçons
j appelles

33
a préfère
b préfères
c préfèrent
d préférons
e préférez
f préfèrent
g préférons
h préférez-vous
i préfères
j préférons

34
a Pour qui tu achètes ces jolies fleurs?
b Nous logeons à l'hôtel.
c Ils enlèvent les ordures deux fois par semaine.
d La femme de chambre nettoie la salle de bains.
e Nous déménageons lundi.

Solutions

f On pèle les concombres pour cette salade.

g Ce livre révèle beaucoup de choses intéressantes.

h Nous levons nos verres à Alice et Jacques.

i Combien de temps vous espérez y rester?

j Le client règle la note en espèces.

35 **a** Ils achètent un four à micro-ondes.

b Le lac gèle en hiver.

c J'enlève mes chaussures, elles sont sales.

d Nous achetons notre pain au supermarché.

e Nous espérons avoir plus de chance la prochaine fois.

f Les enfants m'appellent mamie.

g Vous appelez ça un hôtel de luxe?

h Tu jettes toujours les serviettes par terre.

i Ils me payent *or* Ils me paient à la fin du mois.

j Elle essaye *or* Elle essaie les chaussures noires.

36 **a** ont

b avons

c allons

d a

e fais

f est

g font

h partent

i sommes

j va

37 **a** Tu as l'air triste. **Qu'est-ce qu'il y a?**

b J'ai une sœur ainée. **Comment s'appelle-t-elle?**

c Il fait froid ce matin. **On reste à la maison?**

d Ce soir on a des invités. **On leur fait une tarte aux pommes?**

e Élodie et Luc font des bêtises. **Ils n'ont rien d'intéressant à faire?**

38 **a** Tu as les mains

b Elles ont les cheveux

c J'ai les hanches

d Tu as les cheveux

e Elles ont les mains

f Tu as les mains

g Elle a la jambe

h Il a le cœur

i Tu as les oreilles

j Elles ont les bras

39 **a** Qu'est-ce que vous faites le week-end?

b Tout va bien, merci.

c Elle ne va pas à l'école: elle a trois ans.

d D'habitude nous allons en France, mais cette année nous allons en Italie.

e Qu'est-ce qu'il y a à voir ici? – Rien.

f Lisa est kinésithérapeute.

g Il fait froid, tu vas allumer le chauffage?

h Il n'y a pas de pain, je vais à la boulangerie.

i Je n'ai pas de monnaie. – Ça ne fait rien.

j Le train part dans trois minutes.

40 **a** a

b sont

c fait

d font

e ai

f va

g faites

h a

i vais

j as

41 **a** fait du

b font du

c fais de l'

d faites du

e fait du

f faisons de l'

g font du

h fait de la

i fait du

j faites du

42 **a** Je vais bien.

b Il fait beau.

c Ils ont six ans.

Solutions

d Elle fait du sport.
e J'ai douze ans./J'ai les yeux verts.
f Il est l'heure du déjeuner.
g C'est trop.
h Peut-être.
i Avec eux.
j À l'hôpital.

43 a Elle est artisan-bijoutière. **Elle fait des bagues.**
b Ils sont patissiers. **Ils font des gâteaux.**
c Je suis couturière. **Je fais des robes.**
d Nous sommes potiers. **Nous faisons des poteries.**
e Il est menuisier. **Il fait des fenêtres.**

44 a Ma grand-mère a quatre-vingt-cinq ans.
b Elle est un peu sourde, mais elle va bien.
c Nous faisons une fête pour son anniversaire.
d Tous ses petits-enfants vont être là.
e Elle a quatre petites-filles et cinq petits-fils.
f Le cadet des petits-fils c'est Luc.
g Il a cinq ans.
h Les enfants font des bêtises.
i Je fais un gâteau et une pizza.
j Mes sœurs font un album de photos.

45 a Écoute-moi, Marianne!
b Suivez-moi, les enfants!
c Parles-en à ta mère, Pierre!
d Si vous en avez besoin, demandez-lui!
e Croyez-moi, Monsieur!
f Pardonnez-moi, Madame!
g Prends-en un peu!
h Range ta chambre ce matin!
i Allez vous coucher!
j Excuse-nous!

46 a Partez
b Approche
c Vas-y
d Faites-le
e Réveillez-la
f Prête-leur
g Parlez-en
h commencez

i penses-y
j attendons-la

47 a vos glaces
b la gare
c le tabac/l'engrais
d le rhume
e cette photo
f la voiture
g les pellicules
h de la catastrophe/de l'examen
i ta sœur
j l'argent

48 a Ferme les yeux! **J'ai un cadeau pour toi.**
b Sois courageux! **Ça va faire un peu mal.**
c Soyez patient! **Tout le monde doit attendre.**
d Veuillez les laisser ici. **On va les ranger.**
e Soyons réalistes. **Il n'est pas capable de faire ça.**

49 a Restez là, les enfants!
b Choisissez les plus beaux!
c Attends-les ici!
d Ne me fais pas rire!
e Ne les oubliez pas!
f Parle-leur-en!
g Montrez-les-moi!
h Ne sois pas stupide!
i N'ayez pas peur!
j Ne touche pas à mes affaires!

50 a Remplaçons-les
b aidons-le
c choisissons-les
d goûtons-la
e essayons-la
f finissons-les
g prêtons-les-lui
h N'ayons pas
i Faisons preuve
j allons-y

51 a Enlevez votre manteau, les enfants.
b Finis ton petit déjeuner, Pierre.
c Remplissez le formulaire, s'il vous plaît, monsieur.

Solutions

d Appelons la police.
e Écoutez-moi, les filles.
f Faites moins de bruit, les garcons.
g Suivez-moi!
h Soyons raisonnables.
i Gardez la monnaie!
j Changeons de place.

52 **a** Voilà un autre pantalon. **Essaye-le!**
b Voilà son numéro. **Appelle-le!**
c Voilà Serge. **Attends-le!**
d Voilà l'ordinateur. **Allume-le!**
e Voilà un petit cadeau. **Prends-le!**

53 **a** s'
b te
c s'
d s'
e te
f vous
g me
h te
i se
j se

54 **a** appelles
b t'appelles
c nous arrêtons
d se couchent
e arrêtes
f vous promener
g nous levons
h passe
i se passe
j asseyons-nous

55 **a** D'habitude je me réveille tôt en été.
b Qu'est-ce qui se passe dans la rue?
c Les enfants se couchent bientôt?
d Je me baigne tous les jours.
e On est ici pour se détendre et pour s'amuser.
f Il est tard, tu te lèves?
g L'hôtel se trouve près de la plage.
h Mes amies s'habillent avec beaucoup d'élégance.
i Alors, vous ne vous intéressez pas au sport?
j Nous nous demandons qu'est-ce c'est.

56 **a** Asseyez-vous, Monsieur!
b Ne vous baignez pas après le déjeuner, les enfants!
c Habillez-vous tout de suite, Alain et Michelle!
d Amuse-toi bien à Paris, chérie!
e Ne vous inquiétez pas, Monsieur, tout va bien!
f Ne vous asseyez pas à cette table, s'il vous plaît, Mesdames!
g Détends-toi bien, Laure!
h Reposez-vous au soleil, Mesdames!
i Ne te lève pas, Gaston, reste là!
j Méfie-toi de ce garçon, Florent!

57 **a** te lèves
b vous inquiétez
c te dépêches
d s'appelle
e me détendre
f me demande
g se rappelle
h nous entendons
i s'ennuie
j se disputent

58 **a** t'appelles
b appelle
c appelons
d s'appellent
e appelez
f appeler
g s'appelle
h s'appellent
i appelle
j vous appelez

59 **a** du temps.
b de ma faute.
c du monde.
d bon?
e de nous.
f J'ai chaud.
g de place.
h à temps.
i au pas.
j à merveille./bien./mieux qu'avant.

60 **a** Je travaille dur. **Je me fatigue.**
b Je suis en train de réparer la voiture. **Je me salis.**

Solutions

c Je me renverse de l'eau bouillante sur la main. **Je me brûle.**
d Je joue aux échecs. **Je m'amuse.**
e Je me contrôle. **Je ne dis rien.**

61 a obéissaient
b alliez
c mangeait
d partageais
e finissait
f fournissaient
g nous promenions
h traversais
i arrivait
j vivait

62 a C'était un professeur. **Elle enseignait l'histoire.**
b Ils étaient pauvres. **Ils ne partaient jamais en vacances.**
c Elle était au restaurant. **Elle choisissait son dessert.**
d On était en ville. **On regardait les vitrines des magasins.**
e Le chien aboyait. **Il y avait quelqu'un à la porte.**

63 a arrivait
b préférais
c choisissaient
d vendais
e lancions
f entendait
g commençais
h aviez
i causait
j neigeait

64 a Je regardais la télé.
b Tu te sentais malade hier?
c Je m'occupais de lui quand il était petit.
d Ils finissaient quand nous commencions.
e Elle s'entendait bien avec les autres étudiants.
f Il s'intéressait à la politique.
g Ils se demandaient où aller.
h Le professeur était nul: les enfants ne l'écoutaient pas.
i Il faisait chaud et nous étions en train de nous baigner.
j Vous m'écoutiez, les filles?

65 a Nous choisissions
b repassait
c achetait
d mangeaient
e allais
f finissait
g parliez
h descendait
i refaisaient
j se rasait

66 a Il y a deux ans, je faisais une licence de lettres.
b Une fois à la retraite, nous nous levions plus tard.
c Ils étaient tous les deux professeurs.
d Elle m'en parlait souvent.
e Tu te lavais les cheveux?
f Ça me semblait bizarre.
g Il commençait à faire nuit.
h J'y allais avec eux.
i La police les cherchait.
j À cette époque, je gagnais beaucoup d'argent.

67 a déjeuné.
b les weekends./notre temps libre./ les vacances.
c un SMS./le site web.
d cette personne.
e le train?
f jeune.
g de toi./d'argent./d'un prêt./d'un plombier.
h les yeux bleus.
i quelque fois?
j un chèque.

68 a Il pleuvait. **Il n'y avait personne sur la plage.**
b C'était dimanche après-midi. **La boulangerie était fermée.**
c Il faisait beau. **Les enfants jouaient dehors.**
d Il était au chômage. **Il avait des dettes.**
e Il avait raison. **Nous étions d'accord avec lui.**

Solutions

69 a Je pensais à toi.
b Qu'est-ce que tu faisais cet après-midi?
c J'allais souvent au cinéma quand je vivais à Paris.
d Nous nous entendions bien quand nous étions à l'école.
e Elle se sentait seule et pleurait beaucoup.
f Il perdait toujours ses clés.
g Je me demandais quoi faire.
h Le professeur était sympathique: les enfants l'aimaient beaucoup.
i Il pleuvait et nous nous ennuyions.
j Vous m'attendiez?

70 a pourras
b viendrons
c nettoierai
d partiront
e déménageront
f verrez
g réserverons
h arriverez
i pourra
j enverra

71 a aura
b serons
c pourras
d auront
e sera
f pleuvra
g plaira
h ferai
i fera
j saurez

72 a Sarah et Paul passent une quinzaine de jours à Genève. **Ils y dépenseront beaucoup d'argent.**
b Je vais lui dire que tu dois partir. **Elle en sera désolée.**
c Cet hôtel coûte très cher. **Nous irons ailleurs.**
d L'examen est très difficile. **Je devrai travailler dur.**
e Tu n'es pas sage. **Tu iras bientôt au lit.**

73 a Ils pourront se baigner.
b Je pourrai sortir avec eux mardi.
c Il devra le refaire.
d Il fera beau demain.
e Je lui enverrai un e-mail.
f Elle aura un SMS de son chef.
g Je pense que ça fera mal.
h Est-ce que les filles voudront venir avec nous?
i Le docteur vous verra cet après-midi.
j Vous serez où la semaine prochaine?

74 a fera
b rendrai
c seront
d aurai
e auront
f fera
g retrouveras
h gagnera
i devrez
j comprendront

75 a arriveront *or* arrivent
b arrive
c achèterai
d fera
e savaient
f attendons
g nous attendions
h sera
i s'inquiétera
j voulait

76 a Vous les aurez demain sans faute.
b Le voyage lui coûtera cher.
c Je ne suis pas sûr qu'il pourra y aller l'année prochaine.
d Il y a du vent, le linge séchera vite.
e Vous en aurez peut-être besoin demain.
f Sans doute elle lui en parlera.
g Je les lui enverrai plus tard.
h Cette nouvelle leur fera de la peine.
i À cette heure elle sera déjà au lit.
j Les élèves connaîtront leurs résultats dans trois semaines.

Solutions

77
a Elle est sportive. **Elle participera au marathon.**
b Elle est timide. **Elle ne dira rien.**
c Elle est dépensière. **Elle achètera plein de choses.**
d Elle est curieuse. **Elle nous posera beaucoup de questions.**
e Elle est fiable. **Elle tiendra sa promesse.**

78
a participeras
b partirons
c prêterai
d passeront
e marieront
f offrirez
g nettoierons
h viendrez
i pourra
j rendra

79
a une raquette
b nettoyer la cuisine/attendre le bus
c de l'après-rasage
d un enterrement
e en Chine/aux USA
f un gros rat/ses blessures
g ce musée
h aller en vacances/se parler
i de la poubelle/du facteur
j une grosse bise

80
a pourrais
b voudrais
c devrait
d voudriez
e seraient
f voudrait
g choisirais
h saurais
i feraient
j dirais

81
a Si j'avais le temps, j'irais à la salle de sport.
b Il rirait si tu portais ce pantalon.
c Faire une omelette? Ça ne prendrait pas longtemps.
d S'ils commençaient maintenant, ils finiraient cet après-midi.
e Tu pourrais y arriver si tu faisais un effort.
f Nous aimerions vivre ici.
g Elle serait étonnée si son mari faisait la vaisselle.
h Vous devriez rester plus longtemps.
i Si ça lui faisait mal, elle pleurerait.

82
a aimerait
b ferais
c voudrais
d devrait
e serions
f pourraient
g perdrais
h auraient
i accepteriez
j saurais

83
a Il est tard. **Tu devrais aller au lit.**
b Ces chaussures sont trop petites. **Tu pourrais essayer celles-ci.**
c Tu détestes ton travail? **À ta place j'en chercherais un autre.**
d Tu as mal à la gorge? **Tu ferais mieux d'arrêter de fumer.**
e C'est un bon film. **Il te plairait.**

84
a Ils pourraient peut-être réessayer demain.
b Ça ferait très mal.
c Ce serait dommage s'il ne pouvait pas venir.
d Vous vous attendriez à ça?
e Mes parents s'inquiéteraient.
f Nous viendrions si nous pouvions.
g Elle choisirait le menu le plus cher.
h Si on commençait aujourd'hui, on finirait jeudi.
i Il y aurait plus de monde ici s'il faisait beau.
j Ils trouveraient ce livre ennuyeux.

85
a détesteraient
b refuserais
c garderait
d nous ennuierions
e éteindrais
f réduirait
g prendriez

Solutions

h ignoreraient
i tomberaient
j affaiblerait

86 a voudrais
b devrais
c pourrait
d voudrions
e serait
f voudraient
g proposeriez
h sauraient
i ferait
j oserais

87 a allés
b tombé
c fait
d sorti
e rentrées
f gagné
g pu
h née
i parties
j payé

88 a Nous avons rendu
b as appris
c ont acheté
d ont pris
e sont venus
f t'es entendue
g m'a envoyé
h sont rentrés
i a fallu
j as écrit

89 a Tu vas ranger ta chambre? **Non, je l'ai déjà fait.**
b Demain, c'est l'anniversaire de Catherine. **Je sais: je lui ai acheté des fleurs.**
c Tu t'es couchée tard hier soir, Marie? **Oui, j'ai regardé un film à la télévision.**
d Il vous a demandé un conseil? **Non, il est très sûr de lui.**
e Il a plu pendant la nuit? **Non, le sol est sec.**

90 a Elle lui a donné son adresse.
b J'ai eu une bonne surprise.
c Nous avons perdu 2-1.
d Nous nous sommes promenés dans le parc.
e Elle est sortie avec Richard.
f Il a sorti la poubelle hier soir.
g Il a fini son livre avant de se coucher.
h Nous avons vu un accident sur l'autoroute.
i Claire a perdu son portable.
j Le coût de la vie a augmenté.

91 a ouvertes
b finis
c fermée
d cassé
e perdues
f cuite
g connu
h chargé
i entendu
j habillées

92 a ai
b est
c ont
d a
e est
f suis
g avons
h ai
i êtes
j avez

93 a Il est sorti **de l'hôpital.**
b Il a sorti **le chien.**
c Il nous a promis **de l'aide.**
d Il nous a donné **les pires.**
e Il nous a montré **ses photos.**

94 a J'ai aimé son dernier film.
b À l'époque, j'aimais les voitures rapides.
c Ils allaient souvent dans ce restaurant.
d Les filles sont allées à la salle de sport ce matin.
e Nous avons mangé dehors parce qu'il faisait beau.

Solutions

f Elle gagnait plus d'argent quand elle était à Londres.
g Notre équipe a gagné hier soir.
h Tu portais toujours des jeans.
i J'ai porté cette chemise hier.
j Quand il a dit ça tout le monde a ri.

95
a J'ai rendu
b as passé
c ont déménagé
d a pris
e est venue
f vous êtes amusés
g m'a écrit
h sont descendues
i s'est passé
j a mis

96
a Il n'y avait plus personne. **Tout le monde était parti.**
b Elle était extrêmement pâle. **Elle avait eu un choc.**
c Il s'est mouillé. **Il avait oublié son parapluie.**
d J'étais de mauvaise humeur. **J'avais dû attendre longtemps pour le bus.**
e Les supporters étaient très contents. **Leur équipe avait gagné.**

97
a avait retrouvé
b nous étions couchés
c nous étions entendus
d avait commencé
e s'étaient baignés
f avions voulu
g aviez regardé
h s'étaient attendus
i avais eu
j avait donné

98
a couché
b invité
c pris
d restée
e roulé
f eu
g attendu
h envoyé
i cassé
j allé

99
a Ils s'étaient disputés avant la fête.
b Il avait fait un effort.
c Il avait déjà lu cent pages.
d Je m'étais senti malade la veille.
e Elle s'était demandée si c'était une bonne idée.
f Tu t'étais déjà décidé avant la réunion?
g Mon chef m'en avait déjà parlé.
h J'avais vu le film avant de lire le livre.
i Elle l'avait remarqué à la piscine.
j Ils avaient attendu très longtemps.

100
a avaient
b était
c avait
d avais
e étiez
f avais
g étaient
h avions
i étais
j était

101
a avait acheté
b avais pris
c aviez été
d était allée
e avions lavée
f avais changé
g avais perdu
h étaient partis
i avait cassé
j avait donné

102
a Avant de se faire opérer **il avait fait son testament.**
b Avant de participer au marathon **il s'était entraîné.**
c Avant de donner sa démission **il en avait discuté avec sa copine.**
d Avant d'aller au lit **il avait sorti les poubelles.**
e Avant de gagner à la loterie **il avait eu de gros problèmes financiers.**

103
a Je savais qu'il avait perdu son emploi.
b Ils savaient qu'elle avait volé l'argent.
c Nous savions qu'ils s'étaient mariés.

Solutions

d J'étais sûr que les filles étaient sorties avant moi.

e Il savait qu'elle était devenue bouddhiste.

f J'étais sûr d'avoir fermé la porte à clé.

g Nous savions que nos voisins s'étaient disputés.

h Je savais qu'elle était tombée dans l'escalier.

i J'étais sûr que tout ça s'était passé il y a longtemps.

j Ils étaient sûrs que nous étions devenus fous.

104 a avait oublié

b nous étions levés

c m'étais attendu

d étaient partis

e avions appelés

f avait voulu

g aviez essayé

h était tombée

i avais su

j avait dit

105 a hier soir.

b en 2009.

c accidentellement.

d la semaine dernière.

e sévèrement./par habitude.

f par hasard.

g dans les pharmacies./dans les offices du tourisme./dans les bibliothèques.

h avec du sucre./en dessert.

i mardi prochain.

j par vos admirateurs./pour vos bonnes actions.

106 a construit

b lu

c faites

d vendues

e adorées

f recherché

g écrit

h blessés

i connu

j détruit

107 a Ils avaient été prévenus.

c Le travail sera refait.

d Le problème a été découvert par un technicien.

e La fenêtre devrait être laissée ouverte.

f La maison sera repeinte en octobre.

g Le petit garçon a été retrouvé.

h Le tableau a été volé en 2009.

i Le dossier du siège peut être réglé.

j J'ai été promue en juin.

108 a Ils l'ont licenciée. **Elle a été licenciée.**

b Il les a licenciés. **Ils ont été licenciés.**

c Il a envoyé cette carte de Malte. **Elle a été envoyée de Malte.**

d On va envoyer les billets tout de suite. **Ils seront envoyés ce matin.**

e Tu devrais relire ta dissertation. **Elle devrait être relue.**

109 a Tous les plats seront préparés

b Il est bien payé

c Les lumières sont baissées.

d Les pommes de terre ont été plantées

e ils seront punis *or* elles seront punies

f Vous serez remboursée

g Cette lettre a été écrite

h Plein de choses ont été découvertes

i leur maison sera vendue.

j le lancement du nouveau modèle sera retardé.

110 a On nous a proposé une autre chambre.

b On m'a dit qu'il était en réunion.

c On lui a fait payer deux cents euros.

d On te donnera une carte et des sandwichs, Marcel.

e On lui enverra un e-mail.

f On les couche à neuf heures.

g On m'a conseillé d'aller chez le docteur.

h On leur dit la vérité.

i On leur donne de la nourriture et de l'eau.

Solutions

111
a semées
b enlevées
c fermée
d stérilisé
e portée
f faits
g restauré
h blessées
i publiée
j défendu *or* interdit

112
a Ils étaient coupables. **Ils ont été condamnés à deux ans de prison.**
b Ils étaient les meilleurs. **Ils ont été choisis.**
c Ils étaient suspects. **On les a fouillés.**
d Ils s'étaient mal comportés. **Ils ont été exclus.**
e Ils étaient les gagnants. **On les a félicités.**

113
a est inquiétante
b est agaçant
c est intéressante
d est déprimante
e serait étonnant
f étaient encourageantes
g est choquant
h ont été surprenants
i était dégoûtante
j est tentante

114
a Les enfants sont entrés en hurlant.
b Elle a souri en entendant sa voix.
c Nadège est sortie en claquant la porte.
d Il a pris un café en lisant ses SMS.
e Il s'est cassé le bras en tombant du cheval.
f Elle a fait la vaisselle en écoutant la radio.
g Louis s'est fait mal en tombant dans l'escalier.
h Je me suis remise en forme en allant à la salle de sport tous les jours.
i Il s'est guéri en prenant ce médicament.
j Elle nous a accueillis en souriant.

115
a étant
b croyant
c Ayant
d Sachant
e soupçonnant
f Trouvant
g Laissant
h faisant
i Habitant
j Entendant

116
a En attendant le train **j'ai envoyé un SMS.**
b En traversant la rue **elle a été renversée par une voiture.**
c En regardant son visage **il a compris qu'elle ne disait pas la vérité.**
d En lisant l'e-mail de son petit ami **elle a fondu en larmes.**
e En entendant la sirène **tout le monde est sorti à toute vitesse.**

117
a En attendant
b En préparant
c En faisant
d En cherchant
e En regardant
f En se rasant
g En me racontant
h En me regardant
i En rangeant
j En mangeant

118
a Comme ils ont six petits-enfants, ils vont souvent au magasin de jouets.
b Étant sourde elle parle plutôt fort.
c En ouvrant les rideaux il a vu qu'il pleuvait.
d Envoie-moi un SMS en quittant la maison.
e Ayant peur de prendre l'avion, je préfère voyager en train.
f En lisant l'e-mail ella a commencé à pleurer.
g Alice et Paul se sont rencontrés deux fois la semaine suivante.
h Nous avons entendu des bruits effrayants.
i Étant sans emploi, ces femmes ont droit aux allocations chômage.

Solutions

j Ne sachant pas quoi faire, j'ai appelé Papa.

119 a écrivant
b regardant
c allant
d rasant
e Sachant
f Ayant
g faisant
h passant
i ouvrant
j Étant

120 a en écrivant.
b en dormant.
c en jouant aux échecs./en se rasant.
d en nageant.
e en se reposant.
f en faisant un bénéfice
g en tricotant.
h en l'écoutant avec attention.
i en allumant la lumière.
j en jouant./en tombant.

121 a sachant
b voyant
c Étant
d Ayant
e croyant
f étant
g entendant
h pouvant
i trouvant
j Cherchant

122 a Il y a deux messages pour vous.
b Il y a beaucoup à voir à Paris.
c Il y a eu des manifestations dans plusieurs villes.
d Il n'y avait personne à la réception
e Il y aura beaucoup de circulation sur l'autoroute.
f Il reste encore des problèmes à résoudre.
g Il faut partir tôt.
h Il manque le mode d'emploi.
i Il vaudrait mieux attendre un peu.
j Il apparaît qu'ils ne peuvent pas nous aider.

123 a il fait
b il n'y a pas
c Il sera
d il faut
e Il reste
f il fait
g il faisait
h Il paraît
i Il restait
j Il vaut mieux

124 a Je ne veux pas me baigner. **Il fait froid aujourd'hui.**
b Ce soir je prépare une bonne soupe. **Il y a plein de légumes au frigo.**
c Tout le monde regardait le match à la télévision. **Il n'y avait personne dans les rues.**
d C'est une personne qui ne supporte pas les critiques. **Il vaut mieux ne rien dire.**
e Votre jardin est superbe. **Il y a tellement de jolies fleurs.**

125 a se faire mal.
b circulation.
c la vitesse.
d jour.
e des nuages.
f une heure.
g fais attention.
h parlons pas l'italien.
i nous attend.
j y aller/prenez le train.

126 a ait
b fasses
c soyez
d soient
e ayons
f soit
g soient
h fassiez
i aie
j sois

127 a Est-ce qu'il faudra réserver? **Oui, il y aura beaucoup de monde le 14 février.**

Solutions

b Est-ce qu'il reste du riz? **Oui, il y en a beaucoup.**

c Est-ce qu'il vaut mieux se garer ici? **Oui, au parking de la gare il faut payer.**

d Est-ce qu'il y a des chambres libres? **Oui, il y en a deux.**

e Est-ce qu'il manque quelque chose? **Oui, il n'y a pas de riz.**

128 a il y aura *or* il y a
b il y a
c il y a eu
d il y avait
e il y aurait
f il y a
g il y avait
h il n'y ait
i il y aurait
j Il y a

129 a Il manque un bouton.
b Il reste une crêpe.
c Il y a beaucoup à voir.
d Il manquait trois vis.
e Il y avait des moustiques dans notre chambre.
f Il restait trois bouteilles.
g Il semble qu'il manque des documents importants.
h Il semble qu'il reste des choses dans leur garage.
i Il semble qu'il y ait trois possibilités.
j Il y avait une table à ping-pong, mais il manquait les raquettes.

130 a soyez
b repenses
c donniez
d fasse
e vienne
f puissiez
g suffisent
h ailles
i ait
j prévenions

131 a Vous devez partir avant 10h. **Il faut que vous partiez avant 10h.**
b Ils doivent prendre le train de 10h. **Il faut qu'ils prennent le train de 10h.**

c Vous parlez le grec? J'en suis surpris. **Je suis surpris que vous parliez le grec.**

d Il y a beaucoup de monde? C'est normal. **C'est normal qu'il y ait beaucoup de monde.**

e Peut-être il ne nous entend pas. **Il est possible qu'il ne nous entende pas.**

132 a en désordre/cassé
b des bêtises
c fais tes devoirs
d plus d'argent/s'amuser
e les plus moches/les moins confortables
f ennuyés/contrariés/blessés
g soit gentil
h disiez n'importe quoi
i venions un autre jour
j veuille souffrir/demande les pires

133 a J'espère que vous ayez plus de chance cette fois.
b Il faut que tu remplisses les deux formulaires.
c Ils préfèrent que vous laissiez les clés à la réception.
d Tu aimes mieux que j'attende dehors?
e Elle veut que tu viennes à sa fête.
f Vous croyez que c'est juste?
g J'ai peur qu'elle ne le rende pas.
h Il veut que nous partagions l'appartement avec lui.
i Vous êtes déçus que nous ne choisissions pas des meubles modernes?
j Je regrette que ça te fasse tant de peine.

134 a il faut que tu lises
b il faut que nous prenions
c Il faut que vous finissiez
d il faut qu'elle aille
e il faut que tu choisisses
f il faut que vous reveniez
g Il faut qu'ils nous disent
h Il faut que tu l'apprennes
i Il faut que je fasse
j Il faut qu'elle soit

Solutions

135
a Elle est contente que vous veniez avec nous.
b Je regrette que tu doives partir si tôt.
c Nous sommes surpris qu'il sorte avec elle.
d J'espère qu'elle pourra venir.
e Ses parents sont ravis qu'elle ait un travail.
f Espérons que le traitement lui fera du bien.
g Il est possible qu'il connaisse l'allemand.
h Ses enfants veulent qu'elle prenne sa retraite.
i Ils sont contents qu'elle veuille être professeur.
j Je crois qu'elle a quarante ans.

136
a Ma sœur a de la fièvre. **Je crains qu'elle n'ait la grippe.**
b Ma chatte est disparue. **Je crains qu'elle ne revienne plus.**
c Ma petite amie est sortie en claquant la porte. **Je crains qu'elle ne soit furieuse contre moi.**
d Ma grandmère est gravement malade. **Je crains qu'elle ne meure.**
e Élodie joue mal aujourd'hui. **Je crains qu'elle ne soit pas en forme.**

137
a a
b ait
c dois
d peux
e dit
f dise
g peux
h puisses
i vienne
j vient

138
a Les joueurs doivent être très fatigués.
b Elle déteste repasser.
c Il préfère y aller en train.
d Tu le laisses sortir seul?
e Ils espèrent pouvoir partir en vacances cet année.
f Je t'ai entendu rentrer hier soir.
g Ils vont déménager.
h Qu'est-ce que ça veut dire?

i Elle sait faire les crêpes.
j Laissez-le parler!

139
a de
b à
c de
d à
e de or à
f d'
g de
h à
i d'
j à or de

140
a sommes en train de faire
b est en train de choisir
c sont en train de repeindre
d Je suis en train d'envoyer
e était en train de coucher
f êtes en train de remplir
g est en train de licencier
h est en train de lire
i sommes en train de lancer
j était en train de laver

141
a Le yoga **m'aide à me détendre.**
b Le docteur **te dira d'arrêter de fumer.**
c La voisine **nous a demandé de faire moins de bruit.**
d Mon collègue **m'a demandé de chercher le dossier.**
e Mon petit ami **m'a encouragée à chercher un emploi mieux payé.**

142
a vais les lui envoyer
b va en parler
c va le lire
d allez devoir
e vais le faire
f va partir
g vont avoir
h allons savoir
i vas y aller
j vont pouvoir

143
a Je dois partir.
b le plombier doit revenir.
c je dois l'admettre.
d Elle doit les sortir
e vous devez faire

Solutions

f Tu dois être
g Je dois le finir
h on doit les prévenir.
i Je dois essayer
j Vous devez leur écrire

144 a faire ses bagages.
b s'améliorer./mieux.
c t'aider.
d nager
e leur rendre visite./au chômage.
f rien dire./apprendre l'allemand./ acheter une nouvelle voiture.
g faire ça?/de faire ça?
h d'acheter un billet.
i de pouvoir partir en vacances./de réussir.
j de manger des fruits et des salades./ fumer.

145 a Elle s'est excusée **d'être arrivée en retard.**
b Il y a beaucoup de circulation, elle risque **d'être en retard.**
c Elle a une réunion importante ce matin, elle ne veut pas **être en retard.**
d Elle les a remerciés **d'être arrivés à l'heure.**
e Elle leur avait demandé **d'arriver à l'heure.**

146 a à
b de
c à
d à *or* de
e de
f à
g de
h à
i de
j à

147 a Nos invités ont envie de se baigner.
b J'ai besoin de me faire couper les cheveux.
c Tu ne dois pas le prendre sans demander, Luc.
d Ils sont contents de pouvoir aider.
e Il l'a fait pour me plaire.
f Elle adore jouer au foot.

g Je dois faire réviser ma voiture.
h Mélanger la farine et le sucre.
i Tirer
j Ralentir

148 a Je suis ravi de vous revoir.
b Ils sont désolés de ne pas pouvoir accepter.
c La prochaine fois, je pourrai le faire sans te demander de l'aide.
d Il s'en sert pour aller au travail.
e Tu es content de me voir?
f Elle a peur d'y aller seule.
g Gaspiller de l'argent n'a pas de sens.
h Il y a deux ans on était censé changer le système.
i Je t'appelle pour dire que je n'ai plus envie d'y aller.
j Se laver les mains, c'est important.

149 a Faire du sport, **ça fait maigrir.**
b Apprendre une langue, **c'est découvrir une culture.**
c Gaspiller l'énergie **coûte cher.**
d Faire ses courses sur Internet, **c'est pratique.**
e Voyager seule **ne me tente pas.**

150 a de devoir attendre.
b tu peux le faire?
c d'avoir mal à la tête.
d de s'en moquer.
e de rien voir.
f de choisir.
g oublier.
h se réveiller.
i de pouvoir le faire./ d'avoir de leurs nouvelles.
j de nous ennuyer.

151 a Nous aimons aller en France.
b J'ai envie d'aller en Turquie.
c Il faut que j'achète des piles.
d Ils ont peur de se perdre.
e Tu as besoin d'aller aux toilettes?
f Bronzer n'est pas bon pour la peau.
g Il veut faire réparer ses chaussures.
h Les enfants adorent nager.
i Il a pris le café sans dire merci.
j Nous allons au restaurant pour fêter son anniversaire.

Solutions

152
  a J'ai envie d'aller au cinéma.
  b J'ai besoin d'acheter des timbres.
  c Ne traverse pas la rue sans regarder, Aurélie.
  d Nous sommes prêts à partir.
  e Ils l'ont fait pour nous aider.

  f Ils aiment jouer au foot.
  g Nous devons faire réparer la fenêtre.
  h Je veux me faire couper les cheveux.
  i Pousser
  j Ajouter le lait et les œufs.

main index

Index

For further explanation of grammatical terms, please see pages x-xii.

verb tables

Introduction

The Verb Tables in the following section contain 115 tables of French verbs (some regular and some irregular) in alphabetical order. Each table shows you the following forms: **Present**, **Present Subjunctive**, **Perfect**, **Imperfect**, **Future**, **Conditional**, **Past Historic**, **Pluperfect**, **Imperative** and the **Present** and **Past Participles**. For more information on these tenses and how they are formed you should refer to the main text on pages ????. If you want to find out in more detail how verbs are used in different contexts, the Easy Learning French Grammar will give you additional information.

In order to help you use the verbs shown in the Verb Tables correctly, there are also a number of example phrases on each page to show the verb as it is used in context.

In French there are both **regular** (their forms follow the normal rules) and **irregular** verbs (their forms do not follow the normal rules). The regular verbs in these tables are:

donner (regular **-er** verb, Verb Table 36)
finir (regular **-ir** verb, Verb Table 51)
attendre (regular **-re** verb, Verb Table 12)

The irregular verbs are shown in full.

The **Verb Index** at the end of this section contains over 2000 verbs, each of which is cross-referred to one of the verbs given in the Verb Tables. The table shows the patterns that the verb listed in the index follows.

acheter (to buy)

PRESENT

j'	**achète**
tu	**achètes**
il/elle/on	**achète**
nous	**achetons**
vous	**achetez**
ils/elles	**achètent**

PRESENT SUBJUNCTIVE

j'	**achète**
tu	**achètes**
il/elle/on	**achète**
nous	**achetions**
vous	**achetiez**
ils/elles	**achètent**

PERFECT

j'	**ai acheté**
tu	**as acheté**
il/elle/on	**a acheté**
nous	**avons acheté**
vous	**avez acheté**
ils/elles	**ont acheté**

IMPERFECT

j'	**achetais**
tu	**achetais**
il/elle/on	**achetait**
nous	**achetions**
vous	**achetiez**
ils/elles	**achetaient**

PRESENT PARTICIPLE
achetant

PAST PARTICIPLE
acheté

FUTURE

j'	**achèterai**
tu	**achèteras**
il/elle/on	**achètera**
nous	**achèterons**
vous	**achèterez**
ils/elles	**achèteront**

CONDITIONAL

j'	**achèterais**
tu	**achèterais**
il/elle/on	**achèterait**
nous	**achèterions**
vous	**achèteriez**
ils/elles	**achèteraient**

PAST HISTORIC

j'	**achetai**
tu	**achetas**
il/elle/on	**acheta**
nous	**achetâmes**
vous	**achetâtes**
ils/elles	**achetèrent**

PLUPERFECT

j'	**avais acheté**
tu	**avais acheté**
il/elle/on	**avait acheté**
nous	**avions acheté**
vous	**aviez acheté**
ils/elles	**avaient acheté**

IMPERATIVE
achète / achetons / achetez

EXAMPLE PHRASES

Nous n'**achetons** jamais de chips.
We never buy crisps.

Qu'est-ce que tu **as acheté**?
What did you buy?

Il faut que j'**achète** un cadeau pour son anniversaire.
I must buy a present for his birthday.

Ses parents lui **achetaient** des bonbons.
His parents bought him sweets.

J'**achèterai** des gâteaux à la pâtisserie.
I'll buy some cakes at the cake shop.

Elle **acheta** la robe rouge.
She bought the red dress.

Si j'étais riche j'**achèterais** un voilier.
If I were rich, I'd buy a yacht.

Il lui **avait acheté** une jolie robe, mais elle ne voulait pas la porter.
He'd bought her a nice dress, but she didn't want to wear it.

N'**achète** rien pour moi.
Don't buy anything for me.

je/j' = I **tu** = you **il** = he/it **elle** = she/it **on** = we/one **nous** = we **vous** = you **ils/elles** = they

acquerir (to acquire)

PRESENT

j'	**acquiers**
tu	**acquiers**
il/elle/on	**acquiert**
nous	**acquérons**
vous	**acquérez**
ils/elles	**acquièrent**

PRESENT SUBJUNCTIVE

j'	**acquière**
tu	**acquières**
il/elle/on	**acquière**
nous	**acquérions**
vous	**acquériez**
ils/elles	**acquièrent**

PERFECT

j'	**ai acquis**
tu	**as acquis**
il/elle/on	**a acquis**
nous	**avons acquis**
vous	**avez acquis**
ils/elles	**ont acquis**

IMPERFECT

j'	**acquérais**
tu	**acquérais**
il/elle/on	**acquérait**
nous	**acquérions**
vous	**acquériez**
ils/elles	**acquéraient**

PRESENT PARTICIPLE
acquérant

PAST PARTICIPLE
acquis

FUTURE

j'	**acquerrai**
tu	**acquerras**
il/elle/on	**acquerra**
nous	**acquerrons**
vous	**acquerrez**
ils/elles	**acquerront**

CONDITIONAL

j'	**acquerrais**
tu	**acquerrais**
il/elle/on	**acquerrait**
nous	**acquerrions**
vous	**acquerriez**
ils/elles	**acquerrient**

PAST HISTORIC

j'	**acquis**
tu	**acquis**
il/elle/on	**acquit**
nous	**acquîmes**
vous	**acquîtes**
ils/elles	**acquirent**

PLUPERFECT

j'	**avais acquis**
tu	**avais acquis**
il/elle/on	**avait acquis**
nous	**avions acquis**
vous	**aviez acquis**
ils/elles	**avaient acquis**

IMPERATIVE
acquiers / acquérons / acquérez

EXAMPLE PHRASES

Nous **acquérons** de nouvelles connaissances tous les jours.
We acquire new knowledge every day.

Les mauvaises habitudes s'**acquièrent** facilement.
One easily acquires bad habits.

Elle **a acquis** la nationalité française en 2003.
She acquired French nationality in 2003.

Il faut qu'il **acquière** de l'expérience avant que nous puissions lui offrir un travail.
He has to gain some experience before we can offer him a job.

Elle **acquit** soudain la certitude qu'il lui avait toujours menti.
She suddenly felt certain that he'd always lied to her.

Tu **acquerrais** un peu d'expérience si tu travaillais cet été.
You'd gain some experience if you worked this summer.

Il **avait** mystérieusement **acquis** une superbe voiture de sport.
He had mysteriously acquired a beautiful sportscar.

Le tableau **avait acquis** beaucoup de valeur.
The painting had risen a lot in value.

---

je/j' = I   **tu** = you   **il** = he/it   **elle** = she/it   **on** = we/one   **nous** = we   **vous** = you   **ils/elles** = they

aller (to go)

PRESENT

je	**vais**
tu	**vas**
il/elle/on	**va**
nous	**allons**
vous	**allez**
ils/elles	**vont**

PRESENT SUBJUNCTIVE

j'	**aille**
tu	**ailles**
il/elle/on	**aille**
nous	**allions**
vous	**alliez**
ils/elles	**aillent**

PERFECT

je	**suis allé(e)**
tu	**es allé(e)**
il/elle/on	**est allé(e)**
nous	**sommes allé(e)s**
vous	**êtes allé(e)(s)**
ils/elles	**sont allé(e)s**

IMPERFECT

j'	**allais**
tu	**allais**
il/elle/on	**allait**
nous	**allions**
vous	**alliez**
ils/elles	**allaient**

PRESENT PARTICIPLE
allant

PAST PARTICIPLE
allé

FUTURE

j'	**irai**
tu	**iras**
il/elle/on	**ira**
nous	**irons**
vous	**irez**
ils/elles	**iront**

CONDITIONAL

j'	**irais**
tu	**irais**
il/elle/on	**irait**
nous	**irions**
vous	**iriez**
ils/elles	**iraient**

PAST HISTORIC

j'	**allai**
tu	**allas**
il/elle/on	**alla**
nous	**allâmes**
vous	**allâtes**
ils/elles	**allèrent**

PLUPERFECT

j'	**étais allé(e)**
tu	**étais allé(e)**
il/elle/on	**était allé(e)**
nous	**étions allé(e)s**
vous	**étiez allé(e)(s)**
ils/elles	**étaient allé(e)s**

IMPERATIVE
va / allons / allez

EXAMPLE PHRASES

Vous **allez** souvent au cinéma?
Do you often go to the cinema?

Je **suis allé** à Londres.
I went to London.

Est-ce que tu **es** déjà **allé** en Allemagne?
Have you ever been to Germany?

Il faut que j'**aille** la chercher à la gare.
I have to go and get her at the station.

J'**allais** tous les jours à l'école à pied.
I would walk to school every day.

J'**irai** en ville demain.
I'll go into town tomorrow.

Ils **allèrent** la voir à l'hôpital.
They went to see her at the hospital.

J'**irais** au théâtre avec toi s'il restait des places.
I'd go to the theatre with you if there were any tickets left.

Nous **étions allés** à Paris en avion mais nous étions rentrés par le train.
We'd flown to Paris, but we'd come back by train.

Va voir s'ils sont arrivés.
Go and see whether they have arrived.

je/j' = I   **tu** = you   **il** = he/it   **elle** = she/it   **on** = we/one   **nous** = we   **vous** = you   **ils/elles** = they

s'amuser (to play; to enjoy oneself)

PRESENT

je	**m'amuse**
tu	**t'amuses**
il/elle/on	**s'amuse**
nous	**nous amusons**
vous	**vous amusez**
ils/elles	**s'amusent**

PRESENT SUBJUNCTIVE

je	**m'amuse**
tu	**t'amuses**
il/elle/on	**s'amuse**
nous	**nous amusions**
vous	**vous amusiez**
ils/elles	**s'amusent**

PERFECT

je	**me suis amusé(e)**
tu	**t'es amusé(e)**
il/elle/on	**s'est amusé(e)**
nous	**nous sommes amusé(e)s**
vous	**vous êtes amusé(e)(s)**
ils/elles	**se sont amusé(e)s**

IMPERFECT

je	**m'amusais**
tu	**t'amusais**
il/elle/on	**s'amusait**
nous	**nous amusions**
vous	**vous amusiez**
ils/elles	**s'amusaient**

PRESENT PARTICIPLE

s'amusant

PAST PARTICIPLE

amusé

FUTURE

je	**m'amuserai**
tu	**t'amuseras**
il/elle/on	**s'amusera**
nous	**nous amuserons**
vous	**vous amuserez**
ils/elles	**s'amuseront**

CONDITIONAL

je	**m'amuserais**
tu	**t'amuserais**
il/elle/on	**s'amuserait**
nous	**nous amuserions**
vous	**vous amuseriez**
ils/elles	**s'amuseraient**

PAST HISTORIC

je	**m'amusai**
tu	**t'amusas**
il/elle/on	**s'amusa**
nous	**nous amusâmes**
vous	**vous amusâtes**
ils/elles	**s'amusèrent**

PLUPERFECT

je	**m'étais amusé(e)**
tu	**t'étais amusé(e)**
il/elle/on	**s'était amusé(e)**
nous	**nous étions amusé(e)s**
vous	**vous étiez amusé(e)(s)**
ils/elles	**s'étaient amusé(e)s**

IMPERATIVE

amuse-toi / amusons-nous / amusez-vous

EXAMPLE PHRASES

Les enfants **s'amusent** dehors.
The children are playing outside.

On **s'est** bien **amusés** à cette soirée.
We really enjoyed ourselves at that party.

J'ai peur que personne ne **s'amuse** cet après-midi.
I'm scared nobody enjoys themselves this afternoon.

Ils **s'amusaient** à sauter dans les flaques d'eau.
They had fun jumping in the puddles.

Je suis sûr qu'ils **s'amuseront** comme des fous.
I'm sure they'll have a whale of a time.

Ils **s'amusèrent** à dessiner un monstre.
They had fun drawing a monster.

Tu **t'amuserais** bien si tu venais avec nous.
You'd have fun if you came with us.

Je **m'étais** bien **amusé** à leur mariage.
I'd really enjoyed myself at their wedding.

Amuse-toi bien avec Florence.
Have fun with Florence.

je/j' = I   **tu** = you   **il** = he/it   **elle** = she/it   **on** = we/one   **nous** = we   **vous** = you   **ils/elles** = they

apercevoir (to notice)

PRESENT

j'	**aperçois**
tu	**aperçois**
il/elle/on	**aperçoit**
nous	**apercevons**
vous	**apercevez**
ils/elles	**aperçoivent**

PRESENT SUBJUNCTIVE

j'	**aperçoive**
tu	**aperçoives**
il/elle/on	**aperçoive**
nous	**apercevions**
vous	**aperceviez**
ils/elles	**aperçoivent**

PERFECT

j'	**ai aperçu**
tu	**as aperçu**
il/elle/on	**a aperçu**
nous	**avons aperçu**
vous	**avez aperçu**
ils/elles	**ont aperçu**

IMPERFECT

j'	**apercevais**
tu	**apercevais**
il/elle/on	**apercevait**
nous	**apercevions**
vous	**aperceviez**
ils/elles	**apercevaient**

PRESENT PARTICIPLE

apercevant

PAST PARTICIPLE

aperçu

FUTURE

j'	**apercevrai**
tu	**apercevras**
il/elle/on	**apercevra**
nous	**apercevrons**
vous	**apercevrez**
ils/elles	**apercevront**

CONDITIONAL

j'	**apercevrais**
tu	**apercevrais**
il/elle/on	**apercevrait**
nous	**apercevrions**
vous	**apercevriez**
ils/elles	**apercevraient**

PAST HISTORIC

j'	**aperçus**
tu	**aperçus**
il/elle/on	**aperçut**
nous	**aperçûmes**
vous	**aperçûtes**
ils/elles	**aperçurent**

PLUPERFECT

j'	**avais aperçu**
tu	**avais aperçu**
il/elle/on	**avait aperçu**
nous	**avions aperçu**
vous	**aviez aperçu**
ils/elles	**avaient aperçu**

IMPERATIVE

not used

EXAMPLE PHRASES

J'**aperçois** une lumière là-bas.
I can see a light over there.

Je l'**ai aperçue** hier au marché.
I saw her yesterday at the market.

Ils ont marché longtemps, jusqu'à ce qu'ils **aperçoivent** une maison.
They walked for a long time, until they saw a house.

Je les **apercevais** de temps en temps en allant travailler.
I saw them from time to time on my way to work.

Va jusqu'à l'arrêt du bus et tu **apercevras** le magasin au coin de la rue.
Go up to the bus stop and you'll see the shop on the street corner.

Ils **aperçurent** une silhouette au loin.
They saw a shadow in the distance.

Il l'**avait aperçue** une ou deux fois chez les Duval il y avait très longtemps.
He'd seen her once or twice at the Duvals' a long time before.

Je ne me souvenais pas de l'endroit où je l'**avais aperçu**.
I couldn't remember where I'd seen him.

je/j' = I **tu** = you **il** = he/it **elle** = she/it **on** = we/one **nous** = we **vous** = you **ils/elles** = they

appeler (to call)

PRESENT

j'	**appelle**
tu	**appelles**
il/elle/on	**appelle**
nous	**appelons**
vous	**appelez**
ils/elles	**appellent**

PERFECT

j'	**ai appelé**
tu	**as appelé**
il/elle/on	**a appelé**
nous	**avons appelé**
vous	**avez appelé**
ils/elles	**ont appelé**

PRESENT PARTICIPLE

appelant

FUTURE

j'	**appellerai**
tu	**appelleras**
il/elle/on	**appellera**
nous	**appellerons**
vous	**appellerez**
ils/elles	**appelleront**

PAST HISTORIC

j'	**appelai**
tu	**appelas**
il/elle/on	**appela**
nous	**appelâmes**
vous	**appelâtes**
ils/elles	**appelèrent**

IMPERATIVE

appelle / appelons / appelez

PRESENT SUBJUNCTIVE

j'	**appelle**
tu	**appelles**
il/elle/on	**appelle**
nous	**appelions**
vous	**appeliez**
ils/elles	**appellent**

IMPERFECT

j'	**appelais**
tu	**appelais**
il/elle/on	**appelait**
nous	**appelions**
vous	**appeliez**
ils/elles	**appelaient**

PAST PARTICIPLE

appelé

CONDITIONAL

j'	**appellerais**
tu	**appellerais**
il/elle/on	**appellerait**
nous	**appellerions**
vous	**appelleriez**
ils/elles	**appelleraient**

PLUPERFECT

j'	**avais appelé**
tu	**avais appelé**
il/elle/on	**avait appelé**
nous	**avions appelé**
vous	**aviez appelé**
ils/elles	**avaient appelé**

EXAMPLE PHRASES

Louise! Descends: maman t'**appelle**.
Louise! Go downstairs – Mum's
   calling you.

Comment tu t'**appelles**?
What's your name?

Elle **a appelé** le médecin.
She called the doctor.

Il faut que je l'**appelle** après dîner.
I must ring her after dinner.

Elle **appelait** souvent le soir.
She often rang in the evening.

Je t'**appellerai** demain.
I'll ring you tomorrow.

On **appela** mon nom et je me levai.
My name was called and I stood up.

Je l'**appellerais** si j'étais sûr de ne pas
   le déranger.
I'd ring him if I was sure not to
   disturb him.

Elle m'**avait appelé** mais je ne l'avais
   pas entendue.
She had called me but I hadn't
   heard her.

Appelle-moi sur mon portable.
Ring me on my mobile.

je/j' = I   **tu** = you   **il** = he/it   **elle** = she/it   **on** = we/one   **nous** = we   **vous** = you   **ils/elles** = they

appuyer (to lean; to press)

PRESENT

j'	**appuie**
tu	**appuies**
il/elle/on	**appuie**
nous	**appuyons**
vous	**appuyez**
ils/elles	**appuient**

PRESENT SUBJUNCTIVE

j'	**appuie**
tu	**appuies**
il/elle/on	**appuie**
nous	**appuyions**
vous	**appuyiez**
ils/elles	**appuient**

PERFECT

j'	**ai appuyé**
tu	**as appuyé**
il/elle/on	**a appuyé**
nous	**avons appuyé**
vous	**avez appuyé**
ils/elles	**ont appuyé**

IMPERFECT

j'	**appuyais**
tu	**appuyais**
il/elle/on	**appuyait**
nous	**appuyions**
vous	**appuyiez**
ils/elles	**appuyaient**

PRESENT PARTICIPLE
appuyant

PAST PARTICIPLE
appuyé

FUTURE

j'	**appuierai**
tu	**appuieras**
il/elle/on	**appuiera**
nous	**appuierons**
vous	**appuierez**
ils/elles	**appuieront**

CONDITIONAL

j'	**appuierais**
tu	**appuierais**
il/elle/on	**appuierait**
nous	**appuierions**
vous	**appuieriez**
ils/elles	**appuieraient**

PAST HISTORIC

j'	**appuyai**
tu	**appuyas**
il/elle/on	**appuya**
nous	**appuyâmes**
vous	**appuyâtes**
ils/elles	**appuyèrent**

PLUPERFECT

j'	**avais appuyé**
tu	**avais appuyé**
il/elle/on	**avait appuyé**
nous	**avions appuyé**
vous	**aviez appuyé**
ils/elles	**avaient appuyé**

IMPERATIVE
appuie / appuyons / appuyez

EXAMPLE PHRASES

Elle **a appuyé** son vélo contre le mur.
She leaned her bike against the wall.

Il faut que tu **appuies** fort.
You have to press hard.

J'appuierai trois fois sur la sonnette.
I'll press the bell three times.

Il **appuya** longtemps mais la colle ne tenait pas.
He pressed for a long time but the glue didn't hold.

Il n'**appuierait** pas si fort si tu le laissais faire.
He wouldn't press so hard if you'd let him do it.

Elle n'**avait** pas **appuyé** assez fort et la cloche n'avait pas sonné.
She hadn't pressed hard enough and the bell hadn't rung.

Appuie sur le bouton rouge.
Press the red button.

je/j' = I   **tu** = you   **il** = he/it   **elle** = she/it   **on** = we/one   **nous** = we   **vous** = you   **ils/elles** = they

arriver (to arrive)

PRESENT

j'	**arrive**
tu	**arrives**
il/elle/on	**arrive**
nous	**arrivons**
vous	**arrivez**
ils/elles	**arrivent**

PRESENT SUBJUNCTIVE

j'	**arrive**
tu	**arrives**
il/elle/on	**arrive**
nous	**arrivions**
vous	**arriviez**
ils/elles	**arrivent**

PERFECT

je	**suis arrivé(e)**
tu	**es arrivé(e)**
il/elle/on	**est arrivé(e)**
nous	**sommes arrivé(e)s**
vous	**êtes arrivé(e)(s)**
ils/elles	**sont arrivé(e)s**

IMPERFECT

j'	**arrivais**
tu	**arrivais**
il/elle/on	**arrivait**
nous	**arrivions**
vous	**arriviez**
ils/elles	**arrivaient**

PRESENT PARTICIPLE
arrivant

PAST PARTICIPLE
arrivé

FUTURE

j'	**arriverai**
tu	**arriveras**
il/elle/on	**arrivera**
nous	**arriverons**
vous	**arriverez**
ils/elles	**arriveront**

CONDITIONAL

j'	**arriverais**
tu	**arriverais**
il/elle/on	**arriverait**
nous	**arriverions**
vous	**arriveriez**
ils/elles	**arriveraient**

PAST HISTORIC

j'	**arrivai**
tu	**arrivas**
il/elle/on	**arriva**
nous	**arrivâmes**
vous	**arrivâtes**
ils/elles	**arrivèrent**

PLUPERFECT

j'	**étais arrivé(e)**
tu	**étais arrivé(e)**
il/elle/on	**était arrivé(e)**
nous	**étions arrivé(e)s**
vous	**étiez arrivé(e)(s)**
ils/elles	**étaient arrivé(e)s**

IMPERATIVE
arrive / arrivons / arrivez

EXAMPLE PHRASES

J'**arrive** à l'école à huit heures.
I arrive at school at 8 o'clock.

Qu'est-ce qui **est arrivé** à Aurélie?
What happened to Aurélie?

N'**arrivez** pas en retard demain.
Don't arrive late tomorrow.

Il faut que j'**arrive** à jouer cet air pour la leçon de demain.
I'll have to be able to play this tune for tomorrow's lesson.

Il m'**arrivait** de dormir jusqu'à midi.
I sometimes slept till midday.

Arriveras-tu à l'heure pour ton rendez-vous?
Will you be on time for your appointment?

La réunion était finie depuis longtemps quand il **arriva**.
The meeting had finished long before he arrived.

Je n'**arriverais** jamais à faire tout ce travail sans ton aide.
I would never be able to get all this work done without your help.

Le prof n'**était** pas encore **arrivé**.
The teacher hadn't arrived yet.

je/j' = I **tu** = you **il** = he/it **elle** = she/it **on** = we/one **nous** = we **vous** = you **ils/elles** = they

s'asseoir (to sit down)

PRESENT	
je	**m'assieds/m'assois**
tu	**t'assieds/t'assois**
il/elle/on	**s'assied/s'assoit**
nous	**nous asseyons/ nous assoyons**
vous	**vous asseyez/ vous assoyez**
ils/elles	**s'asseyent/s'assoient**

PRESENT SUBJUNCTIVE	
je	**m'asseye**
tu	**t'asseyes**
il/elle/on	**s'asseye**
nous	**nous asseyions**
vous	**vous asseyiez**
ils/elles	**s'asseyent**

PERFECT	
je	**me suis assis(e)**
tu	**t'es assis(e)**
il/elle/on	**s'est assis(e)**
nous	**nous sommes assis(es)**
vous	**vous êtes assis(e(s))**
ils/elles	**se sont assis(es)**

IMPERFECT	
je	**m'asseyais**
tu	**t'asseyais**
il/elle/on	**s'asseyait**
nous	**nous asseyions**
vous	**vous asseyiez**
ils/elles	**s'asseyaient**

PRESENT PARTICIPLE	**PAST PARTICIPLE**
s'asseyant	assis

FUTURE	
je	**m'assiérai**
tu	**t'assiéras**
il/elle/on	**s'assiéra**
nous	**nous assiérons**
vous	**vous assiérez**
ils/elles	**s'assiéront**

CONDITIONAL	
je	**m'assiérais**
tu	**t'assiérais**
il/elle/on	**s'assiérait**
nous	**nous assiérions**
vous	**vous assiériez**
ils/elles	**s'assiéraient**

PAST HISTORIC	
je	**m'assis**
tu	**t'assis**
il/elle/on	**s'assit**
nous	**nous assîmes**
vous	**vous assîtes**
ils/elles	**s'assirent**

PLUPERFECT	
je	**m'étais assis(e)**
tu	**t'étais assis(e)**
il/elle/on	**s'était assis(e)**
nous	**nous étions assis(es)**
vous	**vous étiez assis(e(s))**
ils/elles	**s'étaient assis(es)**

EXAMPLE PHRASES

Je peux **m'asseoir**?
May I sit down?

Je **me suis assise** sur un chewing-gum!
I've sat on chewing-gum!

On **s'asseyait** toujours l'un à côté de l'autre.
We would always sit next to each other.

Je **m'assiérai** à côté de toi.
I'll sit next to you.

Il **s'assit** en face de moi.
He sat down opposite me.

Je ne **m'assiérais** pas là si j'étais toi.
I wouldn't sit there if I were you.

Elle ne **s'était** pas encore **assise** quand la fillette l'appela à nouveau.
She hadn't even sat down when the little girl called her once again.

Assieds-toi, Nicole.
Sit down, Nicole.

Asseyez-vous, les enfants.
Sit down children.

IMPERATIVE
assieds-toi / asseyons-nous / asseyez-vous

je/j' = I   **tu** = you   **il** = he/it   **elle** = she/it   **on** = we/one   **nous** = we   **vous** = you   **ils/elles** = they

atteindre (to reach)

PRESENT		PRESENT SUBJUNCTIVE	
j'	**atteins**	j'	**atteigne**
tu	**atteins**	tu	**atteignes**
il/elle/on	**atteint**	il/elle/on	**atteigne**
nous	**atteignons**	nous	**atteignions**
vous	**atteignez**	vous	**atteigniez**
ils/elles	**atteignent**	ils/elles	**atteignent**

PERFECT		IMPERFECT	
j'	**ai atteint**	j'	**atteignais**
tu	**as atteint**	tu	**atteignais**
il/elle/on	**a atteint**	il/elle/on	**atteignait**
nous	**avons atteint**	nous	**atteignions**
vous	**avez atteint**	vous	**atteigniez**
ils/elles	**ont atteint**	ils/elles	**atteignaient**

PRESENT PARTICIPLE
atteignant

PAST PARTICIPLE
atteint

FUTURE		CONDITIONAL	
j'	**atteindrai**	j'	**atteindrais**
tu	**atteindras**	tu	**atteindrais**
il/elle/on	**atteindra**	il/elle/on	**atteindrait**
nous	**atteindrons**	nous	**atteindrions**
vous	**atteindrez**	vous	**atteindriez**
ils/elles	**atteindront**	ils/elles	**atteindraient**

PAST HISTORIC		PLUPERFECT	
j'	**atteignis**	j'	**avais atteint**
tu	**atteignis**	tu	**avais atteint**
il/elle/on	**atteignit**	il/elle/on	**avait atteint**
nous	**atteignîmes**	nous	**avions atteint**
vous	**atteignîtes**	vous	**aviez atteint**
ils/elles	**atteignirent**	ils/elles	**avaient atteint**

IMPERATIVE
atteins / atteignons / atteignez

EXAMPLE PHRASES

Je n'arrive pas à **atteindre** ma valise.
I can't reach my suitcase.

Cette Ferrari **atteint** une vitesse de
245 km/h.
This Ferrari reaches a speed of
245km/h.

Ils **ont atteint** le sommet en quatre
heures et demie.
They reached the summit in four and a
half hours.

Ils **atteignaient** Paris quand l'accident
se produisit.
They were nearing Paris when the
accident happened.

Nous **atteindrons** Rouen dans dix
minutes.
We'll reach Rouen in ten minutes.

Il **atteignit** sa destination en trois
semaines.
He reached his destination in three
weeks.

Il se rendit compte qu'il n'**atteindrait**
jamais son but.
He realized that he would never reach
his goal.

Le tableau **avait atteint** un prix
exorbitant.
The painting had reached a prohibitive
price.

je/j' = I   **tu** = you   **il** = he/it   **elle** = she/it   **on** = we/one   **nous** = we   **vous** = you   **ils/elles** = they

attendre (to wait)

PRESENT

j'	**attends**
tu	**attends**
il/elle/on	**attend**
nous	**attendons**
vous	**attendez**
ils/elles	**attendent**

PRESENT SUBJUNCTIVE

j'	**attende**
tu	**attendes**
il/elle/on	**attende**
nous	**attendions**
vous	**attendiez**
ils/elles	**attendent**

PERFECT

j'	**ai attendu**
tu	**as attendu**
il/elle/on	**a attendu**
nous	**avons attendu**
vous	**avez attendu**
ils/elles	**ont attendu**

IMPERFECT

j'	**attendais**
tu	**attendais**
il/elle/on	**attendait**
nous	**attendions**
vous	**attendiez**
ils/elles	**attendaient**

PRESENT PARTICIPLE
attendant

PAST PARTICIPLE
attendu

FUTURE

j'	**attendrai**
tu	**attendras**
il/elle/on	**attendra**
nous	**attendrons**
vous	**attendrez**
ils/elles	**attendront**

CONDITIONAL

j'	**attendrais**
tu	**attendrais**
il/elle/on	**attendrait**
nous	**attendrions**
vous	**attendriez**
ils/elles	**attendraient**

PAST HISTORIC

j'	**attendis**
tu	**attendis**
il/elle/on	**attendit**
nous	**attendîmes**
vous	**attendîtes**
ils/elles	**attendirent**

PLUPERFECT

j'	**avais attendu**
tu	**avais attendu**
il/elle/on	**avait attendu**
nous	**avions attendu**
vous	**aviez attendu**
ils/elles	**avaient attendu**

IMPERATIVE
attends / attendons / attendez

EXAMPLE PHRASES

Tu **attends** depuis longtemps?
Have you been waiting long?

Je l'**ai attendu** à la poste.
I waited for him at the post office.

Elle veut que je l'**attende** dans le hall.
She wants me to wait for her in the hall.

Elle **attendait** un bébé.
She was expecting a baby.

J'**attendrai** qu'il ne pleuve plus.
I'll wait until it's stopped raining.

Nous **attendîmes** en silence.
We waited in silence.

Je t'**attendrais** si tu n'étais pas si lente.
I'd wait for you if you weren't so slow.

Elle m'**avait attendu** patiemment
  devant la poste.
She had patiently waited for me in
  front of the post office.

Attends-moi!
Wait for me!

---

je/j' = I   **tu** = you   **il** = he/it   **elle** = she/it   **on** = we/one   **nous** = we   **vous** = you   **ils/elles** = they

avoir (to have)

PRESENT

j'	**ai**
tu	**as**
il/elle/on	**a**
nous	**avons**
vous	**avez**
ils/elles	**ont**

PRESENT SUBJUNCTIVE

j'	**aie**
tu	**aies**
il/elle/on	**ait**
nous	**ayons**
vous	**ayez**
ils/elles	**aient**

PERFECT

j'	**ai eu**
tu	**as eu**
il/elle/on	**a eu**
nous	**avons eu**
vous	**avez eu**
ils/elles	**ont eu**

IMPERFECT

j'	**avais**
tu	**avais**
il/elle/on	**avait**
nous	**avions**
vous	**aviez**
ils/elles	**avaient**

PRESENT PARTICIPLE
ayant

PAST PARTICIPLE
eu

FUTURE

j'	**aurai**
tu	**auras**
il/elle/on	**aura**
nous	**aurons**
vous	**aurez**
ils/elles	**auront**

CONDITIONAL

j'	**aurais**
tu	**aurais**
il/elle/on	**aurait**
nous	**aurions**
vous	**auriez**
ils/elles	**auraient**

PAST HISTORIC

j'	**eus**
tu	**eus**
il/elle/on	**eut**
nous	**eûmes**
vous	**eûtes**
ils/elles	**eurent**

PLUPERFECT

j'	**avais eu**
tu	**avais eu**
il/elle/on	**avait eu**
nous	**avions eu**
vous	**aviez eu**
ils/elles	**avaient eu**

IMPERATIVE
aie / ayons / ayez

EXAMPLE PHRASES

Il **a** les yeux bleus.
He's got blue eyes.

Quel âge **as**-tu?
How old are you?

Il y **a** beaucoup de monde.
There are lots of people.

Il **a eu** un accident.
He's had an accident.

J'**avais** faim.
I was hungry.

Cloé **aura** cinq ans au mois d'août.
Cloé will be five in August.

J'**eus** soudain l'idée de lui rendre visite.
I suddenly thought of paying him a visit.

Je n'**aurais** pas tant mangé si j'avais su qu'il y avait un dessert.
I wouldn't have eaten so much if I'd known that there was a pudding.

Paul **avait eu** mal au ventre toute la nuit.
Paul had had a sore stomach all night.

je/j' = I **tu** = you **il** = he/it **elle** = she/it **on** = we/one **nous** = we **vous** = you **ils/elles** = they

battre (to beat)

PRESENT

je	**bats**
tu	**bats**
il/elle/on	**bat**
nous	**battons**
vous	**battez**
ils/elles	**battent**

PRESENT SUBJUNCTIVE

je	**batte**
tu	**battes**
il/elle/on	**batte**
nous	**battions**
vous	**battiez**
ils/elles	**battent**

PERFECT

j'	**ai battu**
tu	**as battu**
il/elle/on	**a battu**
nous	**avons battu**
vous	**avez battu**
ils/elles	**ont battu**

IMPERFECT

je	**battais**
tu	**battais**
il/elle/on	**battait**
nous	**battions**
vous	**battiez**
ils/elles	**battaient**

PRESENT PARTICIPLE

battant

PAST PARTICIPLE

battu

FUTURE

je	**battrai**
tu	**battras**
il/elle/on	**battra**
nous	**battrons**
vous	**battrez**
ils/elles	**battront**

CONDITIONAL

je	**battrais**
tu	**battrais**
il/elle/on	**battrait**
nous	**battrions**
vous	**battriez**
ils/elles	**battraient**

PAST HISTORIC

je	**battis**
tu	**battis**
il/elle/on	**battit**
nous	**battîmes**
vous	**battîtes**
ils/elles	**battirent**

PLUPERFECT

j'	**avais battu**
tu	**avais battu**
il/elle/on	**avait battu**
nous	**avions battu**
vous	**aviez battu**
ils/elles	**avaient battu**

IMPERATIVE

bats / battons / battez

EXAMPLE PHRASES

J'ai le cœur qui **bat vite**!
My heart's beating fast!

Arrêtez de vous **battre**!
Stop fighting!

On les **a battus** deux à un.
We beat them two-one.

Elle le **battait** toujours au poker.
She'd always beat him at poker.

Tu ne me **battras** jamais à la course.
You'll never beat me at running.

Elle le **battit** au Scrabble®.
She beat him at Scrabble®.

Ils se **battraient** tout le temps si je les
laissais faire.
They'd fight all the time if I let them.

Elle **avait battu** le record du monde
du saut à la perche.
She'd beaten the world record for the
pole vault.

Bats les cartes, s'il te plaît.
Shuffle the cards please.

je/j' = I   **tu** = you   **il** = he/it   **elle** = she/it   **on** = we/one   **nous** = we   **vous** = you   **ils/elles** = they

boire (to drink)

PRESENT	
je	**bois**
tu	**bois**
il/elle/on	**boit**
nous	**buvons**
vous	**buvez**
ils/elles	**boivent**

PRESENT SUBJUNCTIVE	
je	**boive**
tu	**boives**
il/elle/on	**boive**
nous	**buvions**
vous	**buviez**
ils/elles	**boivent**

PERFECT	
j'	**ai bu**
tu	**as bu**
il/elle/on	**a bu**
nous	**avons bu**
vous	**avez bu**
ils/elles	**ont bu**

IMPERFECT	
je	**buvais**
tu	**buvais**
il/elle/on	**buvait**
nous	**buvions**
vous	**buviez**
ils/elles	**buvaient**

PRESENT PARTICIPLE
buvant

PAST PARTICIPLE
bu

FUTURE	
je	**boirai**
tu	**boiras**
il/elle/on	**boira**
nous	**boirons**
vous	**boirez**
ils/elles	**boiront**

CONDITIONAL	
je	**boirais**
tu	**boirais**
il/elle/on	**boirait**
nous	**boirions**
vous	**boiriez**
ils/elles	**boiraient**

PAST HISTORIC	
je	**bus**
tu	**bus**
il/elle/on	**but**
nous	**bûmes**
vous	**bûtes**
ils/elles	**burent**

PLUPERFECT	
j'	**avais bu**
tu	**avais bu**
il/elle/on	**avait bu**
nous	**avions bu**
vous	**aviez bu**
ils/elles	**avaient bu**

IMPERATIVE
bois / buvons / buvez

EXAMPLE PHRASES

Qu'est-ce que tu veux **boire**?
What would you like to drink?

Il ne **boit** jamais d'alcool.
He never drinks alcohol.

J'**ai bu** un litre d'eau.
I drank a litre of water.

Elle **buvait** un whisky tous les soirs.
She had a whisky every night.

Que **boirez**-vous?
What will you have to drink?

Il **but** son jus d'orange d'un trait.
He drank his orange juice in one gulp.

Je **boirais** bien un cognac.
I'd quite like a brandy.

On voyait qu'il **avait bu**.
He was obviously drunk.

Bois ton café avant de partir.
Drink your coffee before we leave.

je/j' = I   **tu** = you   **il** = he/it   **elle** = she/it   **on** = we/one   **nous** = we   **vous** = you   **ils/elles** = they

bouillir (to boil)

PRESENT

je **bous**
tu **bous**
il/elle/on **bout**
nous **bouillons**
vous **bouillez**
ils/elles **bouillent**

PRESENT SUBJUNCTIVE

je **bouille**
tu **bouilles**
il/elle/on **bouille**
nous **bouillions**
vous **bouilliez**
ils/elles **bouillent**

PERFECT

j' **ai bouilli**
tu **as bouilli**
il/elle/on **a bouilli**
nous **avons bouilli**
vous **avez bouilli**
ils/elles **ont bouilli**

IMPERFECT

je **bouillais**
tu **bouillais**
il/elle/on **bouillait**
nous **bouillions**
vous **bouilliez**
ils/elles **bouillaient**

PRESENT PARTICIPLE
bouillant

PAST PARTICIPLE
bouilli

FUTURE

je **bouillirai**
tu **bouilliras**
il/elle/on **bouillira**
nous **bouillirons**
vous **bouillirez**
ils/elles **bouilliront**

CONDITIONAL

je **bouillirais**
tu **bouillirais**
il/elle/on **bouillirait**
nous **bouillirions**
vous **bouilliriez**
ils/elles **bouilliraient**

PAST HISTORIC

je **bouillis**
tu **bouillis**
il/elle/on **bouillit**
nous **bouillîmes**
vous **bouillîtes**
ils/elles **bouillirent**

PLUPERFECT

j' **avais bouilli**
tu **avais bouilli**
il/elle/on **avait bouilli**
nous **avions bouilli**
vous **aviez bouilli**
ils/elles **avaient bouilli**

IMPERATIVE
bous / bouillons / bouillez

EXAMPLE PHRASES

Tu peux mettre de l'eau à **bouillir**?
Can you boil some water?

Faites **bouillir** pendant quelques
minutes.
Boil for a few minutes.

L'eau **bout**.
The water's boiling.

La soupe **a bouilli** trop longtemps.
The soup had boiled for too long.

Je **bouillais** d'impatience.
I was bursting with impatience.

Quand l'eau **bouillira**, la bouilloire
sifflera.
When the water boils, the kettle will
whistle.

Le lait **bouillit** et déborda.
The milk boiled over.

L'eau n'**avait** pas encore **bouilli**.
The water hadn't boiled yet.

je/j' = I   **tu** = you   **il** = he/it   **elle** = she/it   **on** = we/one   **nous** = we   **vous** = you   **ils/elles** = they

commencer (to start; to begin)

PRESENT

je	**commence**
tu	**commences**
il/elle/on	**commence**
nous	**commençons**
vous	**commencez**
ils/elles	**commencent**

PRESENT SUBJUNCTIVE

je	**commence**
tu	**commences**
il/elle/on	**commence**
nous	**commencions**
vous	**commenciez**
ils/elles	**commencent**

PERFECT

j'	**ai commencé**
tu	**as commencé**
il/elle/on	**a commencé**
nous	**avons commencé**
vous	**avez commencé**
ils/elles	**ont commencé**

IMPERFECT

je	**commençais**
tu	**commençais**
il/elle/on	**commençait**
nous	**commencions**
vous	**commenciez**
ils/elles	**commençaient**

PRESENT PARTICIPLE

commençant

PAST PARTICIPLE

commencé

FUTURE

je	**commencerai**
tu	**commenceras**
il/elle/on	**commencera**
nous	**commencerons**
vous	**commencerez**
ils/elles	**commenceront**

CONDITIONAL

je	**commencerais**
tu	**commencerais**
il/elle/on	**commencerait**
nous	**commencerions**
vous	**commenceriez**
ils/elles	**commenceraient**

PAST HISTORIC

je	**commençai**
tu	**commenças**
il/elle/on	**commença**
nous	**commençâmes**
vous	**commençâtes**
ils/elles	**commencèrent**

PLUPERFECT

j'	**avais commencé**
tu	**avais commencé**
il/elle/on	**avait commencé**
nous	**avions commencé**
vous	**aviez commencé**
ils/elles	**avaient commencé**

IMPERATIVE

commence / commençons / commencez

EXAMPLE PHRASES

Les cours **commencent** à neuf heures.
Lessons start at nine o'clock.

Tu **as** déjà **commencé** à réviser pour tes examens?
Have you started revising for your exams?

Ne **commence** pas à m'embêter.
Don't start annoying me.

J'aimerais que tu **commences** à faire les valises.
I'd like you to start packing the suitcases.

Son attitude **commençait** à m'énerver.
Her attitude had started to annoy me.

Nous ne **commencerons** pas sans toi.
We won't start without you.

C'est quand les nouveaux voisins arrivèrent que les ennuis **commencèrent**.
It's when the new neighbours arrived that the problems started.

Nous **commencerions** une partie de cartes si nous étions sûrs d'avoir le temps de la finir.
We'd start a game of cards if we were sure we'd have time to finish it.

Il **avait commencé** à pleuvoir.
It had started to rain.

je/j' = I **tu** = you **il** = he/it **elle** = she/it **on** = we/one **nous** = we **vous** = you **ils/elles** = they

conclure (to conclude)

PRESENT

je	**conclus**
tu	**conclus**
il/elle/on	**conclut**
nous	**concluons**
vous	**concluez**
ils/elles	**concluent**

PRESENT SUBJUNCTIVE

je	**conclue**
tu	**conclues**
il/elle/on	**conclue**
nous	**concluions**
vous	**concluiez**
ils/elles	**concluent**

PERFECT

j'	**ai conclu**
tu	**as conclu**
il/elle/on	**a conclu**
nous	**avons conclu**
vous	**avez conclu**
ils/elles	**ont conclu**

IMPERFECT

je	**concluais**
tu	**concluais**
il/elle/on	**concluait**
nous	**concluions**
vous	**concluiez**
ils/elles	**concluaient**

PRESENT PARTICIPLE

concluant

PAST PARTICIPLE

conclu

FUTURE

je	**conclurai**
tu	**concluras**
il/elle/on	**conclura**
nous	**conclurons**
vous	**conclurez**
ils/elles	**concluront**

CONDITIONAL

je	**conclurais**
tu	**conclurais**
il/elle/on	**conclurait**
nous	**conclurions**
vous	**concluriez**
ils/elles	**concluraient**

PAST HISTORIC

je	**conclus**
tu	**conclus**
il/elle/on	**conclut**
nous	**conclûmes**
vous	**conclûtes**
ils/elles	**conclurent**

PLUPERFECT

j'	**avais conclu**
tu	**avais conclu**
il/elle/on	**avait conclu**
nous	**avions conclu**
vous	**aviez conclu**
ils/elles	**avaient conclu**

IMPERATIVE

conclus / concluons / concluez

EXAMPLE PHRASES

J'en **conclus** qu'il ne m'a pas dit la vérité.
I conclude from this that he didn't tell me the truth.

Ils **ont conclu** un marché.
They concluded a deal.

Il en **a conclu** qu'il s'était trompé.
He concluded that he had got it wrong.

Il faut que je **conclue** le marché aujourd'hui.
I must conclude the deal today.

Je **conclurai** par ces mots...
I will conclude with these words...

Elle en **conclut** qu'il était parti.
She concluded that he had gone.

Nous n'**avions** encore rien **conclu** quand il est arrivé.
We hadn't concluded anything when he arrived.

Ils **avaient conclu** la soirée par une partie de cartes.
They had concluded the evening with a game of cards.

je/j' = I   **tu** = you   **il** = he/it   **elle** = she/it   **on** = we/one   **nous** = we   **vous** = you   **ils/elles** = they

conduire (to drive)

PRESENT

je	**conduis**
tu	**conduis**
il/elle/on	**conduit**
nous	**conduisons**
vous	**conduisez**
ils/elles	**conduisent**

PRESENT SUBJUNCTIVE

je	**conduise**
tu	**conduises**
il/elle/on	**conduise**
nous	**conduisions**
vous	**conduisiez**
ils/elles	**conduisent**

PERFECT

j'	**ai conduit**
tu	**as conduit**
il/elle/on	**a conduit**
nous	**avons conduit**
vous	**avez conduit**
ils/elles	**ont conduit**

IMPERFECT

je	**conduisais**
tu	**conduisais**
il/elle/on	**conduisait**
nous	**conduisions**
vous	**conduisiez**
ils/elles	**conduisaient**

PRESENT PARTICIPLE
conduisant

PAST PARTICIPLE
conduit

FUTURE

je	**conduirai**
tu	**conduiras**
il/elle/on	**conduira**
nous	**conduirons**
vous	**conduirez**
ils/elles	**conduiront**

CONDITIONAL

je	**conduirais**
tu	**conduirais**
il/elle/on	**conduirait**
nous	**conduirions**
vous	**conduiriez**
ils/elles	**conduiraient**

PAST HISTORIC

je	**conduisis**
tu	**conduisis**
il/elle/on	**conduisit**
nous	**conduisîmes**
vous	**conduisîtes**
ils/elles	**conduisirent**

PLUPERFECT

j'	**avais conduit**
tu	**avais conduit**
il/elle/on	**avait conduit**
nous	**avions conduit**
vous	**aviez conduit**
ils/elles	**avaient conduit**

IMPERATIVE
conduis / conduisons / conduisez

EXAMPLE PHRASES

Elle **conduit** sa fille à l'école tous les matins.
She drives her daughter to school every morning.

Cela fait longtemps que je n'**ai** pas **conduit**.
I haven't driven for a long time.

J'aimerais que tu me **conduises** à la gare.
I'd like you to drive me to the station.

Il **conduisait** lentement quand l'accident est arrivé.
He was driving slowly when the accident happened.

Je te **conduirai** chez le docteur.
I'll drive you to the doctor's.

Elle **conduisit** sans dire un mot.
She drove without saying a word.

Je te **conduirais** en ville si j'avais le temps.
I'd drive you into town if I had time.

Elle **avait conduit** toute la nuit et elle était épuisée.
She'd driven all night and she was exhausted.

Conduis prudemment.
Drive carefully.

je/j' = I   **tu** = you   **il** = he/it   **elle** = she/it   **on** = we/one   **nous** = we   **vous** = you   **ils/elles** = they

connaître (to know)

PRESENT		PRESENT SUBJUNCTIVE
je	**connais**	je **connaisse**
tu	**connais**	tu **connaisses**
il/elle/on	**connaît**	il/elle/on **connaisse**
nous	**connaissons**	nous **connaissions**
vous	**connaissez**	vous **connaissiez**
ils/elles	**connaissent**	ils/elles **connaissent**

PERFECT		IMPERFECT
j'	**ai connu**	je **connaissais**
tu	**as connu**	tu **connaissais**
il/elle/on	**a connu**	il/elle/on **connaissait**
nous	**avons connu**	nous **connaissions**
vous	**avez connu**	vous **connaissiez**
ils/elles	**ont connu**	ils/elles **connaissaient**

PRESENT PARTICIPLE
connaissant

PAST PARTICIPLE
connu

FUTURE		CONDITIONAL
je	**connaîtrai**	je **connaîtrais**
tu	**connaîtras**	tu **connaîtrais**
il/elle/on	**connaîtra**	il/elle/on **connaîtrait**
nous	**connaîtrons**	nous **connaîtrions**
vous	**connaîtrez**	vous **connaîtriez**
ils/elles	**connaîtront**	ils/elles **connaîtraient**

PAST HISTORIC		PLUPERFECT
je	**connus**	j' **avais connu**
tu	**connus**	tu **avais connu**
il/elle/on	**connut**	il/elle/on **avait connu**
nous	**connûmes**	nous **avions connu**
vous	**connûtes**	vous **aviez connu**
ils/elles	**connurent**	ils/elles **avaient connu**

IMPERATIVE
connais / connaissons / connaissez

EXAMPLE PHRASES

Je ne **connais** pas du tout cette région.
I don't know the area at all.

Vous **connaissez** M. Amiot?
Do you know Mr Amiot?

Il n'**a** pas **connu** son grand-père.
He never knew his granddad.

Je **connaissais** bien sa mère.
I knew his mother well.

Je ne la **connaîtrai** jamais bien.
I'll never know her well.

Il **connut** d'abord Laura puis il rencontra Claire.
First he got to know Laura and then he met Claire.

Nous ne nous **connaîtrions** pas s'il ne nous avait pas présentés.
We wouldn't know each other if he hadn't introduced us.

J'aurais gagné si j'**avais connu** la réponse à la dernière question.
I would have won if I had known the answer to the last question.

Ils s'**étaient connus** à Rouen.
They'd first met in Rouen.

je/j' = I   **tu** = you   **il** = he/it   **elle** = she/it   **on** = we/one   **nous** = we   **vous** = you   **ils/elles** = they

continuer (to continue; to go on)

PRESENT

je	**continue**
tu	**continues**
il/elle/on	**continue**
nous	**continuons**
vous	**continuez**
ils/elles	**continuent**

PRESENT SUBJUNCTIVE

je	**continue**
tu	**continues**
il/elle/on	**continue**
nous	**continuions**
vous	**continuiez**
ils/elles	**continuent**

PERFECT

j'	**ai continué**
tu	**as continué**
il/elle/on	**a continué**
nous	**avons continué**
vous	**avez continué**
ils/elles	**ont continué**

IMPERFECT

je	**continuais**
tu	**continuais**
il/elle/on	**continuait**
nous	**continuions**
vous	**continuiez**
ils/elles	**continuaient**

PRESENT PARTICIPLE
continuant

PAST PARTICIPLE
continué

FUTURE

je	**continuerai**
tu	**continueras**
il/elle/on	**continuera**
nous	**continuerons**
vous	**continuerez**
ils/elles	**continueront**

CONDITIONAL

je	**continuerais**
tu	**continuerais**
il/elle/on	**continuerait**
nous	**continuerions**
vous	**continueriez**
ils/elles	**continueraient**

PAST HISTORIC

je	**continuai**
tu	**continuas**
il/elle/on	**continua**
nous	**continuâmes**
vous	**continuâtes**
ils/elles	**continuèrent**

PLUPERFECT

j'	**avais continué**
tu	**avais continué**
il/elle/on	**avait continué**
nous	**avions continué**
vous	**aviez continué**
ils/elles	**avaient continué**

IMPERATIVE
continue / continuons / continuez

EXAMPLE PHRASES

Il **continue** de fumer malgré son asthme.
He keeps on smoking despite his asthma.

Ils **ont continué** à regarder la télé sans me dire bonjour.
They went on watching TV without saying hello to me.

Il faut que tu **continues** à réviser si tu veux réussir à ton examen.
You'll have to carry on revising if you want to do well in your exam.

La phrase **continuait** sur la page suivante.
The sentence continued on the next page.

Nous **continuerons** l'histoire demain.
We'll continue the story tomorrow.

Ils **continuèrent** à la harceler toute la soirée.
They went on harassing her all evening.

Je **continuerais** à regarder ce film si j'avais le temps.
I'd carry on watching this film if I had time.

Ils **avaient continué** à lui rendre visite même après leur déménagement.
They had carried on visiting her even after they had moved house.

je/j' = I **tu** = you **il** = he/it **elle** = she/it **on** = we/one **nous** = we **vous** = you **ils/elles** = they

coudre (to sew)

PRESENT

je	**couds**
tu	**couds**
il/elle/on	**coud**
nous	**cousons**
vous	**cousez**
ils/elles	**cousent**

PRESENT SUBJUNCTIVE

je	**couse**
tu	**couses**
il/elle/on	**couse**
nous	**cousions**
vous	**cousiez**
ils/elles	**cousent**

PERFECT

j'	**ai cousu**
tu	**as cousu**
il/elle/on	**a cousu**
nous	**avons cousu**
vous	**avez cousu**
ils/elles	**ont cousu**

IMPERFECT

je	**cousais**
tu	**cousais**
il/elle/on	**cousait**
nous	**cousions**
vous	**cousiez**
ils/elles	**cousaient**

PRESENT PARTICIPLE
cousant

PAST PARTICIPLE
cousu

FUTURE

je	**coudrai**
tu	**coudras**
il/elle/on	**coudra**
nous	**coudrons**
vous	**coudrez**
ils/elles	**coudront**

CONDITIONAL

je	**coudrais**
tu	**coudrais**
il/elle/on	**coudrait**
nous	**coudrions**
vous	**coudriez**
ils/elles	**coudraient**

PAST HISTORIC

je	**cousus**
tu	**cousus**
il/elle/on	**cousut**
nous	**cousûmes**
vous	**cousûtes**
ils/elles	**cousurent**

PLUPERFECT

j'	**avais cousu**
tu	**avais cousu**
il/elle/on	**avait cousu**
nous	**avions cousu**
vous	**aviez cousu**
ils/elles	**avaient cousu**

IMPERATIVE
couds / cousons / cousez

EXAMPLE PHRASES

Tu sais **coudre**?
Can you sew?

Ma mère **coud** beaucoup.
My mum sews a lot.

J'**ai cousu** toute la soirée hier.
I spent all evening yesterday sewing.

Elle **cousait** tous les soirs après dîner.
She would sew every night after dinner.

Demain, je **coudrai** l'écusson sur ton sweat.
Tomorrow, I'll sew the badge on your sweatshirt.

Elle **cousut** rapidement le bouton.
She quickly sewed the button on.

Je **coudrais** l'ourlet si j'étais sûr de ce que je faisais.
I'd sew the hem if I knew what I was doing.

Je n'**avais** pas bien **cousu** le bouton et je l'avais perdu.
I hadn't sewn the button on properly and I'd lost it.

---

je/j' = I   **tu** = you   **il** = he/it   **elle** = she/it   **on** = we/one   **nous** = we   **vous** = you   **ils/elles** = they

courir (to run)

PRESENT

je	**cours**
tu	**cours**
il/elle/on	**court**
nous	**courons**
vous	**courez**
ils/elles	**courent**

PERFECT

j'	**ai couru**
tu	**as couru**
il/elle/on	**a couru**
nous	**avons couru**
vous	**avez couru**
ils/elles	**ont couru**

PRESENT PARTICIPLE
courant

FUTURE

je	**courrai**
tu	**courras**
il/elle/on	**courra**
nous	**courrons**
vous	**courrez**
ils/elles	**courront**

PAST HISTORIC

je	**courus**
tu	**courus**
il/elle/on	**courut**
nous	**courûmes**
vous	**courûtes**
ils/elles	**coururent**

IMPERATIVE
cours / courons / courez

PRESENT SUBJUNCTIVE

je	**coure**
tu	**coures**
il/elle/on	**coure**
nous	**courions**
vous	**couriez**
ils/elles	**courent**

IMPERFECT

je	**courais**
tu	**courais**
il/elle/on	**courait**
nous	**courions**
vous	**couriez**
ils/elles	**couraient**

PAST PARTICIPLE
couru

CONDITIONAL

je	**courrais**
tu	**courrais**
il/elle/on	**courrait**
nous	**courrions**
vous	**courriez**
ils/elles	**courraient**

PLUPERFECT

j'	**avais couru**
tu	**avais couru**
il/elle/on	**avait couru**
nous	**avions couru**
vous	**aviez couru**
ils/elles	**avaient couru**

EXAMPLE PHRASES

Je ne **cours** pas très vite.
I can't run very fast.

J'**ai couru** jusqu'à l'école.
I ran all the way to school.

Ne **courez** pas dans le couloir.
Don't run in the corridor.

Elle est sortie en **courant**.
She ran out.

L'été prochain, nous **courrons** le marathon de Londres.
Next summer, we'll run the London marathon.

Il **courut** après elle, mais elle était trop rapide.
He ran after her, but she was too fast.

Je **courrais** bien plus vite si je n'étais pas fatigué.
I'd run much faster if I wasn't tired.

J'étais essoufflé parce que j'**avais couru**.
I was out of breath because I'd been running.

je/j' = I **tu** = you **il** = he/it **elle** = she/it **on** = we/one **nous** = we **vous** = you **ils/elles** = they

craindre (to fear)

PRESENT

je	**crains**
tu	**crains**
il/elle/on	**craint**
nous	**craignons**
vous	**craignez**
ils/elles	**craignent**

PRESENT SUBJUNCTIVE

je	**craigne**
tu	**craignes**
il/elle/on	**craigne**
nous	**craignions**
vous	**craigniez**
ils/elles	**craignent**

PERFECT

j'	**ai craint**
tu	**as craint**
il/elle/on	**a craint**
nous	**avons craint**
vous	**avez craint**
ils/elles	**ont craint**

IMPERFECT

je	**craignais**
tu	**craignais**
il/elle/on	**craignait**
nous	**craignions**
vous	**craigniez**
ils/elles	**craignaient**

PRESENT PARTICIPLE

craignant

PAST PARTICIPLE

craint

FUTURE

je	**craindrai**
tu	**craindras**
il/elle/on	**craindra**
nous	**craindrons**
vous	**craindrez**
ils/elles	**craindront**

CONDITIONAL

je	**craindrais**
tu	**craindrais**
il/elle/on	**craindrait**
nous	**craindrions**
vous	**craindriez**
ils/elles	**craindraient**

PAST HISTORIC

je	**craignis**
tu	**craignis**
il/elle/on	**craignit**
nous	**craignîmes**
vous	**craignîtes**
ils/elles	**craignirent**

PLUPERFECT

j'	**avais craint**
tu	**avais craint**
il/elle/on	**avait craint**
nous	**avions craint**
vous	**aviez craint**
ils/elles	**avaient craint**

IMPERATIVE

crains / craignons / craignez

EXAMPLE PHRASES

Tu n'as rien à **craindre**.
You've got nothing to fear.

Je **crains** le pire.
I fear the worst.

Il **craignait** qu'elle ne soit partie.
He feared that she had gone.

Je **craignis** qu'il ne se vexe.
I feared he might get upset.

Je ne le **craindrais** pas tant s'il n'était
pas si irritable.
I wouldn't fear him so much if he wasn't
so irritable.

Si j'étais toi, je **craindrais** sa colère.
If I were you, I'd fear his anger.

Elle **avait craint** sa colère, mais il n'avait
rien dit.
She had feared his anger, but he didn't
say anything.

Ne **craignez** rien, ce chien n'est pas
méchant.
Don't be scared, this dog is harmless.

---

je/j' = I **tu** = you **il** = he/it **elle** = she/it **on** = we/one **nous** = we **vous** = you **ils/elles** = they

créer (to create)

PRESENT		PRESENT SUBJUNCTIVE	
je	**crée**	je	**crée**
tu	**crées**	tu	**crées**
il/elle/on	**crée**	il/elle/on	**crée**
nous	**créons**	nous	**créions**
vous	**créez**	vous	**créiez**
ils/elles	**créent**	ils/elles	**créent**

PERFECT		IMPERFECT	
j'	**ai créé**	je	**créais**
tu	**as créé**	tu	**créais**
il/elle/on	**a créé**	il/elle/on	**créait**
nous	**avons créé**	nous	**créions**
vous	**avez créé**	vous	**créiez**
ils/elles	**ont créé**	ils/elles	**créaient**

PRESENT PARTICIPLE
créant

PAST PARTICIPLE
créé

FUTURE		CONDITIONAL	
je	**créerai**	je	**créerais**
tu	**créeras**	tu	**créerais**
il/elle/on	**créera**	il/elle/on	**créerait**
nous	**créerons**	nous	**créerions**
vous	**créerez**	vous	**créeriez**
ils/elles	**créeront**	ils/elles	**créeraient**

PAST HISTORIC		PLUPERFECT	
je	**créai**	j'	**avais créé**
tu	**créas**	tu	**avais créé**
il/elle/on	**créa**	il/elle/on	**avait créé**
nous	**créâmes**	nous	**avions créé**
vous	**créâtes**	vous	**aviez créé**
ils/elles	**créèrent**	ils/elles	**avaient créé**

IMPERATIVE
crée / créons / créez

EXAMPLE PHRASES

Ce virus **crée** des difficultés dans le monde entier.
This virus is causing problems all over the world.

Il **a créé** une nouvelle recette.
He's created a new recipe.

Nous **avons créé** ce parfum spécialement pour cette occasion.
We've created this perfume specially for this occasion.

Elle **créait** souvent des disputes entre nous.
She would often cause arguments between us.

Le gouvernement **créera** deux mille emplois supplémentaires.
The government will create an extra two thousand jobs.

Les licenciements **créèrent** des tensions dans l'entreprise.
The redundancies created tensions in the firm.

Elle **avait créé** une crème qui allait révolutionner l'industrie des produits cosmétiques.
She had created a cream which was to revolutionize the cosmetics industry.

je/j' = I   **tu** = you   **il** = he/it   **elle** = she/it   **on** = we/one   **nous** = we   **vous** = you   **ils/elles** = they

crier (to shout)

PRESENT

je	**crie**
tu	**cries**
il/elle/on	**crie**
nous	**crions**
vous	**criez**
ils/elles	**crient**

PRESENT SUBJUNCTIVE

je	**crie**
tu	**cries**
il/elle/on	**crie**
nous	**criions**
vous	**criiez**
ils/elles	**crient**

PERFECT

j'	**ai crié**
tu	**as crié**
il/elle/on	**a crié**
nous	**avons crié**
vous	**avez crié**
ils/elles	**ont crié**

IMPERFECT

je	**criais**
tu	**criais**
il/elle/on	**criait**
nous	**criions**
vous	**criiez**
ils/elles	**criaient**

PRESENT PARTICIPLE
criant

PAST PARTICIPLE
crié

FUTURE

je	**crierai**
tu	**crieras**
il/elle/on	**criera**
nous	**crierons**
vous	**crierez**
ils/elles	**crieront**

CONDITIONAL

je	**crierais**
tu	**crierais**
il/elle/on	**crierait**
nous	**crierions**
vous	**crieriez**
ils/elles	**crieraient**

PAST HISTORIC

je	**criai**
tu	**crias**
il/elle/on	**cria**
nous	**criâmes**
vous	**criâtes**
ils/elles	**crièrent**

PLUPERFECT

j'	**avais crié**
tu	**avais crié**
il/elle/on	**avait crié**
nous	**avions crié**
vous	**aviez crié**
ils/elles	**avaient crié**

IMPERATIVE
crie / crions / criez

EXAMPLE PHRASES

La maîtresse **crie** tout le temps après nous.
The teacher's always shouting at us.

Elle **a crié** au secours.
She cried for help.

Je ne veux pas que tu **cries** devant mes copines.
I don't want you to shout in front of my friends.

Il **criait** toujours plus fort que moi.
He would always shout louder than me.

Ton père ne **criera** pas si tu lui expliques ce qui s'est passé.
Your dad won't shout if you explain to him what happened.

"Attention!", **cria**-t-il.
"Watch out!" he shouted.

Elle **crierait** drôlement si tu lui tachais sa robe.
She would really shout if you stained her dress.

Il n'**avait** pas **crié** comme ça depuis longtemps.
He hadn't shouted like that for a long time.

Ne **crie** pas comme ça!
Don't shout!

---

je/j' = I   **tu** = you   **il** = he/it   **elle** = she/it   **on** = we/one   **nous** = we   **vous** = you   **ils/elles** = they

croire (to believe)

PRESENT

je	**crois**
tu	**crois**
il/elle/on	**croit**
nous	**croyons**
vous	**croyez**
ils/elles	**croient**

PRESENT SUBJUNCTIVE

je	**croie**
tu	**croies**
il/elle/on	**croie**
nous	**croyions**
vous	**croyiez**
ils/elles	**croient**

PERFECT

j'	**ai cru**
tu	**as cru**
il/elle/on	**a cru**
nous	**avons cru**
vous	**avez cru**
ils/elles	**ont cru**

IMPERFECT

je	**croyais**
tu	**croyais**
il/elle/on	**croyait**
nous	**croyions**
vous	**croyiez**
ils/elles	**croyaient**

PRESENT PARTICIPLE

croyant

PAST PARTICIPLE

cru

FUTURE

je	**croirai**
tu	**croiras**
il/elle/on	**croira**
nous	**croirons**
vous	**croirez**
ils/elles	**croiront**

CONDITIONAL

je	**croirais**
tu	**croirais**
il/elle/on	**croirait**
nous	**croirions**
vous	**croiriez**
ils/elles	**croiraient**

PAST HISTORIC

je	**crus**
tu	**crus**
il/elle/on	**crut**
nous	**crûmes**
vous	**crûtes**
ils/elles	**crurent**

PLUPERFECT

j'	**avais cru**
tu	**avais cru**
il/elle/on	**avait cru**
nous	**avions cru**
vous	**aviez cru**
ils/elles	**avaient cru**

IMPERATIVE

crois / croyons / croyez

EXAMPLE PHRASES

Je ne te **crois** pas.
I don't believe you.

J'**ai cru** que tu n'allais pas venir.
I thought you weren't going to come.

Il faut que tu me **croies**.
You have to believe me.

Elle **croyait** encore au père Noël.
She still believed in Father Christmas.

Elle ne me **croira** pas si je lui dis que j'ai gagné.
She won't believe me if I tell her that I won.

Il **crut** que je me moquais de lui.
He thought that I was making fun of him.

Elle te **croirait** peut-être si tu lui disais que tu as oublié ton maillot de bain.
She might believe you if you tell her that you forgot your swimming costume.

Au début, il ne m'**avait** pas **cru**, mais plus tard il s'était rendu compte que c'était vrai.
Initially he hadn't believed me, but later he had realized that it was true.

Crois-moi, Mme Leblond est très stricte.
Believe me, Mrs Leblond is very strict.

je/j' = I   **tu** = you   **il** = he/it   **elle** = she/it   **on** = we/one   **nous** = we   **vous** = you   **ils/elles** = they

croître (to grow; to increase)

PRESENT

je	**croîs**
tu	**croîs**
il/elle/on	**croît**
nous	**croissons**
vous	**croissez**
ils/elles	**croissent**

PRESENT SUBJUNCTIVE

je	**croisse**
tu	**croisses**
il/elle/on	**croisse**
nous	**croissions**
vous	**croissiez**
ils/elles	**croissent**

EXAMPLE PHRASES

Les ventes **croissent** de 6% par an.
Sales are growing by 6% per year.

C'est une plante qui **croît** dans les pays chauds.
This plant grows in hot countries.

Le nombre de gens qui partent travailler à l'étranger va **croissant**.
An increasing number of people go and work abroad.

Les problèmes **crûrent** de jour en jour.
Problems increased day after day.

Les dépenses **croîtraient** rapidement si on ne faisait pas attention.
Spending would increase rapidly if we weren't careful.

PERFECT

j'	**ai crû**
tu	**as crû**
il/elle/on	**a crû**
nous	**avons crû**
vous	**avez crû**
ils/elles	**ont crû**

IMPERFECT

je	**croissais**
tu	**croissais**
il/elle/on	**croissait**
nous	**croissions**
vous	**croissiez**
ils/elles	**croissaient**

PRESENT PARTICIPLE

croissant

PAST PARTICIPLE

crû

FUTURE

je	**croîtrai**
tu	**croîtras**
il/elle/on	**croîtra**
nous	**croîtrons**
vous	**croîtrez**
ils/elles	**croîtront**

CONDITIONAL

je	**croîtrais**
tu	**croîtrais**
il/elle/on	**croîtrait**
nous	**croîtrions**
vous	**croîtriez**
ils/elles	**croîtraient**

PAST HISTORIC

je	**crûs**
tu	**crûs**
il/elle/on	**crût**
nous	**crûmes**
vous	**crûtes**
ils/elles	**crûrent**

PLUPERFECT

j'	**avais crû**
tu	**avais crû**
il/elle/on	**avait crû**
nous	**avions crû**
vous	**aviez crû**
ils/elles	**avaient crû**

IMPERATIVE

croîs / croissons / croissez

je/j' = I   **tu** = you   **il** = he/it   **elle** = she/it   **on** = we/one   **nous** = we   **vous** = you   **ils/elles** = they

cueillir (to pick)

PRESENT

je	**cueille**
tu	**cueilles**
il/elle/on	**cueille**
nous	**cueillons**
vous	**cueillez**
ils/elles	**cueillent**

PRESENT SUBJUNCTIVE

je	**cueille**
tu	**cueilles**
il/elle/on	**cueille**
nous	**cueillions**
vous	**cueilliez**
ils/elles	**cueillent**

PERFECT

j'	**ai cueilli**
tu	**as cueilli**
il/elle/on	**a cueilli**
nous	**avons cueilli**
vous	**avez cueilli**
ils/elles	**ont cueilli**

IMPERFECT

je	**cueillais**
tu	**cueillais**
il/elle/on	**cueillait**
nous	**cueillions**
vous	**cueilliez**
ils/elles	**cueillaient**

PRESENT PARTICIPLE

cueillant

PAST PARTICIPLE

cueilli

FUTURE

je	**cueillerai**
tu	**cueilleras**
il/elle/on	**cueillera**
nous	**cueillerons**
vous	**cueillerez**
ils/elles	**cueilleront**

CONDITIONAL

je	**cueillerais**
tu	**cueillerais**
il/elle/on	**cueillerait**
nous	**cueillerions**
vous	**cueilleriez**
ils/elles	**cueilleraient**

PAST HISTORIC

je	**cueillis**
tu	**cueillis**
il/elle/on	**cueillit**
nous	**cueillîmes**
vous	**cueillîtes**
ils/elles	**cueillirent**

PLUPERFECT

j'	**avais cueilli**
tu	**avais cueilli**
il/elle/on	**avait cueilli**
nous	**avions cueilli**
vous	**aviez cueilli**
ils/elles	**avaient cueilli**

IMPERATIVE

cueille / cueillons / cueillez

EXAMPLE PHRASES

Il est interdit de **cueillir** des fleurs
sauvages dans la montagne.
It's forbidden to pick wild flowers in
the mountains.

J'**ai cueilli** quelques fraises dans
le jardin.
I picked a few strawberries in the
garden.

J'aimerais que tu me **cueilles** des mûres
pour faire de la confiture.
I'd like you to pick some blackberries
for me to make jam.

Je **cueillerai** des framboises à la ferme.
I'll pick some raspberries at the farm.

Elle **cueillit** des fraises des bois.
She picked some wild strawberries.

Je **cueillerais** toutes les fleurs de
la terre entière pour toi.
I'd pick all the flowers in the
whole wide world for you.

Il lui **avait cueilli** un beau bouquet de
fleurs.
He'd picked a beautiful bunch of
flowers for her.

Ne **cueille** pas les fleurs dans le parc.
Don't pick the flowers in the park.

je/j' = I   **tu** = you   **il** = he/it   **elle** = she/it   **on** = we/one   **nous** = we   **vous** = you   **ils/elles** = they

cuire (to cook)

PRESENT

je	**cuis**
tu	**cuis**
il/elle/on	**cuit**
nous	**cuisons**
vous	**cuisez**
ils/elles	**cuisent**

PRESENT SUBJUNCTIVE

je	**cuise**
tu	**cuises**
il/elle/on	**cuise**
nous	**cuisions**
vous	**cuisiez**
ils/elles	**cuisent**

PERFECT

j'	**ai cuit**
tu	**as cuit**
il/elle/on	**a cuit**
nous	**avons cuit**
vous	**avez cuit**
ils/elles	**ont cuit**

IMPERFECT

je	**cuisais**
tu	**cuisais**
il/elle/on	**cuisait**
nous	**cuisions**
vous	**cuisiez**
ils/elles	**cuisaient**

PRESENT PARTICIPLE

cuisant

PAST PARTICIPLE

cuit

FUTURE

je	**cuirai**
tu	**cuiras**
il/elle/on	**cuira**
nous	**cuirons**
vous	**cuirez**
ils/elles	**cuiront**

CONDITIONAL

je	**cuirais**
tu	**cuirais**
il/elle/on	**cuirait**
nous	**cuirions**
vous	**cuiriez**
ils/elles	**cuiraient**

PAST HISTORIC

je	**cuisis**
tu	**cuisis**
il/elle/on	**cuisit**
nous	**cuisîmes**
vous	**cuisîtes**
ils/elles	**cuisirent**

PLUPERFECT

j'	**avais cuit**
tu	**avais cuit**
il/elle/on	**avait cuit**
nous	**avions cuit**
vous	**aviez cuit**
ils/elles	**avaient cuit**

IMPERATIVE

cuis / cuisons / cuisez

EXAMPLE PHRASES

Ce gâteau prend environ une heure à **cuire**.
This cake takes about an hour to bake.

En général, je **cuis** les légumes à la vapeur.
I usually steam vegetables.

Je les **ai cuits** au beurre.
I cooked them in butter.

Mon père **cuisait** toujours la viande au barbecue.
My dad always barbecued meat.

Nous **cuirons** les côtelettes sur le gril.
We'll grill the chops.

Elle **cuisit** l'omelette et la servit.
She cooked the omelette and served it.

Je **cuirais** les crêpes plus longtemps si je n'avais pas peur de les faire brûler.
I'd cook the pancakes longer if I wasn't scared of burning them.

Elle **avait cuit** le poisson au four.
She'd baked the fish in the oven.

---

je/j' = I **tu** = you **il** = he/it **elle** = she/it **on** = we/one **nous** = we **vous** = you **ils/elles** = they

se débrouiller (to manage)

PRESENT

je	**me débrouille**
tu	**te débrouilles**
il/elle/on	**se débrouille**
nous	**nous débrouillons**
vous	**vous débrouillez**
ils/elles	**se débrouillent**

PRESENT SUBJUNCTIVE

je	**me débrouille**
tu	**te débrouilles**
il/elle/on	**se débrouille**
nous	**nous débrouillions**
vous	**vous débrouilliez**
ils/elles	**se débrouillent**

PERFECT

je	**me suis débrouillé(e)**
tu	**t'es débrouillé(e)**
il/elle/on	**s'est débrouillé(e)**
nous	**nous sommes débrouillé(e)s**
vous	**vous êtes débrouillé(e)(s)**
ils/elles	**se sont débrouillé(e)s**

IMPERFECT

je	**me débrouillais**
tu	**te débrouillais**
il/elle/on	**se débrouillait**
nous	**nous débrouillions**
vous	**vous débrouilliez**
ils/elles	**se débrouillaient**

PRESENT PARTICIPLE
se débrouillant

PAST PARTICIPLE
débrouillé

FUTURE

je	**me débrouillerai**
tu	**te débrouilleras**
il/elle/on	**se débrouillera**
nous	**nous débrouillerons**
vous	**vous débrouillerez**
ils/elles	**se débrouilleront**

CONDITIONAL

je	**me débrouillerais**
tu	**te débrouillerais**
il/elle/on	**se débrouillerait**
nous	**nous débrouillerions**
vous	**vous débrouilleriez**
ils/elles	**se débrouilleraient**

PAST HISTORIC

je	**me débrouillai**
tu	**te débrouillas**
il/elle/on	**se débrouilla**
nous	**nous débrouillâmes**
vous	**vous débrouillâtes**
ils/elles	**se débrouillèrent**

PLUPERFECT

je	**m'étais débrouillé(e)**
tu	**t'étais débrouillé(e)**
il/elle/on	**s'était débrouillé(e)**
nous	**nous étions débrouillé(e)s**
vous	**vous étiez débrouillé(e)(s)**
ils/elles	**s'étaient débrouillé(e)s**

IMPERATIVE
débrouille-toi / débrouillons-nous / débrouillez-vous

EXAMPLE PHRASES

Elle **se débrouille** bien à l'école.
She gets on well at school.

C'était difficile, mais je ne **me suis** pas trop mal **débrouillé**.
It was difficult, but I managed OK.

Je **me débrouillais** mieux en français qu'en maths.
I got on better in French than in maths.

Nous **nous débrouillerons** bien sans toi.
We'll manage fine without you.

Il **se débrouilla** tant bien que mal pour préparer le dîner.
He just about managed to prepare dinner.

Il **se débrouillerait** bien tout seul s'il était obligé.
He would manage fine by himself if he had to.

Comme mes parents étaient partis, je **m'étais débrouillée** toute seule.
As my parents were away, I had managed by myself.

Débrouille-toi tout seul.
Sort things out for yourself.

je/j' = I   **tu** = you   **il** = he/it   **elle** = she/it   **on** = we/one   **nous** = we   **vous** = you   **ils/elles** = they

descendre (to go down)

PRESENT

je	**descends**
tu	**descends**
il/elle/on	**descend**
nous	**descendons**
vous	**descendez**
ils/elles	**descendent**

PRESENT SUBJUNCTIVE

je	**descende**
tu	**descendes**
il/elle/on	**descende**
nous	**descendions**
vous	**descendiez**
ils/elles	**descendent**

PERFECT

je	**suis descendu(e)**
tu	**es descendu(e)**
il/elle/on	**est descendu(e)**
nous	**sommes descendu(e)s**
vous	**êtes descendu(e)(s)**
ils/elles	**sont descendu(e)s**

IMPERFECT

je	**descendais**
tu	**descendais**
il/elle/on	**descendait**
nous	**descendions**
vous	**descendiez**
ils/elles	**descendaient**

PRESENT PARTICIPLE

descendant

PAST PARTICIPLE

descendu

FUTURE

je	**descendrai**
tu	**descendras**
il/elle/on	**descendra**
nous	**descendrons**
vous	**descendrez**
ils/elles	**descendront**

CONDITIONAL

je	**descendrais**
tu	**descendrais**
il/elle/on	**descendrait**
nous	**descendrions**
vous	**descendriez**
ils/elles	**descendraient**

PAST HISTORIC

je	**descendis**
tu	**descendis**
il/elle/on	**descendit**
nous	**descendîmes**
vous	**descendîtes**
ils/elles	**descendirent**

PLUPERFECT

j'	**étais descendu(e)**
tu	**étais descendu(e)**
il/elle/on	**était descendu(e)**
nous	**étions descendu(e)s**
vous	**étiez descendu(e)(s)**
ils/elles	**étaient descendu(e)s**

IMPERATIVE

descends / descendons / descendez

EXAMPLE PHRASES

Vous pouvez **descendre** ma valise, s'il vous plaît?
Could you get my suitcase down, please?

Reste en bas: je **descends**!
Stay downstairs – I'm coming down!

Nous **sommes descendus** à la station Trocadéro.
We got off at Trocadéro.

Il faut que je **descende** chercher quelque chose à la cave.
I have to go down to the cellar to get something.

Nous **descendrons** dans le Midi au mois de juillet.
We'll go down to the south of France in July.

Il **descendit** les escaliers en courant.
He ran down the stairs.

Si j'étais toi, je ne **descendrais** pas l'escalier si vite.
I wouldn't rush down the stairs if I were you.

Ils **étaient descendus** regarder la télé quand les plombs ont sauté.
They had gone down to watch TV when the fuses blew.

Descendez la rue jusqu'au rond-point.
Go down the street to the roundabout.

je/j' = I   **tu** = you   **il** = he/it   **elle** = she/it   **on** = we/one   **nous** = we   **vous** = you   **ils/elles** = they

devenir (to become)

PRESENT
je	**deviens**
tu	**deviens**
il/elle/on	**devient**
nous	**devenons**
vous	**devenez**
ils/elles	**deviennent**

PRESENT SUBJUNCTIVE
je	**devienne**
tu	**deviennes**
il/elle/on	**devienne**
nous	**devenions**
vous	**deveniez**
ils/elles	**deviennent**

PERFECT
je	**suis devenu(e)**
tu	**es devenu(e)**
il/elle/on	**est devenu(e)**
nous	**sommes devenu(e)s**
vous	**êtes devenu(e)(s)**
ils/elles	**sont devenu(e)s**

IMPERFECT
je	**devenais**
tu	**devenais**
il/elle/on	**devenait**
nous	**devenions**
vous	**deveniez**
ils/elles	**devenaient**

PRESENT PARTICIPLE
devenant

PAST PARTICIPLE
devenu

FUTURE
je	**deviendrai**
tu	**deviendras**
il/elle/on	**deviendra**
nous	**deviendrons**
vous	**deviendrez**
ils/elles	**deviendront**

CONDITIONAL
je	**deviendrais**
tu	**deviendrais**
il/elle/on	**deviendrait**
nous	**deviendrions**
vous	**deviendriez**
ils/elles	**deviendraient**

PAST HISTORIC
je	**devins**
tu	**devins**
il/elle/on	**devint**
nous	**devînmes**
vous	**devîntes**
ils/elles	**devinrent**

PLUPERFECT
j'	**étais devenu(e)**
tu	**étais devenu(e)**
il/elle/on	**était devenu(e)**
nous	**étions devenu(e)s**
vous	**étiez devenu(e)(s)**
ils/elles	**étaient devenu(e)s**

IMPERATIVE
deviens / devenons / devenez

EXAMPLE PHRASES

Ça **devient** de plus en plus difficile.
It's becoming more and more difficult.

Il **est devenu** médecin.
He became a doctor.

Qu'est-ce qu'elle **est devenue**?
What has become of her?

Il ne faut pas que ça **devienne** une corvée.
It mustn't become a chore.

Elle **devenait** de plus en plus exigeante.
She was becoming more and more demanding.

J'espère qu'elle ne **deviendra** pas comme sa mère.
I hope that she won't become like her mother.

Elle **devint** la première femme à traverser l'Atlantique en avion.
She became the first woman to fly across the Atlantic.

Si on les nourrissait trop, les poissons rouges **deviendraient** énormes.
If we overfed them, the goldfish would become enormous.

Je me demandais ce qu'ils **étaient devenus**.
I wondered what had become of them.

---

je/j' = I   **tu** = you   **il** = he/it   **elle** = she/it   **on** = we/one   **nous** = we   **vous** = you   **ils/elles** = they

devoir (to have to; to owe)

PRESENT

je	**dois**
tu	**dois**
il/elle/on	**doit**
nous	**devons**
vous	**devez**
ils/elles	**doivent**

PRESENT SUBJUNCTIVE

je	**doive**
tu	**doives**
il/elle/on	**doive**
nous	**devions**
vous	**deviez**
ils/elles	**doivent**

PERFECT

j'	**ai dû**
tu	**as dû**
il/elle/on	**a dû**
nous	**avons dû**
vous	**avez dû**
ils/elles	**ont dû**

IMPERFECT

je	**devais**
tu	**devais**
il/elle/on	**devait**
nous	**devions**
vous	**deviez**
ils/elles	**devaient**

PRESENT PARTICIPLE
devant

PAST PARTICIPLE
dû (NB: **due, dus, dues**)

FUTURE

je	**devrai**
tu	**devras**
il/elle/on	**devra**
nous	**devrons**
vous	**devrez**
ils/elles	**devront**

CONDITIONAL

je	**devrais**
tu	**devrais**
il/elle/on	**devrait**
nous	**devrions**
vous	**devriez**
ils/elles	**devraient**

PAST HISTORIC

je	**dus**
tu	**dus**
il/elle/on	**dut**
nous	**dûmes**
vous	**dûtes**
ils/elles	**durent**

PLUPERFECT

j'	**avais dû**
tu	**avais dû**
il/elle/on	**avait dû**
nous	**avions dû**
vous	**aviez dû**
ils/elles	**avaient dû**

IMPERATIVE
dois / devons / devez

EXAMPLE PHRASES

Je **dois** aller faire les courses ce matin.
I have to do the shopping this morning.

À quelle heure est-ce que tu **dois** partir?
What time do you have to leave?

J'**ai dû** partir avant la fin du film.
I had to leave before the end of the film.

Il **a dû** changer d'avis.
He must have changed his mind.

Il **devait** prendre le train pour aller travailler.
He had to go to work by train.

Ils **devront** finir leurs devoirs avant de venir.
They'll have to finish their homework before they come.

Elle **dut** lui annoncer elle-même la mauvaise nouvelle.
She had to tell him the bad news herself.

Tu ne **devrais** pas les déranger tout le temps comme ça.
You shouldn't disturb them all the time like that.

Comme il était malade, il **avait dû** arrêter de fumer.
As he was ill, he'd had to stop smoking.

je/j' = I   **tu** = you   **il** = he/it   **elle** = she/it   **on** = we/one   **nous** = we   **vous** = you   **ils/elles** = they

dire (to say; to tell)

PRESENT

je	**dis**
tu	**dis**
il/elle/on	**dit**
nous	**disons**
vous	**dites**
ils/elles	**disent**

PRESENT SUBJUNCTIVE

je	**dise**
tu	**dises**
il/elle/on	**dise**
nous	**disions**
vous	**disiez**
ils/elles	**disent**

PERFECT

j'	**ai dit**
tu	**as dit**
il/elle/on	**a dit**
nous	**avons dit**
vous	**avez dit**
ils/elles	**ont dit**

IMPERFECT

je	**disais**
tu	**disais**
il/elle/on	**disait**
nous	**disions**
vous	**disiez**
ils/elles	**disaient**

PRESENT PARTICIPLE
disant

PAST PARTICIPLE
dit

FUTURE

je	**dirai**
tu	**diras**
il/elle/on	**dira**
nous	**dirons**
vous	**direz**
ils/elles	**diront**

CONDITIONAL

je	**dirais**
tu	**dirais**
il/elle/on	**dirait**
nous	**dirions**
vous	**diriez**
ils/elles	**diraient**

PAST HISTORIC

je	**dis**
tu	**dis**
il/elle/on	**dit**
nous	**dîmes**
vous	**dîtes**
ils/elles	**dirent**

PLUPERFECT

j'	**avais dit**
tu	**avais dit**
il/elle/on	**avait dit**
nous	**avions dit**
vous	**aviez dit**
ils/elles	**avaient dit**

IMPERATIVE
dis / disons / dites

EXAMPLE PHRASES

Qu'est-ce qu'elle **dit**?
What is she saying?

Comment ça se **dit** en anglais?
How do you say that in English?

"Bonjour!", **a**-t-il **dit**.
"Hello!" he said.

Ils m'**ont dit** que le film était nul.
They told me that the film was rubbish.

Je lui **dirai** de venir à midi.
I'll tell him to come at midday.

"Viens ici!", **dit**-il. Mais le chien refusait de bouger.
"Come here!" he said. But the dog refused to move.

On **dirait** qu'il va neiger.
It looks like snow.

On ne m'**avait** pas **dit** que tu serais là.
I hadn't been told that you'd be there.

Ne **dis** pas de bêtises.
Don't talk nonsense.

je/j' = I **tu** = you **il** = he/it **elle** = she/it **on** = we/one **nous** = we **vous** = you **ils/elles** = they

donner (to give)

PRESENT

je	**donne**
tu	**donnes**
il/elle/on	**donne**
nous	**donnons**
vous	**donnez**
ils/elles	**donnent**

PRESENT SUBJUNCTIVE

je	**donne**
tu	**donnes**
il/elle/on	**donne**
nous	**donnions**
vous	**donniez**
ils/elles	**donnent**

PERFECT

j'	**ai donné**
tu	**as donné**
il/elle/on	**a donné**
nous	**avons donné**
vous	**avez donné**
ils/elles	**ont donné**

IMPERFECT

je	**donnais**
tu	**donnais**
il/elle/on	**donnait**
nous	**donnions**
vous	**donniez**
ils/elles	**donnaient**

PRESENT PARTICIPLE
donnant

PAST PARTICIPLE
donné

FUTURE

je	**donnerai**
tu	**donneras**
il/elle/on	**donnera**
nous	**donnerons**
vous	**donnerez**
ils/elles	**donneront**

CONDITIONAL

je	**donnerais**
tu	**donnerais**
il/elle/on	**donnerait**
nous	**donnerions**
vous	**donneriez**
ils/elles	**donneraient**

PAST HISTORIC

je	**donnai**
tu	**donnas**
il/elle/on	**donna**
nous	**donnâmes**
vous	**donnâtes**
ils/elles	**donnèrent**

PLUPERFECT

j'	**avais donné**
tu	**avais donné**
il/elle/on	**avait donné**
nous	**avions donné**
vous	**aviez donné**
ils/elles	**avaient donné**

IMPERATIVE
donne / donnons / donnez

EXAMPLE PHRASES

L'appartement **donne** sur la place.
The flat overlooks the square.

Est-ce que je t'**ai donné** mon adresse?
Did I give you my address?

Il faut que tu me **donnes** plus de détails.
You must give me more details.

Je **donnais** des sucres aux chevaux.
I'd give sugar lumps to the horses.

Je te **donnerai** un ticket de métro.
I'll give you a tube ticket.

Il lui **donna** un vieux livre.
He gave him an old book.

Je lui **donnerais** des nouvelles si j'avais
   son adresse.
I'd give her some news if I had her
   address.

Je lui **avais donné** mon numéro de
   téléphone mais il a dû le perdre.
I had given him my phone number but
   he must have lost it.

Donne-moi la main.
Give me your hand.

je/j' = I   **tu** = you   **il** = he/it   **elle** = she/it   **on** = we/one   **nous** = we   **vous** = you   **ils/elles** = they

dormir (to sleep)

PRESENT

je	**dors**
tu	**dors**
il/elle/on	**dort**
nous	**dormons**
vous	**dormez**
ils/elles	**dorment**

PRESENT SUBJUNCTIVE

je	**dorme**
tu	**dormes**
il/elle/on	**dorme**
nous	**dormions**
vous	**dormiez**
ils/elles	**dorment**

PERFECT

j'	**ai dormi**
tu	**as dormi**
il/elle/on	**a dormi**
nous	**avons dormi**
vous	**avez dormi**
ils/elles	**ont dormi**

IMPERFECT

je	**dormais**
tu	**dormais**
il/elle/on	**dormait**
nous	**dormions**
vous	**dormiez**
ils/elles	**dormaient**

PRESENT PARTICIPLE
dormant

PAST PARTICIPLE
dormi

FUTURE

je	**dormirai**
tu	**dormiras**
il/elle/on	**dormira**
nous	**dormirons**
vous	**dormirez**
ils/elles	**dormiront**

CONDITIONAL

je	**dormirais**
tu	**dormirais**
il/elle/on	**dormirait**
nous	**dormirions**
vous	**dormiriez**
ils/elles	**dormiraient**

PAST HISTORIC

je	**dormis**
tu	**dormis**
il/elle/on	**dormit**
nous	**dormîmes**
vous	**dormîtes**
ils/elles	**dormirent**

PLUPERFECT

j'	**avais dormi**
tu	**avais dormi**
il/elle/on	**avait dormi**
nous	**avions dormi**
vous	**aviez dormi**
ils/elles	**avaient dormi**

IMPERATIVE
dors / dormons / dormez

EXAMPLE PHRASES

Nous **dormons** dans la même chambre.
We sleep in the same bedroom.

Tu **as** bien **dormi**?
Did you sleep well?

Elle m'a fait une tisane pour que je **dorme** bien.
She made me a herbal tea so that I got a good sleep.

À 9 heures, il **dormait** déjà.
He was already asleep by nine.

Ce soir, nous **dormirons** sous la tente.
Tonight we'll sleep in the tent.

Il était si fatigué qu'il **dormit** toute la journée.
He was so tired that he slept all day.

Il **dormirait** mieux s'il buvait moins de café.
He'd sleep better if he didn't drink so much coffee.

J'étais épuisé car je n'**avais** pas **dormi** de la nuit.
I was exhausted as I hadn't slept all night.

Dors bien.
Sleep well.

je/j' = I **tu** = you **il** = he/it **elle** = she/it **on** = we/one **nous** = we **vous** = you **ils/elles** = they

écrire

PRESENT

j'	**écris**
tu	**écris**
il/elle/on	**écrit**
nous	**écrivons**
vous	**écrivez**
ils/elles	**écrivent**

PERFECT

j'	**ai écrit**
tu	**as écrit**
il/elle/on	**a écrit**
nous	**avons écrit**
vous	**avez écrit**
ils/elles	**ont écrit**

PRESENT PARTICIPLE

écrivant

FUTURE

j'	**écrirai**
tu	**écriras**
il/elle/on	**écrira**
nous	**écrirons**
vous	**écrirez**
ils/elles	**écriront**

PAST HISTORIC

j'	**écrivis**
tu	**écrivis**
il/elle/on	**écrivit**
nous	**écrivîmes**
vous	**écrivîtes**
ils/elles	**écrivirent**

IMPERATIVE

écris / écrivons / écrivez

PRESENT SUBJUNCTIVE

j'	**écrive**
tu	**écrives**
il/elle/on	**écrive**
nous	**écrivions**
vous	**écriviez**
ils/elles	**écrivent**

IMPERFECT

j'	**écrivais**
tu	**écrivais**
il/elle/on	**écrivait**
nous	**écrivions**
vous	**écriviez**
ils/elles	**écrivaient**

PAST PARTICIPLE

écrit

CONDITIONAL

j'	**écrirais**
tu	**écrirais**
il/elle/on	**écrirait**
nous	**écririons**
vous	**écririez**
ils/elles	**écriraient**

PLUPERFECT

j'	**avais écrit**
tu	**avais écrit**
il/elle/on	**avait écrit**
nous	**avions écrit**
vous	**aviez écrit**
ils/elles	**avaient écrit**

EXAMPLE PHRASES

Elle **écrit** des romans.
She writes novels.

Tu **as écrit** à ta correspondante récemment?
Have you written to your penfriend recently?

Elle aimerait que tu **écrives** plus souvent.
She'd like you to write more often.

Il ne nous **écrivait** jamais quand il était en France.
He never wrote to us when he was in France.

Demain, j'**écrirai** une lettre au directeur.
Tomorrow, I'll write a letter to the headmaster.

Il **écrivit** un poème à la lueur de la bougie.
He wrote a poem by candlelight.

J'**écrirais** plus souvent si j'avais le temps.
I'd write more often if I had the time.

Comme il n'**avait** encore rien **écrit** sur sa feuille, il se fit disputer par la maîtresse.
As he hadn't written anything on his sheet yet, he was told off by the teacher.

Écrivez votre nom en haut de la feuille.
Write your name at the top of the page.

je/j' = I   **tu** = you   **il** = he/it   **elle** = she/it   **on** = we/one   **nous** = we   **vous** = you   **ils/elles** = they

émouvoir (to move)

PRESENT

j'	**émeus**
tu	**émeus**
il/elle/on	**émeut**
nous	**émouvons**
vous	**émouvez**
ils/elles	**émeuvent**

PRESENT SUBJUNCTIVE

j'	**émeuve**
tu	**émeuves**
il/elle/on	**émeuve**
nous	**émeuvions**
vous	**émeuviez**
ils/elles	**émeuvent**

PERFECT

j'	**ai ému**
tu	**as ému**
il/elle/on	**a ému**
nous	**avons ému**
vous	**avez ému**
ils/elles	**ont ému**

IMPERFECT

j'	**émouvais**
tu	**émouvais**
il/elle/on	**émouvait**
nous	**émouvions**
vous	**émouviez**
ils/elles	**émouvaient**

PRESENT PARTICIPLE
émouvant

PAST PARTICIPLE
ému

FUTURE

j'	**émouvrai**
tu	**émouvras**
il/elle/on	**émouvra**
nous	**émouvrons**
vous	**émouvrez**
ils/elles	**émouvront**

CONDITIONAL

j'	**émouvrais**
tu	**émouvrais**
il/elle/on	**émouvrait**
nous	**émouvrions**
vous	**émouvriez**
ils/elles	**émouvraient**

PAST HISTORIC

j'	**émus**
tu	**émus**
il/elle/on	**émut**
nous	**émûmes**
vous	**émûtes**
ils/elles	**émurent**

PLUPERFECT

j'	**avais ému**
tu	**avais ému**
il/elle/on	**avait ému**
nous	**avions ému**
vous	**aviez ému**
ils/elles	**avaient ému**

IMPERATIVE
émeus / émouvons / émouvez

EXAMPLE PHRASES

Cette histoire m'**émeut** toujours
  beaucoup.
This story always moves me to tears.

Sa fausse gentillesse ne m'**émeut** pas.
I won't be moved by his fake kindness.

Ce film nous **a émus**.
This film moved us.

Cela m'**émouvait** toujours de les voir
  se quitter à la fin de l'été.
It always moved me to see them part
  at the end of the summer.

Sa franchise l'**émut** vraiment.
His frankness really moved her.

Sa lettre l'**avait** beaucoup **émue**.
She had been deeply moved by his
  letter.

je/j' = I **tu** = you **il** = he/it **elle** = she/it **on** = we/one **nous** = we **vous** = you **ils/elles** = they

s'ennuyer (to be bored)

PRESENT

je	**m'ennuie**
tu	**t'ennuies**
il/elle/on	**s'ennuie**
nous	**nous ennuyons**
vous	**vous ennuyez**
ils/elles	**s'ennuient**

PRESENT SUBJUNCTIVE

je	**m'ennuie**
tu	**t'ennuies**
il/elle/on	**s'ennuie**
nous	**nous ennuyions**
vous	**vous ennuyiez**
ils/elles	**s'ennuient**

PERFECT

je	**me suis ennuyé(e)**
tu	**t'es ennuyé(e)**
il/elle/on	**s'est ennuyé(e)**
nous	**nous sommes ennuyé(e)s**
vous	**vous êtes ennuyé(e)(s)**
ils/elles	**se sont ennuyé(e)s**

IMPERFECT

je	**m'ennuyais**
tu	**t'ennuyais**
il/elle/on	**s'ennuyait**
nous	**nous ennuyions**
vous	**vous ennuyiez**
ils/elles	**s'ennuyaient**

PRESENT PARTICIPLE
s'ennuyant

PAST PARTICIPLE
ennuyé

FUTURE

je	**m'ennuierai**
tu	**t'ennuieras**
il/elle/on	**s'ennuiera**
nous	**nous ennuierons**
vous	**vous ennuierez**
ils/elles	**s'ennuieront**

CONDITIONAL

je	**m'ennuierais**
tu	**t'ennuierais**
il/elle/on	**s'ennuierait**
nous	**nous ennuierions**
vous	**vous ennuieriez**
ils/elles	**s'ennuieraient**

PAST HISTORIC

je	**m'ennuyai**
tu	**t'ennuyas**
il/elle/on	**s'ennuya**
nous	**nous ennuyâmes**
vous	**vous ennuyâtes**
ils/elles	**s'ennuyèrent**

PLUPERFECT

je	**m'étais ennuyé(e)**
tu	**t'étais ennuyé(e)**
il/elle/on	**s'était ennuyé(e)**
nous	**nous étions ennuyé(e)s**
vous	**vous étiez ennuyé(e)(s)**
ils/elles	**s'étaient ennuyé(e)s**

IMPERATIVE
ennuie-toi / ennuyons-nous / ennuyez-vous

EXAMPLE PHRASES

Elle **s'ennuie** un peu à l'école.
She's a little bored at school.

Je **me suis ennuyé** quand tu
étais partie.
I got bored when you were away.

Ne **t'ennuie** pas trop cet
après-midi.
Don't get too bored this
afternoon.

Je ne voudrais pas qu'elle
s'ennuie avec moi.
I wouldn't want her to get bored
with me.

On ne **s'ennuyait** jamais avec lui.
We never got bored with him.

Il **s'ennuiera** sûrement quand
ses copains seront partis.
He'll probably be bored when his
friends are away.

Elle **s'ennuya** un peu.
She got a little bored.

Tu ne **t'ennuierais** pas tant si tu
allais jouer avec les autres.
You wouldn't be so bored if you
went to play with the others.

Il **s'était ennuyé** pendant les
vacances et il était content de
retrouver ses copains.
He'd got bored during the
holidays and he was happy to
be with his friends again.

je/j' = I **tu** = you **il** = he/it **elle** = she/it **on** = we/one **nous** = we **vous** = you **ils/elles** = they

entendre (to hear)

PRESENT

j'	**entends**
tu	**entends**
il/elle/on	**entend**
nous	**entendons**
vous	**entendez**
ils/elles	**entendent**

PRESENT SUBJUNCTIVE

j'	**entende**
tu	**entendes**
il/elle/on	**entende**
nous	**entendions**
vous	**entendiez**
ils/elles	**entendent**

PERFECT

j'	**ai entendu**
tu	**as entendu**
il/elle/on	**a entendu**
nous	**avons entendu**
vous	**avez entendu**
ils/elles	**ont entendu**

IMPERFECT

j'	**entendais**
tu	**entendais**
il/elle/on	**entendait**
nous	**entendions**
vous	**entendiez**
ils/elles	**entendaient**

PRESENT PARTICIPLE
entendant

PAST PARTICIPLE
entendu

FUTURE

j'	**entendrai**
tu	**entendras**
il/elle/on	**entendra**
nous	**entendrons**
vous	**entendrez**
ils/elles	**entendront**

CONDITIONAL

j'	**entendrais**
tu	**entendrais**
il/elle/on	**entendrait**
nous	**entendrions**
vous	**entendriez**
ils/elles	**entendraient**

PAST HISTORIC

j'	**entendis**
tu	**entendis**
il/elle/on	**entendit**
nous	**entendîmes**
vous	**entendîtes**
ils/elles	**entendirent**

PLUPERFECT

j'	**avais entendu**
tu	**avais entendu**
il/elle/on	**avait entendu**
nous	**avions entendu**
vous	**aviez entendu**
ils/elles	**avaient entendu**

IMPERATIVE
entends / entendons / entendez

EXAMPLE PHRASES

Il n'**entend** pas bien.
He can't hear very well.

Tu **as entendu** ce que je t'ai dit?
Did you hear what I said to you?

Il ne faut pas qu'elle nous **entende**.
She mustn't hear us.

Elle n'**entendait** jamais le réveil sonner.
She never heard the alarm clock ring.

Tu les **entendras** sûrement rentrer.
You'll probably hear them come back.

Elle **entendit** les oiseaux chanter.
She heard the birds singing.

On **entendrait** moins les voisins si les murs étaient plus épais.
We'd hear the neighbours less if the walls were thicker.

Il ne les **avait** pas **entendus** arriver.
He hadn't heard them arrive.

je/j' = I   **tu** = you   **il** = he/it   **elle** = she/it   **on** = we/one   **nous** = we   **vous** = you   **ils/elles** = they

entrer (to come in; to go in)

PRESENT

j'	**entre**
tu	**entres**
il/elle/on	**entre**
nous	**entrons**
vous	**entrez**
ils/elles	**entrent**

PRESENT SUBJUNCTIVE

j'	**entre**
tu	**entres**
il/elle/on	**entre**
nous	**entrions**
vous	**entriez**
ils/elles	**entrent**

PERFECT

je	**suis entré(e)**
tu	**es entré(e)**
il/elle/on	**est entré(e)**
nous	**sommes entré(e)s**
vous	**êtes entré(e)(s)**
ils/elles	**sont entré(e)s**

IMPERFECT

j'	**entrais**
tu	**entrais**
il/elle/on	**entrait**
nous	**entrions**
vous	**entriez**
ils/elles	**entraient**

PRESENT PARTICIPLE
entrant

PAST PARTICIPLE
entré

FUTURE

j'	**entrerai**
tu	**entreras**
il/elle/on	**entrera**
nous	**entrerons**
vous	**entrerez**
ils/elles	**entreront**

CONDITIONAL

j'	**entrerais**
tu	**entrerais**
il/elle/on	**entrerait**
nous	**entrerions**
vous	**entreriez**
ils/elles	**entreraient**

PAST HISTORIC

j'	**entrai**
tu	**entras**
il/elle/on	**entra**
nous	**entrâmes**
vous	**entrâtes**
ils/elles	**entrèrent**

PLUPERFECT

j'	**étais entré(e)**
tu	**étais entré(e)**
il/elle/on	**était entré(e)**
nous	**étions entré(e)s**
vous	**étiez entré(e)(s)**
ils/elles	**étaient entré(e)s**

IMPERATIVE
entre / entrons / entrez

EXAMPLE PHRASES

Je peux **entrer**?
Can I come in?

Ils **sont** tous **entrés** dans la maison.
They all went inside the house.

Entrez par la porte de derrière.
Come in by the back door.

Essuie-toi les pieds en **entrant**.
Wipe your feet as you come in.

Elle **entrera** en sixième à la rentrée.
She'll go into first year of high school after the summer.

Comme personne ne répondit, il poussa la porte et **entra**.
As nobody answered, he pushed the door and went in.

Je n'**entrerais** pas sans frapper si j'étais toi.
I wouldn't go in without knocking if I were you.

Comme j'avais perdu les clés, j'**étais entré** par la fenêtre.
As I'd lost the keys, I'd gone in through the window.

---

je/j' = I   **tu** = you   **il** = he/it   **elle** = she/it   **on** = we/one   **nous** = we   **vous** = you   **ils/elles** = they

envoyer (to send)

PRESENT

j'	**envoie**
tu	**envoies**
il/elle/on	**envoie**
nous	**envoyons**
vous	**envoyez**
ils/elles	**envoient**

PERFECT

j'	**ai envoyé**
tu	**as envoyé**
il/elle/on	**a envoyé**
nous	**avons envoyé**
vous	**avez envoyé**
ils/elles	**ont envoyé**

PRESENT PARTICIPLE
envoyant

FUTURE

j'	**enverrai**
tu	**enverras**
il/elle/on	**enverra**
nous	**enverrons**
vous	**enverrez**
ils/elles	**enverront**

PAST HISTORIC

j'	**envoyai**
tu	**envoyas**
il/elle/on	**envoya**
nous	**envoyâmes**
vous	**envoyâtes**
ils/elles	**envoyèrent**

IMPERATIVE
envoie / envoyons / envoyez

PRESENT SUBJUNCTIVE

j'	**envoie**
tu	**envoies**
il/elle/on	**envoie**
nous	**envoyions**
vous	**envoyiez**
ils/elles	**envoient**

IMPERFECT

j'	**envoyais**
tu	**envoyais**
il/elle/on	**envoyait**
nous	**envoyions**
vous	**envoyiez**
ils/elles	**envoyaient**

PAST PARTICIPLE
envoyé

CONDITIONAL

j'	**enverrais**
tu	**enverrais**
il/elle/on	**enverrait**
nous	**enverrions**
vous	**enverriez**
ils/elles	**enverraient**

PLUPERFECT

j'	**avais envoyé**
tu	**avais envoyé**
il/elle/on	**avait envoyé**
nous	**avions envoyé**
vous	**aviez envoyé**
ils/elles	**avaient envoyé**

EXAMPLE PHRASES

Ma cousine nous **envoie** toujours des cadeaux pour Noël.
My cousin always sends us presents for Christmas.

J'**ai envoyé** une carte postale à ma tante.
I sent my aunt a postcard.

Il faut que j'**envoie** ce paquet demain.
I must send this parcel away tomorrow.

Elle m'**envoyait** toujours une carte pour mon anniversaire.
She would always send me a card for my birthday.

J'**enverrai** Julie te chercher à l'aéroport.
I'll send Julie to fetch you at the airport.

Sa mère l'**envoya** chercher du pain.
His mother sent him to get some bread.

Je lui **enverrais** un cadeau si j'étais sûr de lui faire plaisir.
I'd send her a present if I thought it would make her happy.

Je ne lui **avais** pas **envoyé** mes vœux et elle était très vexée.
I hadn't sent her a Christmas card and she was very upset.

Envoie-moi un e-mail.
Send me an email.

je/j' = I   **tu** = you   **il** = he/it   **elle** = she/it   **on** = we/one   **nous** = we   **vous** = you   **ils/elles** = they

espérer (to hope)

PRESENT

j'	**espère**
tu	**espères**
il/elle/on	**espère**
nous	**espérons**
vous	**espérez**
ils/elles	**espèrent**

PRESENT SUBJUNCTIVE

j'	**espère**
tu	**espères**
il/elle/on	**espère**
nous	**espérions**
vous	**espériez**
ils/elles	**espèrent**

PERFECT

j'	**ai espéré**
tu	**as espéré**
il/elle/on	**a espéré**
nous	**avons espéré**
vous	**avez espéré**
ils/elles	**ont espéré**

IMPERFECT

j'	**espérais**
tu	**espérais**
il/elle/on	**espérait**
nous	**espérions**
vous	**espériez**
ils/elles	**espéraient**

PRESENT PARTICIPLE
espérant

PAST PARTICIPLE
espéré

FUTURE

j'	**espérerai**
tu	**espéreras**
il/elle/on	**espérera**
nous	**espérerons**
vous	**espérerez**
ils/elles	**espéreront**

CONDITIONAL

j'	**espérerais**
tu	**espérerais**
il/elle/on	**espérerait**
nous	**espérerions**
vous	**espéreriez**
ils/elles	**espéreraient**

PAST HISTORIC

j'	**espérai**
tu	**espéras**
il/elle/on	**espéra**
nous	**espérâmes**
vous	**espérâtes**
ils/elles	**espérèrent**

PLUPERFECT

j'	**avais espéré**
tu	**avais espéré**
il/elle/on	**avait espéré**
nous	**avions espéré**
vous	**aviez espéré**
ils/elles	**avaient espéré**

IMPERATIVE
espère / espérons / espérez

EXAMPLE PHRASES

J'**espère** que tu vas bien.
I hope you're well.

Tu penses réussir tes examens? –
 J'**espère** bien!
Do you think you'll pass your exams? –
 I hope so!

Il **espérait** pouvoir venir.
He was hoping he'd be able to come.

Elle **espérait** qu'il n'était pas déjà parti.
She was hoping that he hadn't already
 left.

Il **espéra** qu'ils se reverraient bientôt.
He hoped that they would see each
 other again soon.

Si j'étais toi, je n'**espérerais** pas trop
 qu'il vienne: tu risques d'être déçu.
If I were you, I wouldn't put too much
 hope in him coming – you could be
 disappointed.

J'**avais espéré** que tu pourrais venir.
I had hoped that you would be able
 to come.

je/j' = I   **tu** = you   **il** = he/it   **elle** = she/it   **on** = we/one   **nous** = we   **vous** = you   **ils/elles** = they

essayer (to try)

PRESENT

j' **essaie**
tu **essaies**
il/elle/on **essaie**
nous **essayons**
vous **essayez**
ils/elles **essaient**

PERFECT

j' **ai essayé**
tu **as essayé**
il/elle/on **a essayé**
nous **avons essayé**
vous **avez essayé**
ils/elles **ont essayé**

PRESENT PARTICIPLE
essayant

FUTURE

j' **essaierai**
tu **essaieras**
il/elle/on **essaiera**
nous **essaierons**
vous **essaierez**
ils/elles **essaieront**

PAST HISTORIC

j' **essayai**
tu **essayas**
il/elle/on **essaya**
nous **essayâmes**
vous **essayâtes**
ils/elles **essayèrent**

IMPERATIVE
essaie / essayons / essayez

PRESENT SUBJUNCTIVE

j' **essaie**
tu **essaies**
il/elle/on **essaie**
nous **essayions**
vous **essayiez**
ils/elles **essaient**

IMPERFECT

j' **essayais**
tu **essayais**
il/elle/on **essayait**
nous **essayions**
vous **essayiez**
ils/elles **essayaient**

PAST PARTICIPLE
essayé

CONDITIONAL

j' **essaierais**
tu **essaierais**
il/elle/on **essaierait**
nous **essaierions**
vous **essaieriez**
ils/elles **essaieraient**

PLUPERFECT

j' **avais essayé**
tu **avais essayé**
il/elle/on **avait essayé**
nous **avions essayé**
vous **aviez essayé**
ils/elles **avaient essayé**

EXAMPLE PHRASES

Elle adorait **essayer** mes vêtements.
She loved trying on my clothes.

J'**ai essayé** de t'appeler hier soir.
I tried to ring you last night.

Il faut que j'**essaie** cette nouvelle recette.
I must try this new recipe.

Il **essayait** de la comprendre, mais il n'y arrivait pas.
He tried to understand her, but he couldn't.

J'**essaierai** d'aller le voir après le travail demain.
I'll try to go and see him after work tomorrow.

Ils **essayèrent** de la rattraper.
They tried to catch up with her.

Je n'**essaierais** pas de lui parler tout de suite si j'étais toi.
I wouldn't try to speak to her right now if I were you.

Elle **avait essayé** la robe, mais elle ne lui allait pas.
She'd tried on the dress, but it didn't fit her.

Essaie de ne pas t'énerver.
Try not to get all worked up.

je/j' = I **tu** = you **il** = he/it **elle** = she/it **on** = we/one **nous** = we **vous** = you **ils/elles** = they

éteindre (to switch off)

PRESENT

j'	**éteins**
tu	**éteins**
il/elle/on	**éteint**
nous	**éteignons**
vous	**éteignez**
ils/elles	**éteignent**

PRESENT SUBJUNCTIVE

j'	**éteigne**
tu	**éteignes**
il/elle/on	**éteigne**
nous	**éteignions**
vous	**éteigniez**
ils/elles	**éteignent**

PERFECT

j'	**ai éteint**
tu	**as éteint**
il/elle/on	**a éteint**
nous	**avons éteint**
vous	**avez éteint**
ils/elles	**ont éteint**

IMPERFECT

j'	**éteignais**
tu	**éteignais**
il/elle/on	**éteignait**
nous	**éteignions**
vous	**éteigniez**
ils/elles	**éteignaient**

PRESENT PARTICIPLE
éteignant

PAST PARTICIPLE
éteint

FUTURE

j'	**éteindrai**
tu	**éteindras**
il/elle/on	**éteindra**
nous	**éteindrons**
vous	**éteindrez**
ils/elles	**éteindront**

CONDITIONAL

j'	**éteindrais**
tu	**éteindrais**
il/elle/on	**éteindrait**
nous	**éteindrions**
vous	**éteindriez**
ils/elles	**éteindraient**

PAST HISTORIC

j'	**éteignis**
tu	**éteignis**
il/elle/on	**éteignit**
nous	**éteignîmes**
vous	**éteignîtes**
ils/elles	**éteignirent**

PLUPERFECT

j'	**avais éteint**
tu	**avais éteint**
il/elle/on	**avait éteint**
nous	**avions éteint**
vous	**aviez éteint**
ils/elles	**avaient éteint**

IMPERATIVE
éteins / éteignons / éteignez

EXAMPLE PHRASES

N'oubliez pas d'**éteindre** la lumière en sortant.
Don't forget to switch off the light when you leave.

Elle n'**éteint** jamais la lumière dans sa chambre.
She never switches off her bedroom light.

Tu **as éteint** la lumière dans la salle de bain?
Have you switched off the bathroom light?

J'**éteindrai** tout avant de partir.
I'll switch everything off before I leave.

Elle **éteignit** la lumière et s'endormit.
She switched off the light and fell asleep.

Il **éteindrait** sa cigarette s'il savait que la fumée te dérange.
He'd put out his cigarette if he knew that the smoke bothers you.

Il **avait éteint** son portable en entrant dans le cinéma.
He'd switched off his mobile on the way into the cinema.

Karine, **éteins** la télé, s'il te plaît.
Switch off the TV please, Karine.

je/j' = I   **tu** = you   **il** = he/it   **elle** = she/it   **on** = we/one   **nous** = we   **vous** = you   **ils/elles** = they

être (to be)

PRESENT

je	**suis**
tu	**es**
il/elle/on	**est**
nous	**sommes**
vous	**êtes**
ils/elles	**sont**

PRESENT SUBJUNCTIVE

je	**sois**
tu	**sois**
il/elle/on	**soit**
nous	**soyons**
vous	**soyez**
ils/elles	**soient**

PERFECT

j'	**ai été**
tu	**as été**
il/elle/on	**a été**
nous	**avons été**
vous	**avez été**
ils/elles	**ont été**

IMPERFECT

j'	**étais**
tu	**étais**
il/elle/on	**était**
nous	**étions**
vous	**étiez**
ils/elles	**étaient**

PRESENT PARTICIPLE
étant

PAST PARTICIPLE
été

FUTURE

je	**serai**
tu	**seras**
il/elle/on	**sera**
nous	**serons**
vous	**serez**
ils/elles	**seront**

CONDITIONAL

je	**serais**
tu	**serais**
il/elle/on	**serait**
nous	**serions**
vous	**seriez**
ils/elles	**seraient**

PAST HISTORIC

je	**fus**
tu	**fus**
il/elle/on	**fut**
nous	**fûmes**
vous	**fûtes**
ils/elles	**furent**

PLUPERFECT

j'	**avais été**
tu	**avais été**
il/elle/on	**avait été**
nous	**avions été**
vous	**aviez été**
ils/elles	**avaient été**

IMPERATIVE
sois / soyons / soyez

EXAMPLE PHRASES

Quelle heure **est**-il? – Il **est** dix heures.
What time is it? – It's ten o'clock.

Ils ne **sont** pas encore arrivés.
They haven't arrived yet.

Je veux que vous **soyez** particulièrement sages aujourd'hui.
I want you to behave particularly well today.

Il **était** professeur de maths dans mon lycée.
He was a maths teacher in my school.

Je **serai** chez moi à partir de midi.
I'll be at home from midday onwards.

Il **fut** tellement vexé qu'il ne lui parla pas de la soirée.
He was so upset that he didn't speak to her all evening.

Nous **serions** contents de vous voir si vous aviez le temps de passer.
We'd be happy to see you if you had time to drop by.

Nous étions punis parce que nous n'**avions** pas **été** sages.
We were punished because we hadn't been good.

Sois courageux.
Be brave.

je/j' = I   **tu** = you   **il** = he/it   **elle** = she/it   **on** = we/one   **nous** = we   **vous** = you   **ils/elles** = they

faillir (faire qch to almost do sth)

PRESENT

je	**faillis**
tu	**faillis**
il/elle/on	**faillit**
nous	**faillissons**
vous	**faillissez**
ils/elles	**faillissent**

PERFECT

j'	**ai failli**
tu	**as failli**
il/elle/on	**a failli**
nous	**avons failli**
vous	**avez failli**
ils/elles	**ont failli**

PRESENT PARTICIPLE
faillissant

FUTURE

je	**faillirai**
tu	**failliras**
il/elle/on	**faillira**
nous	**faillirons**
vous	**faillirez**
ils/elles	**failliront**

PAST HISTORIC

je	**faillis**
tu	**faillis**
il/elle/on	**faillit**
nous	**faillîmes**
vous	**faillîtes**
ils/elles	**faillirent**

IMPERATIVE
not used

PRESENT SUBJUNCTIVE

je	**faillisse**
tu	**faillisses**
il/elle/on	**faillisse**
nous	**faillissions**
vous	**faillissiez**
ils/elles	**faillissent**

IMPERFECT

je	**faillissais**
tu	**faillissais**
il/elle/on	**faillissait**
nous	**faillissions**
vous	**faillissiez**
ils/elles	**faillissaient**

PAST PARTICIPLE
failli

CONDITIONAL

je	**faillirais**
tu	**faillirais**
il/elle/on	**faillirait**
nous	**faillirions**
vous	**failliriez**
ils/elles	**failliraient**

PLUPERFECT

j'	**avais failli**
tu	**avais failli**
il/elle/on	**avait failli**
nous	**avions failli**
vous	**aviez failli**
ils/elles	**avaient failli**

EXAMPLE PHRASES

J'**ai failli** tomber.
I nearly fell.

Il **a failli** s'énerver.
He nearly got angry.

Nous **avons failli** rater notre train.
We nearly missed our train.

Ils **ont failli** ne pas venir.
They nearly didn't come.

Il **faillit** s'en aller sans dire au revoir.
He nearly left without saying goodbye.

Elle **faillit** pleurer quand ils lui annoncèrent la nouvelle.
She nearly cried when they told her the news.

Nous **avions failli** nous perdre en venant vous voir ce jour-là.
We had nearly got lost on our way to see you that day.

Ils **avaient failli** se battre, mais la cloche avait sonné au bon moment.
They had nearly had a fight, but the bell had rung at the right time.

---

je/j' = I   **tu** = you   **il** = he/it   **elle** = she/it   **on** = we/one   **nous** = we   **vous** = you   **ils/elles** = they

faire (to do; to make)

PRESENT

je	**fais**
tu	**fais**
il/elle/on	**fait**
nous	**faisons**
vous	**faites**
ils/elles	**font**

PRESENT SUBJUNCTIVE

je	**fasse**
tu	**fasses**
il/elle/on	**fasse**
nous	**fassions**
vous	**fassiez**
ils/elles	**fassent**

PERFECT

j'	**ai fait**
tu	**as fait**
il/elle/on	**a fait**
nous	**avons fait**
vous	**avez fait**
ils/elles	**ont fait**

IMPERFECT

je	**faisais**
tu	**faisais**
il/elle/on	**faisait**
nous	**faisions**
vous	**faisiez**
ils/elles	**faisaient**

PRESENT PARTICIPLE
faisant

PAST PARTICIPLE
fait

FUTURE

je	**ferai**
tu	**feras**
il/elle/on	**fera**
nous	**ferons**
vous	**ferez**
ils/elles	**feront**

CONDITIONAL

je	**ferais**
tu	**ferais**
il/elle/on	**ferait**
nous	**ferions**
vous	**feriez**
ils/elles	**feraient**

PAST HISTORIC

je	**fis**
tu	**fis**
il/elle/on	**fit**
nous	**fîmes**
vous	**fîtes**
ils/elles	**firent**

PLUPERFECT

j'	**avais fait**
tu	**avais fait**
il/elle/on	**avait fait**
nous	**avions fait**
vous	**aviez fait**
ils/elles	**avaient fait**

IMPERATIVE
fais / faisons / faites

EXAMPLE PHRASES

Qu'est-ce que tu **fais**?
What are you doing?

Qu'est-ce qu'il **a fait**?
What has he done?

Il s'**est fait** couper les cheveux.
He's had his hair cut.

J'aimerais que tu **fasses** la vaisselle plus souvent.
I'd like you to wash the dishes more often.

Il ne **faisait** jamais son lit.
He would never make his bed.

Demain, nous **ferons** une promenade sur la plage.
Tomorrow, we'll go for a walk on the beach.

Il **fit** semblant de ne pas comprendre.
He pretended not to understand.

Si je gagnais à la loterie, je **ferais** le tour du monde.
If I won the lottery, I would take a trip round the world.

Elle **avait fait** un gâteau.
She'd made a cake.

Ne **fais** pas l'idiot.
Don't behave like an idiot.

je/j' = I **tu** = you **il** = he/it **elle** = she/it **on** = we/one **nous** = we **vous** = you **ils/elles** = they

falloir (to be necessary)

PRESENT	**PRESENT SUBJUNCTIVE**
il **faut**	il **faille**
PERFECT	**IMPERFECT**
il **a fallu**	il **fallait**
PRESENT PARTICIPLE	**PAST PARTICIPLE**
not used	**fallu**
FUTURE	**CONDITIONAL**
il **faudra**	il **faudrait**
PAST HISTORIC	**PLUPERFECT**
il **fallut**	il **avait fallu**
IMPERATIVE	
not used	

EXAMPLE PHRASES

Il **faut** se dépêcher!
We have to hurry up!

Il ne **faut** pas paniquer.
Let's not panic.

Il **a fallu** que je lui prête ma voiture.
I had to lend her my car.

Il me **fallait** de l'argent.
I needed money.

Il **faudra** que tu sois là à 8 heures.
You'll have to be there at 8.

Il **fallut** qu'ils partent de très bonne heure.
They had to leave very early.

Il **faudrait** t'arrêter de fumer.
You should stop smoking.

Il **avait fallu** nettoyer toute la maison.
We'd had to clean the whole house.

je/j' = I   **tu** = you   **il** = he/it   **elle** = she/it   **on** = we/one   **nous** = we   **vous** = you   **ils/elles** = they

finir (to finish)

PRESENT
je	**finis**
tu	**finis**
il/elle/on	**finit**
nous	**finissons**
vous	**finissez**
ils/elles	**finissent**

PRESENT SUBJUNCTIVE
je	**finisse**
tu	**finisses**
il/elle/on	**finisse**
nous	**finissions**
vous	**finissiez**
ils/elles	**finissent**

PERFECT
j'	**ai fini**
tu	**as fini**
il/elle/on	**a fini**
nous	**avons fini**
vous	**avez fini**
ils/elles	**ont fini**

IMPERFECT
je	**finissais**
tu	**finissais**
il/elle/on	**finissait**
nous	**finissions**
vous	**finissiez**
ils/elles	**finissaient**

PRESENT PARTICIPLE
finissant

PAST PARTICIPLE
fini

FUTURE
je	**finirai**
tu	**finiras**
il/elle/on	**finira**
nous	**finirons**
vous	**finirez**
ils/elles	**finiront**

CONDITIONAL
je	**finirais**
tu	**finirais**
il/elle/on	**finirait**
nous	**finirions**
vous	**finiriez**
ils/elles	**finiraient**

PAST HISTORIC
je	**finis**
tu	**finis**
il/elle/on	**finit**
nous	**finîmes**
vous	**finîtes**
ils/elles	**finirent**

PLUPERFECT
j'	**avais fini**
tu	**avais fini**
il/elle/on	**avait fini**
nous	**avions fini**
vous	**aviez fini**
ils/elles	**avaient fini**

IMPERATIVE
finis / finissons / finissez

EXAMPLE PHRASES

Je **finis** mes cours à 17h.
I finish my lessons at 5pm.

J'**ai fini**!
I've finished!

Finis ta soupe!
Finish your soup!

Il faut que je **finisse** mon livre avant de commencer celui-là.
I have to finish my book before I start this one.

Elle **finissait** toujours en retard.
She'd always finish late.

Je **finirai** mes devoirs demain.
I'll finish my homework tomorrow.

Il **finit** son dîner et alla se coucher.
He finished his dinner and went to bed.

Si on l'ignorait, elle **finirait** par comprendre.
If we ignored her, she'd eventually understand.

Elle n'**avait** pas **fini** de manger quand nous sommes arrivés.
She hadn't finished eating when we arrived.

je/j' = I   **tu** = you   **il** = he/it   **elle** = she/it   **on** = we/one   **nous** = we   **vous** = you   **ils/elles** = they

fuir (to flee; to leak)

PRESENT

je	**fuis**
tu	**fuis**
il/elle/on	**fuit**
nous	**fuyons**
vous	**fuyez**
ils/elles	**fuient**

PRESENT SUBJUNCTIVE

je	**fuie**
tu	**fuies**
il/elle/on	**fuie**
nous	**fuyions**
vous	**fuyiez**
ils/elles	**fuient**

PERFECT

j'	**ai fui**
tu	**as fui**
il/elle/on	**a fui**
nous	**avons fui**
vous	**avez fui**
ils/elles	**ont fui**

IMPERFECT

je	**fuyais**
tu	**fuyais**
il/elle/on	**fuyait**
nous	**fuyions**
vous	**fuyiez**
ils/elles	**fuyaient**

PRESENT PARTICIPLE
fuyant

PAST PARTICIPLE
fui

FUTURE

je	**fuirai**
tu	**fuiras**
il/elle/on	**fuira**
nous	**fuirons**
vous	**fuirez**
ils/elles	**fuiront**

CONDITIONAL

je	**fuirais**
tu	**fuirais**
il/elle/on	**fuirait**
nous	**fuirions**
vous	**fuiriez**
ils/elles	**fuiraient**

PAST HISTORIC

je	**fuis**
tu	**fuis**
il/elle/on	**fuit**
nous	**fuîmes**
vous	**fuîtes**
ils/elles	**fuirent**

PLUPERFECT

j'	**avais fui**
tu	**avais fui**
il/elle/on	**avait fui**
nous	**avions fui**
vous	**aviez fui**
ils/elles	**avaient fui**

IMPERATIVE
fuis / fuyons / fuyez

EXAMPLE PHRASES

J'ai un stylo qui **fuit**.
My pen leaks.

Ils **ont fui** leur pays.
They fled their country.

Il ne faut pas que tu le **fuies** comme ça.
You mustn't run away from him like
   that.

Le robinet **fuyait**.
The tap was dripping.

Il **fuira** toujours les responsabilités.
He will always run away from
   responsibilities.

Beaucoup de gens **fuirent** vers le sud.
A lot of people fled south.

La machine à laver **fuirait** si on la
   remplissait trop.
The washing machine would leak if we
   overloaded it.

Ils **avaient fui** leur village et s'étaient
   réfugiés dans les montagnes.
They had fled from their village and had
   taken refuge in the mountains.

je/j' = I   **tu** = you   **il** = he/it   **elle** = she/it   **on** = we/one   **nous** = we   **vous** = you   **ils/elles** = they

haïr (to hate)

PRESENT

je	**hais**
tu	**hais**
il/elle/on	**hait**
nous	**haïssons**
vous	**haïssez**
ils/elles	**haïssent**

PRESENT SUBJUNCTIVE

je	**haïsse**
tu	**haïsses**
il/elle/on	**haïsse**
nous	**haïssions**
vous	**haïssiez**
ils/elles	**haïssent**

PERFECT

j'	**ai haï**
tu	**as haï**
il/elle/on	**a haï**
nous	**avons haï**
vous	**avez haï**
ils/elles	**ont haï**

IMPERFECT

je	**haïssais**
tu	**haïssais**
il/elle/on	**haïssait**
nous	**haïssions**
vous	**haïssiez**
ils/elles	**haïssaient**

PRESENT PARTICIPLE
haïssant

PAST PARTICIPLE
haï

FUTURE

je	**haïrai**
tu	**haïras**
il/elle/on	**haïra**
nous	**haïrons**
vous	**haïrez**
ils/elles	**haïront**

CONDITIONAL

je	**haïrais**
tu	**haïrais**
il/elle/on	**haïrait**
nous	**haïrions**
vous	**haïriez**
ils/elles	**haïraient**

PAST HISTORIC

je	**haïs**
tu	**haïs**
il/elle/on	**haït**
nous	**haïmes**
vous	**haïtes**
ils/elles	**haïrent**

PLUPERFECT

j'	**avais haï**
tu	**avais haï**
il/elle/on	**avait haï**
nous	**avions haï**
vous	**aviez haï**
ils/elles	**avaient haï**

IMPERATIVE
hais / haïssons / haïssez

EXAMPLE PHRASES

Je te **hais**!
I hate you!

Ils se **haïssent**.
They hate each other.

Il ne faut pas que tu le **haïsses** pour ça.
You mustn't hate him for that.

Elle **haïssait** tout le monde.
She hated everyone.

Je la **haïrai** toujours.
I'll always hate her.

Elle le **haït** pour ce qu'il venait de dire.
She hated him for what he'd just said.

Elle me **haïrait** si je n'allais pas voir ses parents avec elle.
She'd hate me if I didn't go and see her parents with her.

Elle m'**avait haï** durant toutes ces années et maintenant nous étions les meilleures amies du monde.
She had hated me all these years and now we were the best of friends.

je/j' = I   **tu** = you   **il** = he/it   **elle** = she/it   **on** = we/one   **nous** = we   **vous** = you   **ils/elles** = they

s'inquiéter (to worry)

PRESENT
je	**m'inquiète**
tu	**t'inquiètes**
il/elle/on	**s'inquiète**
nous	**nous inquiétons**
vous	**vous inquiétez**
ils/elles	**s'inquiètent**

PRESENT SUBJUNCTIVE
je	**m'inquiète**
tu	**t'inquiètes**
il/elle/on	**s'inquiète**
nous	**nous inquiétions**
vous	**vous inquiétiez**
ils/elles	**s'inquiètent**

PERFECT
je	**me suis inquiété(e)**
tu	**t'es inquiété(e)**
il/elle/on	**s'est inquiété(e)**
nous	**nous sommes inquiété(e)s**
vous	**vous êtes inquiété(e)(s)**
ils/elles	**se sont inquiété(e)s**

IMPERFECT
je	**m'inquiétais**
tu	**t'inquiétais**
il/elle/on	**s'inquiétait**
nous	**nous inquiétions**
vous	**vous inquiétiez**
ils/elles	**s'inquiétaient**

PRESENT PARTICIPLE
s'inquiétant

PAST PARTICIPLE
inquiété

FUTURE
je	**m'inquiéterai**
tu	**t'inquiéteras**
il/elle/on	**s'inquiétera**
nous	**nous inquiéterons**
vous	**vous inquiéterez**
ils/elles	**s'inquiéteront**

CONDITIONAL
je	**m'inquiéterais**
tu	**t'inquiéterais**
il/elle/on	**s'inquiéterait**
nous	**nous inquiéterions**
vous	**vous inquiéteriez**
ils/elles	**s'inquiéteraient**

PAST HISTORIC
je	**m'inquiétai**
tu	**t'inquiétas**
il/elle/on	**s'inquiéta**
nous	**nous inquiétâmes**
vous	**vous inquiétâtes**
ils/elles	**s'inquiétèrent**

PLUPERFECT
je	**m'étais inquiété(e)**
tu	**t'étais inquiété(e)**
il/elle/on	**s'était inquiété(e)**
nous	**nous étions inquiété(e)s**
vous	**vous étiez inquiété(e)(s)**
ils/elles	**s'étaient inquiété(e)s**

IMPERATIVE
inquiète-toi / inquiétons-nous / inquiétez-vous

EXAMPLE PHRASES

Elle **s'inquiète** toujours si je suis en retard.
She always worries if I'm late.

Comme je savais où tu étais, je ne **me suis** pas **inquiétée**.
As I knew where you were, I didn't worry.

Ne **t'inquiète** pas, je ne rentrerai pas tard.
Don't worry, I'll not be late coming home.

Je ne veux pas qu'ils **s'inquiètent**.
I don't want them to worry.

Ça **m'inquiétait** un peu que tu ne nous aies pas téléphoné.
I was a little worried that you hadn't phoned us.

Mes parents **s'inquiéteront** si j'y vais toute seule.
My parents will worry if I go there on my own.

Il **s'inquiéta** pour elle.
He worried about her.

Je **m'inquiéterais** moins si tu n'étais pas si loin.
I'd worry less if you weren't so far away.

Comme ils savaient qu'elle était avec Vincent, ils ne **s'étaient** pas **inquiétés**.
As they knew that she was with Vincent, they hadn't worried.

je/j' = I   **tu** = you   **il** = he/it   **elle** = she/it   **on** = we/one   **nous** = we   **vous** = you   **ils/elles** = they

interdire (to forbid)

PRESENT

j'	**interdis**
tu	**interdis**
il/elle/on	**interdit**
nous	**interdisons**
vous	**interdisez**
ils/elles	**interdisent**

PRESENT SUBJUNCTIVE

j'	**interdise**
tu	**interdises**
il/elle/on	**interdise**
nous	**interdisions**
vous	**interdisiez**
ils/elles	**interdisent**

PERFECT

j'	**ai interdit**
tu	**as interdit**
il/elle/on	**a interdit**
nous	**avons interdit**
vous	**avez interdit**
ils/elles	**ont interdit**

IMPERFECT

j'	**interdisais**
tu	**interdisais**
il/elle/on	**interdisait**
nous	**interdisions**
vous	**interdisiez**
ils/elles	**interdisaient**

PRESENT PARTICIPLE
interdisant

PAST PARTICIPLE
interdit

FUTURE

j'	**interdirai**
tu	**interdiras**
il/elle/on	**interdira**
nous	**interdirons**
vous	**interdirez**
ils/elles	**interdiront**

CONDITIONAL

j'	**interdirais**
tu	**interdirais**
il/elle/on	**interdirait**
nous	**interdirions**
vous	**interdiriez**
ils/elles	**interdiraient**

PAST HISTORIC

j'	**interdis**
tu	**interdis**
il/elle/on	**interdit**
nous	**interdîmes**
vous	**interdîtes**
ils/elles	**interdirent**

PLUPERFECT

j'	**avais interdit**
tu	**avais interdit**
il/elle/on	**avait interdit**
nous	**avions interdit**
vous	**aviez interdit**
ils/elles	**avaient interdit**

IMPERATIVE
interdis / interdisons / interdisez

EXAMPLE PHRASES

Je t'**interdis** de toucher à ça.
I forbid you to touch this.

Ses parents lui **ont interdit** de sortir.
His parents have forbidden him to go
   out.

Interdisons-leur de regarder la télé ce
   week-end.
Let's ban them from watching TV over
   the weekend.

Elle nous **interdisait** de jouer avec lui.
She forbade us to play with him.

Si vous n'êtes pas raisonnables, je vous
   interdirai de sortir du jardin.
If you're not sensible, I'll forbid you to
   leave the garden.

À partir de ce jour, ils nous **interdirent**
   de la voir.
From that day on, they forbade us
   to see her.

Si ma fille me parlait comme ça, je lui
   interdirais de sortir avec ses copines.
If my daughter spoke to me like that,
   I'd ban her from going out with her
   friends.

Elle nous **avait interdit** de lui en parler.
She had forbidden us to tell him
   about it.

je/j' = I   **tu** = you   **il** = he/it   **elle** = she/it   **on** = we/one   **nous** = we   **vous** = you   **ils/elles** = they

jeter (to throw)

PRESENT		
je	**jette**	
tu	**jettes**	
il/elle/on	**jette**	
nous	**jetons**	
vous	**jetez**	
ils/elles	**jettent**	

PRESENT SUBJUNCTIVE

je	**jette**
tu	**jettes**
il/elle/on	**jette**
nous	**jetions**
vous	**jetiez**
ils/elles	**jettent**

PERFECT

j'	**ai jeté**
tu	**as jeté**
il/elle/on	**a jeté**
nous	**avons jeté**
vous	**avez jeté**
ils/elles	**ont jeté**

IMPERFECT

je	**jetais**
tu	**jetais**
il/elle/on	**jetait**
nous	**jetions**
vous	**jetiez**
ils/elles	**jetaient**

PRESENT PARTICIPLE
jetant

PAST PARTICIPLE
jeté

FUTURE

je	**jetterai**
tu	**jetteras**
il/elle/on	**jettera**
nous	**jetterons**
vous	**jetterez**
ils/elles	**jetteront**

CONDITIONAL

je	**jetterais**
tu	**jetterais**
il/elle/on	**jetterait**
nous	**jetterions**
vous	**jetteriez**
ils/elles	**jetteraient**

PAST HISTORIC

je	**jetai**
tu	**jetas**
il/elle/on	**jeta**
nous	**jetâmes**
vous	**jetâtes**
ils/elles	**jetèrent**

PLUPERFECT

j'	**avais jeté**
tu	**avais jeté**
il/elle/on	**avait jeté**
nous	**avions jeté**
vous	**aviez jeté**
ils/elles	**avaient jeté**

IMPERATIVE
jette / jetons / jetez

EXAMPLE PHRASES

Ils ne **jettent** jamais rien.
They never throw anything away.

Elle **a jeté** son chewing-gum par
   la fenêtre.
She threw her chewing gum out of
   the window.

Il faut qu'on **jette** tous ces vieux jouets
   cassés.
We'll have to throw away all these old
   broken toys.

Il **jetait** toujours ses vêtements par
   terre.
He'd always throw his clothes on
   the floor.

Je **jetterai** tout ça à la poubelle.
I'll throw all this in the bin.

Il **jeta** sa veste sur la chaise et répondit
   au téléphone.
He threw his jacket on the chair and
   answered the phone.

Je **jetterais** bien tous ces vieux
   magazines.
I'd quite like to throw all these old
   magazines away.

Elle jurait qu'elle n'**avait** rien **jeté**.
She swore she hadn't thrown anything
   away.

Ne **jette** pas de papiers par terre.
Don't throw litter on the ground.

je/j' = I   **tu** = you   **il** = he/it   **elle** = she/it   **on** = we/one   **nous** = we   **vous** = you   **ils/elles** = they

joindre (to join)

PRESENT

je	**joins**
tu	**joins**
il/elle/on	**joint**
nous	**joignons**
vous	**joignez**
ils/elles	**joignent**

PRESENT SUBJUNCTIVE

je	**joigne**
tu	**joignes**
il/elle/on	**joigne**
nous	**joignions**
vous	**joigniez**
ils/elles	**joignent**

PERFECT

j'	**ai joint**
tu	**as joint**
il/elle/on	**a joint**
nous	**avons joint**
vous	**avez joint**
ils/elles	**ont joint**

IMPERFECT

je	**joignais**
tu	**joignais**
il/elle/on	**joignait**
nous	**joignions**
vous	**joigniez**
ils/elles	**joignaient**

PRESENT PARTICIPLE
joignant

PAST PARTICIPLE
joint

FUTURE

je	**joindrai**
tu	**joindras**
il/elle/on	**joindra**
nous	**joindrons**
vous	**joindrez**
ils/elles	**joindront**

CONDITIONAL

je	**joindrais**
tu	**joindrais**
il/elle/on	**joindrait**
nous	**joindrions**
vous	**joindriez**
ils/elles	**joindraient**

PAST HISTORIC

je	**joignis**
tu	**joignis**
il/elle/on	**joignit**
nous	**joignîmes**
vous	**joignîtes**
ils/elles	**joignirent**

PLUPERFECT

j'	**avais joint**
tu	**avais joint**
il/elle/on	**avait joint**
nous	**avions joint**
vous	**aviez joint**
ils/elles	**avaient joint**

IMPERATIVE
joins / joignons / joignez

EXAMPLE PHRASES

Où est-ce qu'on peut te **joindre** ce week-end?
Where can we contact you this weekend?

Il n'est pas facile à **joindre**.
He's not easy to contact.

Je vous **ai joint** un plan de la ville.
I have enclosed a map of the town.

Il **joignit** les mains et se mit à prier.
He put his hands together and started to pray.

On **avait joint** les deux tables.
We'd put the two tables together.

Nous **avions joint** nos efforts.
It had been a joint effort.

je/j' = I   **tu** = you   **il** = he/it   **elle** = she/it   **on** = we/one   **nous** = we   **vous** = you   **ils/elles** = they

lever (to lift)

PRESENT

je	**lève**
tu	**lèves**
il/elle/on	**lève**
nous	**levons**
vous	**levez**
ils/elles	**lèvent**

PRESENT SUBJUNCTIVE

je	**lève**
tu	**lèves**
il/elle/on	**lève**
nous	**levions**
vous	**leviez**
ils/elles	**lèvent**

PERFECT

j'	**ai levé**
tu	**as levé**
il/elle/on	**a levé**
nous	**avons levé**
vous	**avez levé**
ils/elles	**ont levé**

IMPERFECT

je	**levais**
tu	**levais**
il/elle/on	**levait**
nous	**levions**
vous	**leviez**
ils/elles	**levaient**

PRESENT PARTICIPLE
levant

PAST PARTICIPLE
levé

FUTURE

je	**lèverai**
tu	**lèveras**
il/elle/on	**lèvera**
nous	**lèverons**
vous	**lèverez**
ils/elles	**lèveront**

CONDITIONAL

je	**lèverais**
tu	**lèverais**
il/elle/on	**lèverait**
nous	**lèverions**
vous	**lèveriez**
ils/elles	**lèveraient**

PAST HISTORIC

je	**levai**
tu	**levas**
il/elle/on	**leva**
nous	**levâmes**
vous	**levâtes**
ils/elles	**levèrent**

PLUPERFECT

j'	**avais levé**
tu	**avais levé**
il/elle/on	**avait levé**
nous	**avions levé**
vous	**aviez levé**
ils/elles	**avaient levé**

IMPERATIVE
lève / levons / levez

EXAMPLE PHRASES

Je me **lève** tous les matins à sept heures.
I get up at seven every day.

Elle **a levé** la main pour répondre à la question.
She put her hand up to answer the question.

Je ne **lèverai** pas le petit doigt pour l'aider.
I won't lift a finger to help him.

Elle **leva** les yeux et vit qu'il était en train de tricher.
She looked up and saw that he was cheating.

Si mon père était encore là, il **lèverait** les bras au ciel.
If my dad were still here, he'd throw his arms up in despair.

Levez le doigt!
Put your hand up!

Levons notre verre à ta réussite.
Let's raise our glasses to your success.

je/j' = I   **tu** = you   **il** = he/it   **elle** = she/it   **on** = we/one   **nous** = we   **vous** = you   **ils/elles** = they

lire (to read)

PRESENT

je	**lis**
tu	**lis**
il/elle/on	**lit**
nous	**lisons**
vous	**lisez**
ils/elles	**lisent**

PRESENT SUBJUNCTIVE

je	**lise**
tu	**lises**
il/elle/on	**lise**
nous	**lisions**
vous	**lisiez**
ils/elles	**lisent**

PERFECT

j'	**ai lu**
tu	**as lu**
il/elle/on	**a lu**
nous	**avons lu**
vous	**avez lu**
ils/elles	**ont lu**

IMPERFECT

je	**lisais**
tu	**lisais**
il/elle/on	**lisait**
nous	**lisions**
vous	**lisiez**
ils/elles	**lisaient**

PRESENT PARTICIPLE

lisant

PAST PARTICIPLE

lu

FUTURE

je	**lirai**
tu	**liras**
il/elle/on	**lira**
nous	**lirons**
vous	**lirez**
ils/elles	**liront**

CONDITIONAL

je	**lirais**
tu	**lirais**
il/elle/on	**lirait**
nous	**lirions**
vous	**liriez**
ils/elles	**liraient**

PAST HISTORIC

je	**lus**
tu	**lus**
il/elle/on	**lut**
nous	**lûmes**
vous	**lûtes**
ils/elles	**lurent**

PLUPERFECT

j'	**avais lu**
tu	**avais lu**
il/elle/on	**avait lu**
nous	**avions lu**
vous	**aviez lu**
ils/elles	**avaient lu**

IMPERATIVE

lis / lisons / lisez

EXAMPLE PHRASES

Il **lit** beaucoup.
He reads a lot.

Vous **avez lu** "Madame Bovary"?
Have you read "Madame Bovary"?

J'aimerais que tu **lises** ce livre.
I'd like you to read this book.

Elle lui **lisait** une histoire.
She was reading him a story.

Je le **lirai** dans l'avion.
I'll read it on the plane.

Il **lut** la lettre à haute voix.
He read the letter aloud.

Je **lirais** plus si j'avais le temps.
I'd read more if I had time.

La maîtresse s'aperçut qu'il n'**avait** pas **lu** le livre.
The teacher realized that he hadn't read the book.

Lisez bien les instructions.
Read the instructions carefully.

je/j' = I **tu** = you **il** = he/it **elle** = she/it **on** = we/one **nous** = we **vous** = you **ils/elles** = they

manger (to eat)

PRESENT

je	**mange**
tu	**manges**
il/elle/on	**mange**
nous	**mangeons**
vous	**mangez**
ils/elles	**mangent**

PERFECT

j'	**ai mangé**
tu	**as mangé**
il/elle/on	**a mangé**
nous	**avons mangé**
vous	**avez mangé**
ils/elles	**ont mangé**

PRESENT PARTICIPLE
mangeant

FUTURE

je	**mangerai**
tu	**mangeras**
il/elle/on	**mangera**
nous	**mangerons**
vous	**mangerez**
ils/elles	**mangeront**

PAST HISTORIC

je	**mangeai**
tu	**mangeas**
il/elle/on	**mangea**
nous	**mangeâmes**
vous	**mangeâtes**
ils/elles	**mangèrent**

IMPERATIVE
mange / mangeons / mangez

PRESENT SUBJUNCTIVE

je	**mange**
tu	**manges**
il/elle/on	**mange**
nous	**mangions**
vous	**mangiez**
ils/elles	**mangent**

IMPERFECT

je	**mangeais**
tu	**mangeais**
il/elle/on	**mangeait**
nous	**mangions**
vous	**mangiez**
ils/elles	**mangeaient**

PAST PARTICIPLE
mangé

CONDITIONAL

je	**mangerais**
tu	**mangerais**
il/elle/on	**mangerait**
nous	**mangerions**
vous	**mangeriez**
ils/elles	**mangeraient**

PLUPERFECT

j'	**avais mangé**
tu	**avais mangé**
il/elle/on	**avait mangé**
nous	**avions mangé**
vous	**aviez mangé**
ils/elles	**avaient mangé**

EXAMPLE PHRASES

Nous ne **mangeons** pas souvent ensemble.
We don't often eat together.

Tu **as** assez **mangé**?
Have you had enough to eat?

Il faut que je **mange** avant de partir.
I have to eat before I leave.

Ils **mangeaient** en regardant la télé.
They were eating while watching TV.

Je **mangerai** plus tard.
I'll eat later on.

Il **mangea** rapidement et retourna travailler.
He ate quickly and went back to work.

Je **mangerais** bien le reste si je n'avais pas peur de grossir.
I'd gladly eat the rest if I wasn't afraid of putting on weight.

Comme ils **avaient** bien **mangé** le midi, ils ont tenu jusqu'au soir.
As they had had a good lunch, they kept going until dinner time.

Mange ta soupe.
Eat your soup.

je/j' = I   **tu** = you   **il** = he/it   **elle** = she/it   **on** = we/one   **nous** = we   **vous** = you   **ils/elles** = they

maudire (to curse)

PRESENT

je	**maudis**
tu	**maudis**
il/elle/on	**maudit**
nous	**maudissons**
vous	**maudissez**
ils/elles	**maudissent**

PRESENT SUBJUNCTIVE

je	**maudisse**
tu	**maudisses**
il/elle/on	**maudisse**
nous	**maudissions**
vous	**maudissiez**
ils/elles	**maudissent**

PERFECT

j'	**ai maudit**
tu	**as maudit**
il/elle/on	**a maudit**
nous	**avons maudit**
vous	**avez maudit**
ils/elles	**ont maudit**

IMPERFECT

je	**maudissais**
tu	**maudissais**
il/elle/on	**maudissait**
nous	**maudissions**
vous	**maudissiez**
ils/elles	**maudissaient**

PRESENT PARTICIPLE

maudissant

PAST PARTICIPLE

maudit

FUTURE

je	**maudirai**
tu	**maudiras**
il/elle/on	**maudira**
nous	**maudirons**
vous	**maudirez**
ils/elles	**maudiront**

CONDITIONAL

je	**maudirais**
tu	**maudirais**
il/elle/on	**maudirait**
nous	**maudirions**
vous	**maudiriez**
ils/elles	**maudiraient**

PAST HISTORIC

je	**maudis**
tu	**maudis**
il/elle/on	**maudit**
nous	**maudîmes**
vous	**maudîtes**
ils/elles	**maudirent**

PLUPERFECT

j'	**avais maudit**
tu	**avais maudit**
il/elle/on	**avait maudit**
nous	**avions maudit**
vous	**aviez maudit**
ils/elles	**avaient maudit**

IMPERATIVE

maudis / maudissons / maudissez

EXAMPLE PHRASES

Ils **maudissent** leurs ennemis.
They curse their enemies.

Je **maudis** le jour où je l'ai rencontrée.
I curse the day I met her.

Elle me **maudissait** en nettoyant mon
   manteau couvert de boue.
She cursed me as she was cleaning my
   muddy coat.

Ce **maudit** stylo ne marche pas!
This blasted pen doesn't work!

Je les **maudirai** jusqu'à ma mort.
I'll curse them to the day I die.

Il la **maudit** pour sa stupidité.
He cursed her for her stupidity.

Je te **maudirais** si tu arrivais en retard.
I'd curse you if you arrived late.

Nous les **avions maudits** de nous avoir
   laissés les attendre sous la pluie.
We had cursed them for making us
   wait for them in the rain.

---

je/j' = I   **tu** = you   **il** = he/it   **elle** = she/it   **on** = we/one   **nous** = we   **vous** = you   **ils/elles** = they

mentir (to lie)

PRESENT

je	**mens**
tu	**mens**
il/elle/on	**ment**
nous	**mentons**
vous	**mentez**
ils/elles	**mentent**

PRESENT SUBJUNCTIVE

je	**mente**
tu	**mentes**
il/elle/on	**mente**
nous	**mentions**
vous	**mentiez**
ils/elles	**mentent**

PERFECT

j'	**ai menti**
tu	**as menti**
il/elle/on	**a menti**
nous	**avons menti**
vous	**avez menti**
ils/elles	**ont menti**

IMPERFECT

je	**mentais**
tu	**mentais**
il/elle/on	**mentait**
nous	**mentions**
vous	**mentiez**
ils/elles	**mentaient**

PRESENT PARTICIPLE
mentant

PAST PARTICIPLE
menti

FUTURE

je	**mentirai**
tu	**mentiras**
il/elle/on	**mentira**
nous	**mentirons**
vous	**mentirez**
ils/elles	**mentiront**

CONDITIONAL

je	**mentirais**
tu	**mentirais**
il/elle/on	**mentirait**
nous	**mentirions**
vous	**mentiriez**
ils/elles	**mentiraient**

PAST HISTORIC

je	**mentis**
tu	**mentis**
il/elle/on	**mentit**
nous	**mentîmes**
vous	**mentîtes**
ils/elles	**mentirent**

PLUPERFECT

j'	**avais menti**
tu	**avais menti**
il/elle/on	**avait menti**
nous	**avions menti**
vous	**aviez menti**
ils/elles	**avaient menti**

IMPERATIVE
mens / mentons / mentez

EXAMPLE PHRASES

Je ne **mens** jamais.
I never lie.

Il lui **a menti**.
He lied to her.

Je ne veux pas que tu me **mentes**.
I don't want you to lie to me.

Elle savait qu'il **mentait**.
She knew that he was lying.

Je **mentirai** s'il le faut.
I'll lie if I have to.

Il **mentit** pour qu'on le laisse tranquille.
He lied so that he'd be left alone.

Elle ne **mentirait** pas si tu ne lui faisais
  pas aussi peur.
She wouldn't lie if you didn't frighten
  her so much.

Il **avait menti** pour ne pas la contrarier.
He had lied in order not to upset her.

Ne **mens** pas, s'il te plaît.
Please don't lie.

je/j' = I   **tu** = you   **il** = he/it   **elle** = she/it   **on** = we/one   **nous** = we   **vous** = you   **ils/elles** = they

mettre (to put)

PRESENT

je	**mets**
tu	**mets**
il/elle/on	**met**
nous	**mettons**
vous	**mettez**
ils/elles	**mettent**

PRESENT SUBJUNCTIVE

je	**mette**
tu	**mettes**
il/elle/on	**mette**
nous	**mettions**
vous	**mettiez**
ils/elles	**mettent**

PERFECT

j'	**ai mis**
tu	**as mis**
il/elle/on	**a mis**
nous	**avons mis**
vous	**avez mis**
ils/elles	**ont mis**

IMPERFECT

je	**mettais**
tu	**mettais**
il/elle/on	**mettait**
nous	**mettions**
vous	**mettiez**
ils/elles	**mettaient**

PRESENT PARTICIPLE
mettant

PAST PARTICIPLE
mis

FUTURE

je	**mettrai**
tu	**mettras**
il/elle/on	**mettra**
nous	**mettrons**
vous	**mettrez**
ils/elles	**mettront**

CONDITIONAL

je	**mettrais**
tu	**mettrais**
il/elle/on	**mettrait**
nous	**mettrions**
vous	**mettriez**
ils/elles	**mettraient**

PAST HISTORIC

je	**mis**
tu	**mis**
il/elle/on	**mit**
nous	**mîmes**
vous	**mîtes**
ils/elles	**mirent**

PLUPERFECT

j'	**avais mis**
tu	**avais mis**
il/elle/on	**avait mis**
nous	**avions mis**
vous	**aviez mis**
ils/elles	**avaient mis**

IMPERATIVE
mets / mettons / mettez

EXAMPLE PHRASES

Il **met** du gel dans ses cheveux.
He puts gel in his hair.

Où est-ce que tu **as mis** les clés?
Where have you put the keys?

Il faut que je **mette** le gâteau au four.
I have to put the cake in the oven.

Elle **mettait** toujours des heures
  à s'habiller.
She would always take hours to get
  dressed.

Je **mettrai** ma robe rose demain.
I'll put on my pink dress tomorrow.

Elle **mit** la bouilloire à chauffer.
She put the kettle on.

Je **mettrais** une robe si tu en mettais
  une aussi.
I'd put on a dress if you'd put one on too.

J'**avais mis** le livre sur la table.
I had put the book on the table.

Mets ton manteau!
Put your coat on!

je/j' = I **tu** = you **il** = he/it **elle** = she/it **on** = we/one **nous** = we **vous** = you **ils/elles** = they

monter (to go up; to take up)

PRESENT

je	**monte**
tu	**montes**
il/elle/on	**monte**
nous	**montons**
vous	**montez**
ils/elles	**montent**

PRESENT SUBJUNCTIVE

je	**monte**
tu	**montes**
il/elle/on	**monte**
nous	**montions**
vous	**montiez**
ils/elles	**montent**

PERFECT

je	**suis monté(e)**
tu	**es monté(e)**
il/elle/on	**est monté(e)**
nous	**sommes monté(e)s**
vous	**êtes monté(e)(s)**
ils/elles	**sont monté(e)s**

IMPERFECT

je	**montais**
tu	**montais**
il/elle/on	**montait**
nous	**montions**
vous	**montiez**
ils/elles	**montaient**

PRESENT PARTICIPLE

montant

PAST PARTICIPLE

monté

FUTURE

je	**monterai**
tu	**monteras**
il/elle/on	**montera**
nous	**monterons**
vous	**monterez**
ils/elles	**monteront**

CONDITIONAL

je	**monterais**
tu	**monterais**
il/elle/on	**monterait**
nous	**monterions**
vous	**monteriez**
ils/elles	**monteraient**

PAST HISTORIC

je	**montai**
tu	**montas**
il/elle/on	**monta**
nous	**montâmes**
vous	**montâtes**
ils/elles	**montèrent**

PLUPERFECT

j'	**étais monté(e)**
tu	**étais monté(e)**
il/elle/on	**était monté(e)**
nous	**étions monté(e)s**
vous	**étiez monté(e)(s)**
ils/elles	**étaient monté(e)s**

IMPERATIVE

monte / montons / montez

In the perfect and the pluperfect, use the auxiliary **avoir** when there is a direct object.

je/j' = I **tu** = you **il** = he/it **elle** = she/it **on** = we/one **nous** = we **vous** = you **ils/elles** = they

EXAMPLE PHRASES

Je **monte** ces escaliers cent fois par jour.
I go up these stairs a hundred times a day.

Hier, je **suis montée** à cheval pour la première fois.
Yesterday, I went horse riding for the first time.

Monte dans la voiture, je t'y emmène.
Get into the car, I'll take you there.

Il s'est tordu la cheville en **montant** à une échelle.
He twisted his ankle going up a ladder.

Je **monterai** lui dire bonsoir dans cinq minutes.
I'll go up to say goodnight to her in five minutes.

Il **monta** les escaliers en courant et sonna à la porte.
He ran up the stairs and rang the bell.

Je **monterais** en haut de la tour si je n'avais pas tant le vertige.
I'd go up the tower if I wasn't so scared of heights.

Comme elle était malade, je lui **avais monté** son dîner.
As she was ill, I had taken her dinner up to her.

mordre (to bite)

PRESENT	**PRESENT SUBJUNCTIVE**
je **mords**	je **morde**
tu **mords**	tu **mordes**
il/elle/on **mord**	il/elle/on **morde**
nous **mordons**	nous **mordions**
vous **mordez**	vous **mordiez**
ils/elles **mordent**	ils/elles **mordent**

PERFECT	**IMPERFECT**
j' **ai mordu**	je **mordais**
tu **as mordu**	tu **mordais**
il/elle/on **a mordu**	il/elle/on **mordait**
nous **avons mordu**	nous **mordions**
vous **avez mordu**	vous **mordiez**
ils/elles **ont mordu**	ils/elles **mordaient**

PRESENT PARTICIPLE	**PAST PARTICIPLE**
mordant	**mordu**

FUTURE	**CONDITIONAL**
je **mordrai**	je **mordrais**
tu **mordras**	tu **mordrais**
il/elle/on **mordra**	il/elle/on **mordrait**
nous **mordrons**	nous **mordrions**
vous **mordrez**	vous **mordriez**
ils/elles **mordront**	ils/elles **mordraient**

PAST HISTORIC	**PLUPERFECT**
je **mordis**	j' **avais mordu**
tu **mordis**	tu **avais mordu**
il/elle/on **mordit**	il/elle/on **avait mordu**
nous **mordîmes**	nous **avions mordu**
vous **mordîtes**	vous **aviez mordu**
ils/elles **mordirent**	ils/elles **avaient mordu**

IMPERATIVE
mords / mordons / mordez

EXAMPLE PHRASES

Il ne va pas te **mordre**!
He won't bite you!

Attention, il **mord**!
Watch out, he bites!

Le chien m'**a mordue**.
The dog bit me.

Je me **suis mordu** la langue.
I bit my tongue.

Il ne te **mordra** pas.
He won't bite you.

Elle lui **mordit** le doigt et partit se cacher.
She bit his finger and ran off to hide.

Il ne **mordrait** jamais personne.
He would never bite anybody.

Le chien l'**avait mordu** au mollet.
The dog had bitten him on the shin.

je/j' = I   **tu** = you   **il** = he/it   **elle** = she/it   **on** = we/one   **nous** = we   **vous** = you   **ils/elles** = they

moudre (to grind)

PRESENT

je	**mouds**
tu	**mouds**
il/elle/on	**moud**
nous	**moulons**
vous	**moulez**
ils/elles	**moulent**

PRESENT SUBJUNCTIVE

je	**moule**
tu	**moules**
il/elle/on	**moule**
nous	**moulions**
vous	**mouliez**
ils/elles	**moulent**

PERFECT

j'	**ai moulu**
tu	**as moulu**
il/elle/on	**a moulu**
nous	**avons moulu**
vous	**avez moulu**
ils/elles	**ont moulu**

IMPERFECT

je	**moulais**
tu	**moulais**
il/elle/on	**moulait**
nous	**moulions**
vous	**mouliez**
ils/elles	**moulaient**

PRESENT PARTICIPLE

moulant

PAST PARTICIPLE

moulu

FUTURE

je	**moudrai**
tu	**moudras**
il/elle/on	**moudra**
nous	**moudrons**
vous	**moudrez**
ils/elles	**moudront**

CONDITIONAL

je	**moudrais**
tu	**moudrais**
il/elle/on	**moudrait**
nous	**moudrions**
vous	**moudriez**
ils/elles	**moudraient**

PAST HISTORIC

je	**moulus**
tu	**moulus**
il/elle/on	**moulut**
nous	**moulûmes**
vous	**moulûtes**
ils/elles	**moulurent**

PLUPERFECT

j'	**avais moulu**
tu	**avais moulu**
il/elle/on	**avait moulu**
nous	**avions moulu**
vous	**aviez moulu**
ils/elles	**avaient moulu**

IMPERATIVE

mouds / moulons / moulez

EXAMPLE PHRASES

"Qui va m'aider à **moudre** ce grain?", demanda la petite poule rousse.
"Who will help me to grind this grain?" asked the little red hen.

Il **moud** toujours son café lui-même.
He always grinds his coffee himself.

J'**ai moulu** du café pour demain matin.
I've ground some coffee for tomorrow morning.

Le meunier **moulait** le blé à la meule.
The miller ground the wheat with the millstone.

Je **moudrai** du café tout à l'heure.
I'll grind some coffee in a moment.

Elle **moulut** un peu de poivre sur le rôti.
She ground some pepper over the roast.

Si j'avais le temps je **moudrais** mon café moi-même.
If I had time, I'd grind my coffee myself.

Il mesura le café qu'il **avait moulu**.
He measured the coffee that he'd ground.

---

je/j' = I   **tu** = you   **il** = he/it   **elle** = she/it   **on** = we/one   **nous** = we   **vous** = you   **ils/elles** = they

mourir (to die)

PRESENT

je	**meurs**
tu	**meurs**
il/elle/on	**meurt**
nous	**mourons**
vous	**mourez**
ils/elles	**meurent**

PRESENT SUBJUNCTIVE

je	**meure**
tu	**meures**
il/elle/on	**meure**
nous	**mourions**
vous	**mouriez**
ils/elles	**meurent**

PERFECT

je	**suis mort(e)**
tu	**es mort(e)**
il/elle/on	**est mort(e)**
nous	**sommes mort(e)s**
vous	**êtes mort(e)(s)**
ils/elles	**sont mort(e)s**

IMPERFECT

je	**mourais**
tu	**mourais**
il/elle/on	**mourait**
nous	**mourions**
vous	**mouriez**
ils/elles	**mouraient**

PRESENT PARTICIPLE

mourant

PAST PARTICIPLE

mort

FUTURE

je	**mourrai**
tu	**mourras**
il/elle/on	**mourra**
nous	**mourrons**
vous	**mourrez**
ils/elles	**mourront**

CONDITIONAL

je	**mourrais**
tu	**mourrais**
il/elle/on	**mourrait**
nous	**mourrions**
vous	**mourriez**
ils/elles	**mourraient**

PAST HISTORIC

je	**mourus**
tu	**mourus**
il/elle/on	**mourut**
nous	**mourûmes**
vous	**mourûtes**
ils/elles	**moururent**

PLUPERFECT

j'	**étais mort(e)**
tu	**étais mort(e)**
il/elle/on	**était mort(e)**
nous	**étions mort(e)s**
vous	**étiez mort(e)(s)**
ils/elles	**étaient mort(e)s**

IMPERATIVE

meurs / mourons / mourez

EXAMPLE PHRASES

On **meurt** de froid ici!
We're freezing to death here!

Elle **est morte** en 1998.
She died in 1998.

Ils **sont morts**.
They're dead.

Je ne veux pas qu'il **meure**.
I don't want him to die.

Nous **mourions** de froid.
We were freezing to death.

Si tu t'en vas, j'en **mourrai** de chagrin.
If you go, I'll die of sorrow.

Il **mourut** quelques heures plus tard.
He died a few hours later.

Je **mourrais** de honte si tu le lui disais.
I'd die of shame if you told him about it.

Nous **étions morts** de peur.
We were scared to death.

je/j' = I   **tu** = you   **il** = he/it   **elle** = she/it   **on** = we/one   **nous** = we   **vous** = you   **ils/elles** = they

naître (to be born)

PRESENT

je	**nais**
tu	**nais**
il/elle/on	**naît**
nous	**naissons**
vous	**naissez**
ils/elles	**naissent**

PRESENT SUBJUNCTIVE

je	**naisse**
tu	**naisses**
il/elle/on	**naisse**
nous	**naissions**
vous	**naissiez**
ils/elles	**naissent**

PERFECT

je	**suis né(e)**
tu	**es né(e)**
il/elle/on	**est né(e)**
nous	**sommes né(e)s**
vous	**êtes né(e)(s)**
ils/elles	**sont né(e)s**

IMPERFECT

je	**naissais**
tu	**naissais**
il/elle/on	**naissait**
nous	**naissions**
vous	**naissiez**
ils/elles	**naissaient**

PRESENT PARTICIPLE
naissant

PAST PARTICIPLE
né

FUTURE

je	**naîtrai**
tu	**naîtras**
il/elle/on	**naîtra**
nous	**naîtrons**
vous	**naîtrez**
ils/elles	**naîtront**

CONDITIONAL

je	**naîtrais**
tu	**naîtrais**
il/elle/on	**naîtrait**
nous	**naîtrions**
vous	**naîtriez**
ils/elles	**naîtraient**

PAST HISTORIC

je	**naquis**
tu	**naquis**
il/elle/on	**naquit**
nous	**naquîmes**
vous	**naquîtes**
ils/elles	**naquirent**

PLUPERFECT

j'	**étais né(e)**
tu	**étais né(e)**
il/elle/on	**était né(e)**
nous	**étions né(e)s**
vous	**étiez né(e)(s)**
ils/elles	**étaient né(é)s**

IMPERATIVE
nais / naissons / naissez

EXAMPLE PHRASES

Il a l'air innocent comme l'agneau qui vient de **naître**.
He looks as innocent as a newborn lamb.

Quand est-ce que tu **es né**?
When were you born?

Je **suis née** le 12 février.
I was born on the 12th of February.

Je ne **suis** pas **né** de la dernière pluie.
I wasn't born yesterday.

Le bébé de Delphine **naîtra** en mars.
Delphine is going to have a baby in March.

Il **naquit** le 5 juillet 1909.
He was born on 5 July 1909.

Ses enfants n'**étaient** pas **nés** en Écosse.
Her children weren't born in Scotland.

je/j' = I   **tu** = you   **il** = he/it   **elle** = she/it   **on** = we/one   **nous** = we   **vous** = you   **ils/elles** = they

nettoyer (to clean)

PRESENT

je	**nettoie**
tu	**nettoies**
il/elle/on	**nettoie**
nous	**nettoyons**
vous	**nettoyez**
ils/elles	**nettoient**

PRESENT SUBJUNCTIVE

je	**nettoie**
tu	**nettoies**
il/elle/on	**nettoie**
nous	**nettoyions**
vous	**nettoyiez**
ils/elles	**nettoient**

PERFECT

j'	**ai nettoyé**
tu	**as nettoyé**
il/elle/on	**a nettoyé**
nous	**avons nettoyé**
vous	**avez nettoyé**
ils/elles	**ont nettoyé**

IMPERFECT

je	**nettoyais**
tu	**nettoyais**
il/elle/on	**nettoyait**
nous	**nettoyions**
vous	**nettoyiez**
ils/elles	**nettoyaient**

PRESENT PARTICIPLE
nettoyant

PAST PARTICIPLE
nettoyé

FUTURE

je	**nettoierai**
tu	**nettoieras**
il/elle/on	**nettoiera**
nous	**nettoierons**
vous	**nettoierez**
ils/elles	**nettoieront**

CONDITIONAL

je	**nettoierais**
tu	**nettoierais**
il/elle/on	**nettoierait**
nous	**nettoierions**
vous	**nettoieriez**
ils/elles	**nettoieraient**

PAST HISTORIC

je	**nettoyai**
tu	**nettoyas**
il/elle/on	**nettoya**
nous	**nettoyâmes**
vous	**nettoyâtes**
ils/elles	**nettoyèrent**

PLUPERFECT

j'	**avais nettoyé**
tu	**avais nettoyé**
il/elle/on	**avait nettoyé**
nous	**avions nettoyé**
vous	**aviez nettoyé**
ils/elles	**avaient nettoyé**

IMPERATIVE
nettoie / nettoyons / nettoyez

EXAMPLE PHRASES

Je ne **nettoie** pas souvent mes lunettes.
I don't clean my glasses very often.

Richard **a nettoyé** tout l'appartement.
Richard has cleaned the whole flat.

Nettoie tes chaussures avant de les ranger.
Clean your shoes before putting them away.

J'aimerais que vous **nettoyiez** ta chambre.
I'd like you to clean your room.

Elle **nettoyait** le sol en écoutant la radio.
She was cleaning the floor while listening to the radio.

Je **nettoierai** tout ça ce soir.
I'll clean everything this evening.

Elle **nettoya** le miroir et s'y regarda longuement.
She cleaned the mirror and looked at herself for a long time.

Il **nettoierait** sa chambre tout seul si je l'encourageais à le faire.
He'd clean his bedroom himself if I encouraged him to do it.

Quand je suis rentrée , ils **avaient** tout **nettoyé**.
When I got back, they'd cleaned everything up.

je/j' = I   **tu** = you   **il** = he/it   **elle** = she/it   **on** = we/one   **nous** = we   **vous** = you   **ils/elles** = they

obéir (to obey)

PRESENT

j'	**obéis**
tu	**obéis**
il/elle/on	**obéit**
nous	**obéissons**
vous	**obéissez**
ils/elles	**obéissent**

PRESENT SUBJUNCTIVE

j'	**obéisse**
tu	**obéisses**
il/elle/on	**obéisse**
nous	**obéissions**
vous	**obéissiez**
ils/elles	**obéissent**

PERFECT

j'	**ai obéi**
tu	**as obéi**
il/elle/on	**a obéi**
nous	**avons obéi**
vous	**avez obéi**
ils/elles	**ont obéi**

IMPERFECT

j'	**obéissais**
tu	**obéissais**
il/elle/on	**obéissait**
nous	**obéissions**
vous	**obéissiez**
ils/elles	**obéissaient**

PRESENT PARTICIPLE
obéissant

PAST PARTICIPLE
obéi

FUTURE

j'	**obéirai**
tu	**obéiras**
il/elle/on	**obéira**
nous	**obéirons**
vous	**obéirez**
ils/elles	**obéiront**

CONDITIONAL

j'	**obéirais**
tu	**obéirais**
il/elle/on	**obéirait**
nous	**obéirions**
vous	**obéiriez**
ils/elles	**obéiraient**

PAST HISTORIC

j'	**obéis**
tu	**obéis**
il/elle/on	**obéit**
nous	**obéîmes**
vous	**obéîtes**
ils/elles	**obéirent**

PLUPERFECT

j'	**avais obéi**
tu	**avais obéi**
il/elle/on	**avait obéi**
nous	**avions obéi**
vous	**aviez obéi**
ils/elles	**avaient obéi**

IMPERATIVE
obéis / obéissons / obéissez

EXAMPLE PHRASES

Je n'**obéis** pas toujours à mes parents.
I don't always obey my parents.

J'aimerais que tu **obéisses** quand je te
demande de faire quelque chose.
I'd like you to do it when I ask you to do
something.

Mon chien n'**obéissait** jamais.
My dog never obeyed commands.

Il n'**obéira** jamais si tu lui parles
comme ça.
He'll never obey if you speak to him
like that.

Ils **obéirent** sans se plaindre.
They obeyed without complaining.

Ils ne lui **obéiraient** pas s'ils ne
l'aimaient pas.
They wouldn't obey her if they didn't
like her.

Comme elle n'avait pas le choix,
elle **avait obéi** à ses ordres.
As she didn't have any choice, she'd
obeyed his orders.

je/j' = I **tu** = you **il** = he/it **elle** = she/it **on** = we/one **nous** = we **vous** = you **ils/elles** = they

offrir (to offer)

PRESENT

j'	**offre**
tu	**offres**
il/elle/on	**offre**
nous	**offrons**
vous	**offrez**
ils/elles	**offrent**

PERFECT

j'	**ai offert**
tu	**as offert**
il/elle/on	**a offert**
nous	**avons offert**
vous	**avez offert**
ils/elles	**ont offert**

PRESENT PARTICIPLE
offrant

FUTURE

j'	**offrirai**
tu	**offriras**
il/elle/on	**offrira**
nous	**offrirons**
vous	**offrirez**
ils/elles	**offriront**

PAST HISTORIC

j'	**offris**
tu	**offris**
il/elle/on	**offrit**
nous	**offrîmes**
vous	**offrîtes**
ils/elles	**offrirent**

IMPERATIVE
offre / offrons / offrez

PRESENT SUBJUNCTIVE

j'	**offre**
tu	**offres**
il/elle/on	**offre**
nous	**offrions**
vous	**offriez**
ils/elles	**offrent**

IMPERFECT

j'	**offrais**
tu	**offrais**
il/elle/on	**offrait**
nous	**offrions**
vous	**offriez**
ils/elles	**offraient**

PAST PARTICIPLE
offert

CONDITIONAL

j'	**offrirais**
tu	**offrirais**
il/elle/on	**offrirait**
nous	**offririons**
vous	**offririez**
ils/elles	**offriraient**

PLUPERFECT

j'	**avais offert**
tu	**avais offert**
il/elle/on	**avait offert**
nous	**avions offert**
vous	**aviez offert**
ils/elles	**avaient offert**

EXAMPLE PHRASES

Viens, je t'**offre** à boire.
Come on, I'll buy you a drink.

Paul m'**a offert** du parfum pour mon anniversaire.
Paul gave me some perfume for my birthday.

Offre-lui des fleurs.
Give her some flowers.

Il **offrait** souvent de me raccompagner.
He would often offer me a lift back.

Je lui **offrirai** une voiture pour ses 21 ans.
I'll buy her a car for her 21st birthday.

Il lui **offrit** de l'aider.
He offered to help her.

S'il était plus aimable, je lui **offrirais** de l'aider.
If he were more pleasant, I'd offer to help him.

On lui **avait offert** un poste de secrétaire.
They had offered her a secretarial post.

ouvrir (to open)

PRESENT

j'	**ouvre**
tu	**ouvres**
il/elle/on	**ouvre**
nous	**ouvrons**
vous	**ouvrez**
ils/elles	**ouvrent**

PRESENT SUBJUNCTIVE

j'	**ouvre**
tu	**ouvres**
il/elle/on	**ouvre**
nous	**ouvrions**
vous	**ouvriez**
ils/elles	**ouvrent**

PERFECT

j'	**ai ouvert**
tu	**as ouvert**
il/elle/on	**a ouvert**
nous	**avons ouvert**
vous	**avez ouvert**
ils/elles	**ont ouvert**

IMPERFECT

j'	**ouvrais**
tu	**ouvrais**
il/elle/on	**ouvrait**
nous	**ouvrions**
vous	**ouvriez**
ils/elles	**ouvraient**

PRESENT PARTICIPLE
ouvrant

PAST PARTICIPLE
ouvert

FUTURE

j'	**ouvrirai**
tu	**ouvriras**
il/elle/on	**ouvrira**
nous	**ouvrirons**
vous	**ouvrirez**
ils/elles	**ouvriront**

CONDITIONAL

j'	**ouvrirais**
tu	**ouvrirais**
il/elle/on	**ouvrirait**
nous	**ouvririons**
vous	**ouvririez**
ils/elles	**ouvriraient**

PAST HISTORIC

j'	**ouvris**
tu	**ouvris**
il/elle/on	**ouvrit**
nous	**ouvrîmes**
vous	**ouvrîtes**
ils/elles	**ouvrirent**

PLUPERFECT

j'	**avais ouvert**
tu	**avais ouvert**
il/elle/on	**avait ouvert**
nous	**avions ouvert**
vous	**aviez ouvert**
ils/elles	**avaient ouvert**

IMPERATIVE
ouvre / ouvrons / ouvrez

EXAMPLE PHRASES

Est-ce que tu pourrais **ouvrir** la fenêtre?
Could you open the window?

Elle **a ouvert** la porte.
She opened the door.

La porte s'**est ouverte**.
The door opened.

Je me suis coupé en **ouvrant** une boîte de conserve.
I cut myself opening a tin.

J'**ouvrirai** la fenêtre tout à l'heure.
I'll open the window in a moment.

Elle **ouvrit** les yeux et lui sourit.
She opened her eyes and smiled at him.

J'**ouvrirais** la fenêtre s'il ne faisait pas si froid.
I would open the window if it weren't so cold.

Ils **avaient ouvert** tous leurs cadeaux de Noël.
They had opened all their Christmas presents.

Ouvre la porte, s'il te plaît.
Open the door, please.

Ouvrez vos livres à la page 10.
Open your books at page 10.

je/j' = I   **tu** = you   **il** = he/it   **elle** = she/it   **on** = we/one   **nous** = we   **vous** = you   **ils/elles** = they

paraître (to appear)

PRESENT

je	**parais**
tu	**parais**
il/elle/on	**paraît**
nous	**paraissons**
vous	**paraissez**
ils/elles	**paraissent**

PRESENT SUBJUNCTIVE

je	**paraisse**
tu	**paraisses**
il/elle/on	**paraisse**
nous	**paraissions**
vous	**paraissiez**
ils/elles	**paraissent**

PERFECT

j'	**ai paru**
tu	**as paru**
il/elle/on	**a paru**
nous	**avons paru**
vous	**avez paru**
ils/elles	**ont paru**

IMPERFECT

je	**paraissais**
tu	**paraissais**
il/elle/on	**paraissait**
nous	**paraissions**
vous	**paraissiez**
ils/elles	**paraissaient**

PRESENT PARTICIPLE
paraissant

PAST PARTICIPLE
paru

FUTURE

je	**paraîtrai**
tu	**paraîtras**
il/elle/on	**paraîtra**
nous	**paraîtrons**
vous	**paraîtrez**
ils/elles	**paraîtront**

CONDITIONAL

je	**paraîtrais**
tu	**paraîtrais**
il/elle/on	**paraîtrait**
nous	**paraîtrions**
vous	**paraîtriez**
ils/elles	**paraîtraient**

PAST HISTORIC

je	**parus**
tu	**parus**
il/elle/on	**parut**
nous	**parûmes**
vous	**parûtes**
ils/elles	**parurent**

PLUPERFECT

j'	**avais paru**
tu	**avais paru**
il/elle/on	**avait paru**
nous	**avions paru**
vous	**aviez paru**
ils/elles	**avaient paru**

IMPERATIVE
parais / paraissons / paraissez

EXAMPLE PHRASES

Gisèle **paraît** plus jeune que son âge.
Gisèle doesn't look her age.

Il **paraît** qu'il fait chaud toute l'année là-bas.
Apparently it's hot all year round over there.

Il m'**a paru** angoissé.
I thought he looked stressed.

Elle **paraissait** fatiguée.
She seemed tired.

Cet article **paraîtra** le mois prochain.
This article will be published next month.

Il **parut** gêné.
He looked embarrassed.

Cela **paraîtrait** étrange si je venais sans mon mari.
It would look strange if I came without my husband.

Il **avait paru** pressé de partir.
He had seemed in a hurry to leave.

je/j' = I **tu** = you **il** = he/it **elle** = she/it **on** = we/one **nous** = we **vous** = you **ils/elles** = they

partir (to go; to leave)

PRESENT

je	**pars**
tu	**pars**
il/elle/on	**part**
nous	**partons**
vous	**partez**
ils/elles	**partent**

PRESENT SUBJUNCTIVE

je	**parte**
tu	**partes**
il/elle/on	**parte**
nous	**partions**
vous	**partiez**
ils/elles	**partent**

PERFECT

je	**suis parti(e)**
tu	**es parti(e)**
il/elle/on	**est parti(e)**
nous	**sommes parti(e)s**
vous	**êtes parti(e)(s)**
ils/elles	**sont parti(e)s**

IMPERFECT

je	**partais**
tu	**partais**
il/elle/on	**partait**
nous	**partions**
vous	**partiez**
ils/elles	**partaient**

PRESENT PARTICIPLE
partant

PAST PARTICIPLE
parti

FUTURE

je	**partirai**
tu	**partiras**
il/elle/on	**partira**
nous	**partirons**
vous	**partirez**
ils/elles	**partiront**

CONDITIONAL

je	**partirais**
tu	**partirais**
il/elle/on	**partirait**
nous	**partirions**
vous	**partiriez**
ils/elles	**partiraient**

PAST HISTORIC

je	**partis**
tu	**partis**
il/elle/on	**partit**
nous	**partîmes**
vous	**partîtes**
ils/elles	**partirent**

PLUPERFECT

j'	**étais parti(e)**
tu	**étais parti(e)**
il/elle/on	**était parti(e)**
nous	**étions parti(e)s**
vous	**étiez parti(e)(s)**
ils/elles	**étaient parti(e)s**

IMPERATIVE
pars / partons / partez

EXAMPLE PHRASES

On **part** en vacances le 15 août.
We're going on holiday on the 15th of
August.

Elle **est partie** tôt ce matin.
She left early this morning.

Il faut qu'on **parte** de bonne heure.
We have to leave early.

Il **partait** à huit heures tous les matins.
He left at eight o'clock every morning.

Nous **partirons** demain.
We'll leave tomorrow.

Il **partit** sans rien dire.
He left without saying a word.

Je ne **partirais** pas sans dire au revoir.
I wouldn't leave without saying
goodbye.

Quand je suis arrivée, ils **étaient** déjà
partis.
When I arrived, they had already left.

Ne **partez** pas sans moi!
Don't leave without me!

---

je/j' = I   **tu** = you   **il** = he/it   **elle** = she/it   **on** = we/one   **nous** = we   **vous** = you   **ils/elles** = they

passer (to pass)

PRESENT

je	**passe**
tu	**passes**
il/elle/on	**passe**
nous	**passons**
vous	**passez**
ils/elles	**passent**

PRESENT SUBJUNCTIVE

je	**passe**
tu	**passes**
il/elle/on	**passe**
nous	**passions**
vous	**passiez**
ils/elles	**passent**

PERFECT

je	**suis passé(e)**
tu	**es passé(e)**
il/elle/on	**est passé(e)**
nous	**sommes passé(e)s**
vous	**êtes passé(e)(s)**
ils/elles	**sont passé(e)s**

IMPERFECT

je	**passais**
tu	**passais**
il/elle/on	**passait**
nous	**passions**
vous	**passiez**
ils/elles	**passaient**

PRESENT PARTICIPLE

passant

PAST PARTICIPLE

passé

FUTURE

je	**passerai**
tu	**passeras**
il/elle/on	**passera**
nous	**passerons**
vous	**passerez**
ils/elles	**passeront**

CONDITIONAL

je	**passerais**
tu	**passerais**
il/elle/on	**passerait**
nous	**passerions**
vous	**passeriez**
ils/elles	**passeraient**

PAST HISTORIC

je	**passai**
tu	**passas**
il/elle/on	**passa**
nous	**passâmes**
vous	**passâtes**
ils/elles	**passèrent**

PLUPERFECT

j'	**étais passé(e)**
tu	**étais passé(e)**
il/elle/on	**était passé(e)**
nous	**étions passé(e)s**
vous	**étiez passé(e)(s)**
ils/elles	**étaient passé(e)s**

IMPERATIVE

passe / passons / passez

In the perfect and the pluperfect, use the auxiliary **avoir** when there is a direct object.

EXAMPLE PHRASES

Je vais **passer** les vacances chez mes grands-parents.
I'm going to spend the holidays at my grandparents' house.

L'histoire se **passe** au Mexique.
The story takes place in Mexico.

Il **a passé** son examen en juin.
He sat his exam in June.

Elle **est passée** me dire bonjour.
She came by to say hello.

Ils **passaient** leur temps à regarder la télé.
They spent their time watching TV.

Je **passerai** te voir ce soir.
I'll come to see you tonight.

Elle **passa** la soirée à emballer les cadeaux de Noël.
She spent the evening wrapping up the Christmas presents.

Ils **passeraient** plus de temps à jouer dehors s'il faisait moins mauvais.
They'd spend more time playing outside if the weather weren't so bad.

Les mois **avaient passé**.
Months had passed.

Passe-moi le pain, s'il te plaît.
Pass me the bread please.

---

je/j' = I   **tu** = you   **il** = he/it   **elle** = she/it   **on** = we/one   **nous** = we   **vous** = you   **ils/elles** = they

payer (to pay)

PRESENT

je	**paye**
tu	**payes**
il/elle/on	**paye**
nous	**payons**
vous	**payez**
ils/elles	**payent**

PRESENT SUBJUNCTIVE

je	**paye**
tu	**payes**
il/elle/on	**paye**
nous	**payions**
vous	**payiez**
ils/elles	**payent**

PERFECT

j'	**ai payé**
tu	**as payé**
il/elle/on	**a payé**
nous	**avons payé**
vous	**avez payé**
ils/elles	**ont payé**

IMPERFECT

je	**payais**
tu	**payais**
il/elle/on	**payait**
nous	**payions**
vous	**payiez**
ils/elles	**payaient**

PRESENT PARTICIPLE

payant

PAST PARTICIPLE

payé

FUTURE

je	**payerai**
tu	**payeras**
il/elle/on	**payera**
nous	**payerons**
vous	**payerez**
ils/elles	**payeront**

CONDITIONAL

je	**payerais**
tu	**payerais**
il/elle/on	**payerait**
nous	**payerions**
vous	**payeriez**
ils/elles	**payeraient**

PAST HISTORIC

je	**payai**
tu	**payas**
il/elle/on	**paya**
nous	**payâmes**
vous	**payâtes**
ils/elles	**payèrent**

PLUPERFECT

j'	**avais payé**
tu	**avais payé**
il/elle/on	**avait payé**
nous	**avions payé**
vous	**aviez payé**
ils/elles	**avaient payé**

IMPERATIVE

paye / payons / payez

EXAMPLE PHRASES

Les étudiants **payent** moitié prix.
Students pay half price.

Tu l'**as payé** combien?
How much did you pay for it?

Il faut que je **paye** l'électricien.
I have to pay the electrician.

Il ne **payait** jamais son loyer.
He never paid his rent.

Je vous **payerai** demain.
I'll pay you tomorrow.

Il **paya** la note et partit.
He paid the bill and left.

Je lui ai dit que je le **payerais** la
prochaine fois.
I told him that I would pay him the next
time.

Sa patronne ne l'**avait** pas **payée** depuis
deux mois.
Her boss hadn't paid her for the last two
months.

je/j' = I **tu** = you **il** = he/it **elle** = she/it **on** = we/one **nous** = we **vous** = you **ils/elles** = they

peindre (to paint)

PRESENT

je **peins**
tu **peins**
il/elle/on **peint**
nous **peignons**
vous **peignez**
ils/elles **peignent**

PERFECT

j' **ai peint**
tu **as peint**
il/elle/on **a peint**
nous **avons peint**
vous **avez peint**
ils/elles **ont peint**

PRESENT PARTICIPLE
peignant

FUTURE

je **peindrai**
tu **peindras**
il/elle/on **peindra**
nous **peindrons**
vous **peindrez**
ils/elles **peindront**

PAST HISTORIC

je **peignis**
tu **peignis**
il/elle/on **peignit**
nous **peignîmes**
vous **peignîtes**
ils/elles **peignirent**

IMPERATIVE
peins / peignons / peignez

PRESENT SUBJUNCTIVE

je **peigne**
tu **peignes**
il/elle/on **peigne**
nous **peignions**
vous **peigniez**
ils/elles **peignent**

IMPERFECT

je **peignais**
tu **peignais**
il/elle/on **peignait**
nous **peignions**
vous **peigniez**
ils/elles **peignaient**

PAST PARTICIPLE
peint

CONDITIONAL

je **peindrais**
tu **peindrais**
il/elle/on **peindrait**
nous **peindrions**
vous **peindriez**
ils/elles **peindraient**

PLUPERFECT

j' **avais peint**
tu **avais peint**
il/elle/on **avait peint**
nous **avions peint**
vous **aviez peint**
ils/elles **avaient peint**

EXAMPLE PHRASES

Il ne **peint** plus depuis son opération.
He hasn't painted since his operation.

On **a peint** l'entrée en bleu clair.
We painted the hall light blue.

Ce tableau **a été peint** en 1913.
This picture was painted in 1913.

Il **peignait** toujours des paysages.
He always painted landscapes.

Je **peindrai** le plafond demain.
I'll paint the ceiling tomorrow.

Il **peignit** les volets en rose.
He painted the shutters pink.

Si j'étais toi, je **peindrais** les murs avant de poser le carrelage.
If I were you, I would paint the walls before laying the tiles.

Elle n'**avait peint** que la moitié de la pièce.
She'd only painted half of the room.

je/j' = I   **tu** = you   **il** = he/it   **elle** = she/it   **on** = we/one   **nous** = we   **vous** = you   **ils/elles** = they

perdre (to lose)

PRESENT

je	**perds**
tu	**perds**
il/elle/on	**perd**
nous	**perdons**
vous	**perdez**
ils/elles	**perdent**

PRESENT SUBJUNCTIVE

je	**perde**
tu	**perdes**
il/elle/on	**perde**
nous	**perdions**
vous	**perdiez**
ils/elles	**perdent**

PERFECT

j'	**ai perdu**
tu	**as perdu**
il/elle/on	**a perdu**
nous	**avons perdu**
vous	**avez perdu**
ils/elles	**ont perdu**

IMPERFECT

je	**perdais**
tu	**perdais**
il/elle/on	**perdait**
nous	**perdions**
vous	**perdiez**
ils/elles	**perdaient**

PRESENT PARTICIPLE
perdant

PAST PARTICIPLE
perdu

FUTURE

je	**perdrai**
tu	**perdras**
il/elle/on	**perdra**
nous	**perdrons**
vous	**perdrez**
ils/elles	**perdront**

CONDITIONAL

je	**perdrais**
tu	**perdrais**
il/elle/on	**perdrait**
nous	**perdrions**
vous	**perdriez**
ils/elles	**perdraient**

PAST HISTORIC

je	**perdis**
tu	**perdis**
il/elle/on	**perdit**
nous	**perdîmes**
vous	**perdîtes**
ils/elles	**perdirent**

PLUPERFECT

j'	**avais perdu**
tu	**avais perdu**
il/elle/on	**avait perdu**
nous	**avions perdu**
vous	**aviez perdu**
ils/elles	**avaient perdu**

IMPERATIVE
perds / perdons / perdez

EXAMPLE PHRASES

Si tu te **perds**, appelle-moi.
Call me if you get lost.

L'Italie **a perdu** un à zéro.
Italy lost one-nil.

J'**ai perdu** mon porte-monnaie dans le métro.
I lost my purse on the underground.

Il ne faut pas que je **perde** son adresse.
I mustn't lose his address.

Il **perdait** toujours ses affaires.
He was always losing his things.

Je **perdrai** forcément contre lui.
I'll obviously lose against him.

Il **perdit** patience et se mit à crier.
He lost his patience and began to shout.

Tu ne **perdrais** pas tes affaires si tu faisais plus attention.
You wouldn't lose your things if you were more careful.

Elle **avait perdu** la mémoire depuis son accident.
She had lost her memory after her accident.

Ne **perds** pas encore tes gants.
Don't lose your gloves again.

je/j' = I   **tu** = you   **il** = he/it   **elle** = she/it   **on** = we/one   **nous** = we   **vous** = you   **ils/elles** = they

plaire (to please)

PRESENT

je	**plais**
tu	**plais**
il/elle/on	**plaît**
nous	**plaisons**
vous	**plaisez**
ils/elles	**plaisent**

PRESENT SUBJUNCTIVE

je	**plaise**
tu	**plaises**
il/elle/on	**plaise**
nous	**plaisions**
vous	**plaisiez**
ils/elles	**plaisent**

PERFECT

j'	**ai plu**
tu	**as plu**
il/elle/on	**a plu**
nous	**avons plu**
vous	**avez plu**
ils/elles	**ont plu**

IMPERFECT

je	**plaisais**
tu	**plaisais**
il/elle/on	**plaisait**
nous	**plaisions**
vous	**plaisiez**
ils/elles	**plaisaient**

PRESENT PARTICIPLE

plaisant

PAST PARTICIPLE

plu

FUTURE

je	**plairai**
tu	**plairas**
il/elle/on	**plaira**
nous	**plairons**
vous	**plairez**
ils/elles	**plairont**

CONDITIONAL

je	**plairais**
tu	**plairais**
il/elle/on	**plairait**
nous	**plairions**
vous	**plairiez**
ils/elles	**plairaient**

PAST HISTORIC

je	**plus**
tu	**plus**
il/elle/on	**plut**
nous	**plûmes**
vous	**plûtes**
ils/elles	**plurent**

PLUPERFECT

j'	**avais plu**
tu	**avais plu**
il/elle/on	**avait plu**
nous	**avions plu**
vous	**aviez plu**
ils/elles	**avaient plu**

IMPERATIVE

plais / plaisons / plaisez

EXAMPLE PHRASES

Le menu ne me **plaît** pas.
I don't like the menu.

s'il te **plaît**
please

s'il vous **plaît**
please

Ça t'**a plu**, le film?
Did you like the film?

La robe noire me **plaisait** beaucoup.
I really liked the black dress.

Ce film ne lui **plaira** pas.
He won't like this film.

Elle lui **plut** immédiatement.
He liked her straight away.

Ça te **plairait** d'aller à la mer?
Would you like to go to the seaside?

Cette remarque ne lui **avait** pas **plu**.
He hadn't liked that remark.

---

je/j' = I   **tu** = you   **il** = he/it   **elle** = she/it   **on** = we/one   **nous** = we   **vous** = you   **ils/elles** = they

pleuvoir (to rain)

PRESENT
> il **pleut**

PRESENT SUBJUNCTIVE
> il **pleuve**

PERFECT
> il **a plu**

IMPERFECT
> il **pleuvait**

PRESENT PARTICIPLE
pleuvant

PAST PARTICIPLE
plu

FUTURE
> il **pleuvra**

CONDITIONAL
> il **pleuvrait**

PAST HISTORIC
> il **plut**

PLUPERFECT
> il **avait plu**

IMPERATIVE
not used

EXAMPLE PHRASES

Il **pleut** beaucoup à Glasgow.
It rains a lot in Glasgow.

Il **a plu** toute la journée.
It rained all day long.

J'ai peur qu'il **pleuve** cet après-midi.
I'm afraid it might rain this afternoon.

Il **pleuvait** tellement qu'ils décidèrent de rester chez eux.
It rained so much that they decided to stay at home.

J'espère qu'il ne **pleuvra** pas demain.
I hope it won't rain tomorrow.

Il **plut** pendant quarante jours et quarante nuits.
It rained for forty days and forty nights.

Il **pleuvrait** probablement si je ne prenais pas mon parapluie.
It would probably rain if I didn't take my umbrella.

Il n'**avait** pas **plu** de tout l'été.
It hadn't rained all summer.

---

je/j' = I   **tu** = you   **il** = he/it   **elle** = she/it   **on** = we/one   **nous** = we   **vous** = you   **ils/elles** = they

pouvoir (to be able)

PRESENT

je	**peux**
tu	**peux**
il/elle/on	**peut**
nous	**pouvons**
vous	**pouvez**
ils/elles	**peuvent**

PRESENT SUBJUNCTIVE

je	**puisse**
tu	**puisses**
il/elle/on	**puisse**
nous	**puissions**
vous	**puissiez**
ils/elles	**puissent**

PERFECT

j'	**ai pu**
tu	**as pu**
il/elle/on	**a pu**
nous	**avons pu**
vous	**avez pu**
ils/elles	**ont pu**

IMPERFECT

je	**pouvais**
tu	**pouvais**
il/elle/on	**pouvait**
nous	**pouvions**
vous	**pouviez**
ils/elles	**pouvaient**

PRESENT PARTICIPLE

pouvant

PAST PARTICIPLE

pu

FUTURE

je	**pourrai**
tu	**pourras**
il/elle/on	**pourra**
nous	**pourrons**
vous	**pourrez**
ils/elles	**pourront**

CONDITIONAL

je	**pourrais**
tu	**pourrais**
il/elle/on	**pourrait**
nous	**pourrions**
vous	**pourriez**
ils/elles	**pourraient**

PAST HISTORIC

je	**pus**
tu	**pus**
il/elle/on	**put**
nous	**pûmes**
vous	**pûtes**
ils/elles	**purent**

PLUPERFECT

j'	**avais pu**
tu	**avais pu**
il/elle/on	**avait pu**
nous	**avions pu**
vous	**aviez pu**
ils/elles	**avaient pu**

IMPERATIVE

not used

EXAMPLE PHRASES

Je **peux** vous aider?
Can I help you?

J'ai fait tout ce que j'**ai pu**.
I did all I could.

Nous avons changé la date du baptême de Clara pour que tu **puisses** venir.
We've changed the date of Clara's christening so that you're able to come.

Elle ne **pouvait** pas s'empêcher de rire.
She couldn't help laughing.

Je ne **pourrai** pas venir samedi.
I won't be able to come on Saturday.

Il ne **put** se souvenir de son nom.
He couldn't remember her name.

Je **pourrais** te prêter ma robe si tu voulais.
I could lend you my dress if you like.

Il n'**avait** pas **pu** les rejoindre.
He hadn't been able to join them.

je/j' = I **tu** = you **il** = he/it **elle** = she/it **on** = we/one **nous** = we **vous** = you **ils/elles** = they

prendre (to take)

PRESENT

je	**prends**
tu	**prends**
il/elle/on	**prend**
nous	**prenons**
vous	**prenez**
ils/elles	**prennent**

PRESENT SUBJUNCTIVE

je	**prenne**
tu	**prennes**
il/elle/on	**prenne**
nous	**prenions**
vous	**preniez**
ils/elles	**prennent**

PERFECT

j'	**ai pris**
tu	**as pris**
il/elle/on	**a pris**
nous	**avons pris**
vous	**avez pris**
ils/elles	**ont pris**

IMPERFECT

je	**prenais**
tu	**prenais**
il/elle/on	**prenait**
nous	**prenions**
vous	**preniez**
ils/elles	**prenaient**

PRESENT PARTICIPLE

prenant

PAST PARTICIPLE

pris

FUTURE

je	**prendrai**
tu	**prendras**
il/elle/on	**prendra**
nous	**prendrons**
vous	**prendrez**
ils/elles	**prendront**

CONDITIONAL

je	**prendrais**
tu	**prendrais**
il/elle/on	**prendrait**
nous	**prendrions**
vous	**prendriez**
ils/elles	**prendraient**

PAST HISTORIC

je	**pris**
tu	**pris**
il/elle/on	**prit**
nous	**prîmes**
vous	**prîtes**
ils/elles	**prirent**

PLUPERFECT

j'	**avais pris**
tu	**avais pris**
il/elle/on	**avait pris**
nous	**avions pris**
vous	**aviez pris**
ils/elles	**avaient pris**

IMPERATIVE

prends / prenons / prenez

EXAMPLE PHRASES

N'oublie pas de **prendre** ton passeport.
Don't forget to take your passport.

Pour qui est-ce qu'il se **prend**?
Who does he think he is?

J'**ai pris** plein de photos.
I took lots of pictures.

Il faut que je **prenne** mes affaires de gym.
I have to take my gym kit.

Il **prenait** le bus à huit heures le matin.
He got the bus at eight in the morning.

Il **prendra** le train de 8h20.
He'll take the 8.20 train.

Elle **prit** son sac et partit.
She took her bag and left.

Si j'habitais ici, je **prendrais** le bus pour aller travailler.
If I lived here, I'd take the bus to work.

Il n'**avait** jamais **pris** l'avion.
He'd never travelled by plane.

Prends ton appareil photo.
Take your camera.

je/j' = I   **tu** = you   **il** = he/it   **elle** = she/it   **on** = we/one   **nous** = we   **vous** = you   **ils/elles** = they

protéger (to protect)

PRESENT

je	**protège**
tu	**protèges**
il/elle/on	**protège**
nous	**protégeons**
vous	**protégez**
ils/elles	**protègent**

PRESENT SUBJUNCTIVE

je	**protège**
tu	**protèges**
il/elle/on	**protège**
nous	**protégions**
vous	**protégiez**
ils/elles	**protègent**

PERFECT

j'	**ai protégé**
tu	**as protégé**
il/elle/on	**a protégé**
nous	**avons protégé**
vous	**avez protégé**
ils/elles	**ont protégé**

IMPERFECT

je	**protégeais**
tu	**protégeais**
il/elle/on	**protégeait**
nous	**protégions**
vous	**protégiez**
ils/elles	**protégeaient**

PRESENT PARTICIPLE
protégeant

PAST PARTICIPLE
protégé

FUTURE

je	**protégerai**
tu	**protégeras**
il/elle/on	**protégera**
nous	**protégerons**
vous	**protégerez**
ils/elles	**protégeront**

CONDITIONAL

je	**protégerais**
tu	**protégerais**
il/elle/on	**protégerait**
nous	**protégerions**
vous	**protégeriez**
ils/elles	**protégeraient**

PAST HISTORIC

je	**protégeai**
tu	**protégeas**
il/elle/on	**protégea**
nous	**protégeâmes**
vous	**protégeâtes**
ils/elles	**protégèrent**

PLUPERFECT

j'	**avais protégé**
tu	**avais protégé**
il/elle/on	**avait protégé**
nous	**avions protégé**
vous	**aviez protégé**
ils/elles	**avaient protégé**

IMPERATIVE
protège / protégeons / protégez

EXAMPLE PHRASES

Ne crains rien, je te **protège**.
Don't be scared, I'm looking after you.

Le champ **est protégé** du vent par
la colline.
The field is sheltered from the wind
by the hill.

Je voudrais une tente qui **protège** bien
contre le froid.
I'd like a tent which protects you from
the cold.

Il me **protégeait** contre tous ceux qui
m'embêtaient.
He protected me from all those who
annoyed me.

Ce manteau te **protégera** bien du froid.
This coat will protect you from the cold.

Il se **protégea** le visage avec ses mains.
He protected his face with his hands.

Cette crème te **protégerait** mieux les
mains.
This cream would protect your hands
better.

Il **avait** toujours **protégé** sa petite sœur
à l'école.
He'd always protected his little sister
at school.

Protège ton livre de la pluie.
Protect your book from the rain.

je/j' = I **tu** = you **il** = he/it **elle** = she/it **on** = we/one **nous** = we **vous** = you **ils/elles** = they

recevoir (to receive)

PRESENT

je	**reçois**
tu	**reçois**
il/elle/on	**reçoit**
nous	**recevons**
vous	**recevez**
ils/elles	**reçoivent**

PRESENT SUBJUNCTIVE

je	**reçoive**
tu	**reçoives**
il/elle/on	**reçoive**
nous	**recevions**
vous	**receviez**
ils/elles	**reçoivent**

PERFECT

j'	**ai reçu**
tu	**as reçu**
il/elle/on	**a reçu**
nous	**avons reçu**
vous	**avez reçu**
ils/elles	**ont reçu**

IMPERFECT

je	**recevais**
tu	**recevais**
il/elle/on	**recevait**
nous	**recevions**
vous	**receviez**
ils/elles	**recevaient**

PRESENT PARTICIPLE

recevant

PAST PARTICIPLE

reçu

FUTURE

je	**recevrai**
tu	**recevras**
il/elle/on	**recevra**
nous	**recevrons**
vous	**recevrez**
ils/elles	**recevront**

CONDITIONAL

je	**recevrais**
tu	**recevrais**
il/elle/on	**recevrait**
nous	**recevrions**
vous	**recevriez**
ils/elles	**recevraient**

PAST HISTORIC

je	**reçus**
tu	**reçus**
il/elle/on	**reçut**
nous	**reçûmes**
vous	**reçûtes**
ils/elles	**reçurent**

PLUPERFECT

j'	**avais reçu**
tu	**avais reçu**
il/elle/on	**avait reçu**
nous	**avions reçu**
vous	**aviez reçu**
ils/elles	**avaient reçu**

IMPERATIVE

reçois / recevons / recevez

EXAMPLE PHRASES

Je ne **reçois** jamais de courrier.
I never get any mail.

Elle **a reçu** une lettre de Charlotte.
She received a letter from Charlotte.

J'attendais que tu **reçoives** l'invitation
   pour t'emmener choisir un cadeau.
I was waiting for you to get the
   invitation before I took you to choose
   a present.

Il **recevait** d'étranges messages.
He was getting strange messages.

Elle **recevra** une réponse la semaine
   prochaine.
She'll get an answer next week.

Il **reçut** une lettre anonyme.
He received an anonymous letter.

Tu ne **recevrais** pas autant de monde si
   ta maison n'était pas aussi grande.
You wouldn't entertain so many people
   if your house weren't so big.

Cela faisait une semaine qu'il n'**avait**
   pas **reçu** de courrier.
He hadn't had any mail for a week.

Recevez, Monsieur, mes salutations.
Yours sincerely.

je/j' = I   **tu** = you   **il** = he/it   **elle** = she/it   **on** = we/one   **nous** = we   **vous** = you   **ils/elles** = they

réfléchir (to think)

PRESENT

je	**réfléchis**
tu	**réfléchis**
il/elle/on	**réfléchit**
nous	**réfléchissons**
vous	**réfléchissez**
ils/elles	**réfléchissent**

PRESENT SUBJUNCTIVE

je	**réfléchisse**
tu	**réfléchisses**
il/elle/on	**réfléchisse**
nous	**réfléchissions**
vous	**réfléchissiez**
ils/elles	**réfléchissent**

PERFECT

j'	**ai réfléchi**
tu	**as réfléchi**
il/elle/on	**a réfléchi**
nous	**avons réfléchi**
vous	**avez réfléchi**
ils/elles	**ont réfléchi**

IMPERFECT

je	**réfléchissais**
tu	**réfléchissais**
il/elle/on	**réfléchissait**
nous	**réfléchissions**
vous	**réfléchissiez**
ils/elles	**réfléchissaient**

PRESENT PARTICIPLE
réfléchissant

PAST PARTICIPLE
réfléchi

FUTURE

je	**réfléchirai**
tu	**réfléchiras**
il/elle/on	**réfléchira**
nous	**réfléchirons**
vous	**réfléchirez**
ils/elles	**réfléchiront**

CONDITIONAL

je	**réfléchirais**
tu	**réfléchirais**
il/elle/on	**réfléchirait**
nous	**réfléchirions**
vous	**réfléchiriez**
ils/elles	**réfléchiraient**

PAST HISTORIC

je	**réfléchis**
tu	**réfléchis**
il/elle/on	**réfléchit**
nous	**réfléchîmes**
vous	**réfléchîtes**
ils/elles	**réfléchirent**

PLUPERFECT

j'	**avais réfléchi**
tu	**avais réfléchi**
il/elle/on	**avait réfléchi**
nous	**avions réfléchi**
vous	**aviez réfléchi**
ils/elles	**avaient réfléchi**

IMPERATIVE
réfléchis / réfléchissons / réfléchissez

EXAMPLE PHRASES

Il est en train de **réfléchir**.
He's thinking.

Je vais **réfléchir** à ta proposition.
I'll think about your suggestion.

Il faut que j'y **réfléchisse**.
I'll have to think about it.

J'y **réfléchirai** et nous en reparlerons
   lors de notre prochaine réunion.
I'll think about it and we'll talk about it
   at our next meeting.

Il **réfléchit** longuement avant de parler.
He thought for a long time before he
   spoke.

Si j'étais toi, j'y **réfléchirais** encore un
   peu.
If I were you, I'd give it more thought.

Ils **avaient** bien **réfléchi** et ils avaient
   décidé de vendre la maison.
They had thought it over and they had
   decided to sell the house.

Réfléchissez avant de répondre.
Think before answering.

---

je/j' = I   **tu** = you   **il** = he/it   **elle** = she/it   **on** = we/one   **nous** = we   **vous** = you   **ils/elles** = they

rentrer (to go back; to go in)

PRESENT

je	**rentre**
tu	**rentres**
il/elle/on	**rentre**
nous	**rentrons**
vous	**rentrez**
ils/elles	**rentrent**

PRESENT SUBJUNCTIVE

je	**rentre**
tu	**rentres**
il/elle/on	**rentre**
nous	**rentrions**
vous	**rentriez**
ils/elles	**rentrent**

PERFECT

je	**suis rentré(e)**
tu	**es rentré(e)**
il/elle/on	**est rentré(e)**
nous	**sommes rentré(e)s**
vous	**êtes rentré(e)(s)**
ils/elles	**sont rentré(e)s**

IMPERFECT

je	**rentrais**
tu	**rentrais**
il/elle/on	**rentrait**
nous	**rentrions**
vous	**rentriez**
ils/elles	**rentraient**

PRESENT PARTICIPLE

rentrant

PAST PARTICIPLE

rentré

FUTURE

je	**rentrerai**
tu	**rentreras**
il/elle/on	**rentrera**
nous	**rentrerons**
vous	**rentrerez**
ils/elles	**rentreront**

CONDITIONAL

je	**rentrerais**
tu	**rentrerais**
il/elle/on	**rentrerait**
nous	**rentrerions**
vous	**rentreriez**
ils/elles	**rentreraient**

PAST HISTORIC

je	**rentrai**
tu	**rentras**
il/elle/on	**rentra**
nous	**rentrâmes**
vous	**rentrâtes**
ils/elles	**rentrèrent**

PLUPERFECT

j'	**étais rentré(e)**
tu	**étais rentré(e)**
il/elle/on	**était rentré(e)**
nous	**étions rentré(e)s**
vous	**étiez rentré(e)(s)**
ils/elles	**étaient rentré(e)s**

IMPERATIVE

rentre / rentrons / rentrez

In the perfect and the pluperfect, use the auxiliary **avoir** when there is a direct object.

je/j' = I   **tu** = you   **il** = he/it   **elle** = she/it   **on** = we/one   **nous** = we   **vous** = you   **ils/elles** = they

---

EXAMPLE PHRASES

Je **rentre** déjeuner à midi.
I go home for lunch.

À quelle heure est-ce qu'elle **est rentrée**?
What time did she get in?

Il faut que je **rentre** de bonne heure aujourd'hui.
I have to go home early today.

Il ne **rentrait** jamais avant neuf heures le soir.
He never came home before nine in the evening.

Nous ne **rentrerons** pas tard.
We won't come home late.

Il **rentra** chez lui en courant.
He ran all the way home.

Si je n'avais pas peur de me perdre, je **rentrerais** sans toi.
If I weren't afraid I'd get lost, I'd go home without you.

Ils **étaient rentrés** dans le magasin.
They'd gone into the shop.

Il **avait** déjà **rentré** la voiture dans le garage.
He'd already put the car into the garage.

Ne **rentre** pas trop tard.
Don't come home too late.

répondre (to answer)

PRESENT

je	**réponds**
tu	**réponds**
il/elle/on	**répond**
nous	**répondons**
vous	**répondez**
ils/elles	**répondent**

PRESENT SUBJUNCTIVE

je	**réponde**
tu	**répondes**
il/elle/on	**réponde**
nous	**répondions**
vous	**répondiez**
ils/elles	**répondent**

EXAMPLE PHRASES

Ça ne **répond** pas.
There's no reply.

C'est elle qui **a répondu** au téléphone.
She answered the phone.

Lisez le texte et **répondez** aux questions.
Read the text and answer the questions.

J'attendais que tu **répondes** à ma lettre.
I was waiting for you to reply to my letter.

Il ne **répondait** jamais au téléphone le soir.
He never answered the phone in the evening.

Je **répondrai** à son message ce soir.
I'll reply to his message this evening.

"Je ne sais pas," **répondit**-elle.
I don't know, she answered.

Il ne te **répondrait** pas comme ça si tu étais plus stricte.
He wouldn't answer back like that if you were stricter.

Je n'**avais** pas encore **répondu** à son invitation.
I hadn't replied to her invitation yet.

PERFECT

j'	**ai répondu**
tu	**as répondu**
il/elle/on	**a répondu**
nous	**avons répondu**
vous	**avez répondu**
ils/elles	**ont répondu**

IMPERFECT

je	**répondais**
tu	**répondais**
il/elle/on	**répondait**
nous	**répondions**
vous	**répondiez**
ils/elles	**répondaient**

PRESENT PARTICIPLE
répondant

PAST PARTICIPLE
répondu

FUTURE

je	**répondrai**
tu	**répondras**
il/elle/on	**répondra**
nous	**répondrons**
vous	**répondrez**
ils/elles	**répondront**

CONDITIONAL

je	**répondrais**
tu	**répondrais**
il/elle/on	**répondrait**
nous	**répondrions**
vous	**répondriez**
ils/elles	**répondraient**

PAST HISTORIC

je	**répondis**
tu	**répondis**
il/elle/on	**répondit**
nous	**répondîmes**
vous	**répondîtes**
ils/elles	**répondirent**

PLUPERFECT

j'	**avais répondu**
tu	**avais répondu**
il/elle/on	**avait répondu**
nous	**avions répondu**
vous	**aviez répondu**
ils/elles	**avaient répondu**

IMPERATIVE
réponds / répondons / répondez

je/j' = I   **tu** = you   **il** = he/it   **elle** = she/it   **on** = we/one   **nous** = we   **vous** = you   **ils/elles** = they

résoudre (to solve; to resolve)

PRESENT

je	**résous**
tu	**résous**
il/elle/on	**résout**
nous	**résolvons**
vous	**résolvez**
ils/elles	**résolvent**

PRESENT SUBJUNCTIVE

je	**résolve**
tu	**résolves**
il/elle/on	**résolve**
nous	**résolvions**
vous	**résolviez**
ils/elles	**résolvent**

PERFECT

j'	**ai résolu**
tu	**as résolu**
il/elle/on	**a résolu**
nous	**avons résolu**
vous	**avez résolu**
ils/elles	**ont résolu**

IMPERFECT

je	**résolvais**
tu	**résolvais**
il/elle/on	**résolvait**
nous	**résolvions**
vous	**résolviez**
ils/elles	**résolvaient**

PRESENT PARTICIPLE
résolvant

PAST PARTICIPLE
résolu

FUTURE

je	**résoudrai**
tu	**résoudras**
il/elle/on	**résoudra**
nous	**résoudrons**
vous	**résoudrez**
ils/elles	**résoudront**

CONDITIONAL

je	**résoudrais**
tu	**résoudrais**
il/elle/on	**résoudrait**
nous	**résoudrions**
vous	**résoudriez**
ils/elles	**résoudraient**

PAST HISTORIC

je	**résolus**
tu	**résolus**
il/elle/on	**résolut**
nous	**résolûmes**
vous	**résolûtes**
ils/elles	**résolurent**

PLUPERFECT

j'	**avais résolu**
tu	**avais résolu**
il/elle/on	**avait résolu**
nous	**avions résolu**
vous	**aviez résolu**
ils/elles	**avaient résolu**

IMPERATIVE
résous / résolvons / résolvez

EXAMPLE PHRASES

C'est un problème qui sera difficile à **résoudre**.
This problem will be difficult to solve.

La violence ne **résout** rien.
Violence doesn't solve anything.

J'**ai résolu** le problème.
I've solved the problem.

J'aimerais que vous **résolviez** la question aujourd'hui.
I'd like you to resolve the question today.

Son refus de s'excuser ne **résoudra** pas la querelle.
His refusal to apologize won't resolve the quarrel.

Il **résolut** l'énigme en quelques minutes.
He solved the riddle in a few minutes.

C'est un problème qui se **résoudrait** rapidement s'il n'y avait pas déjà d'autres problèmes.
This problem could be solved quickly if there weren't already other problems.

À la fin de la réunion, nous **avions résolu** la question.
By the end of the meeting, we had resolved the question.

je/j' = I **tu** = you **il** = he/it **elle** = she/it **on** = we/one **nous** = we **vous** = you **ils/elles** = they

rester (to stay)

PRESENT

je	**reste**
tu	**restes**
il/elle/on	**reste**
nous	**restons**
vous	**restez**
ils/elles	**restent**

PERFECT

je	**suis resté(e)**
tu	**es resté(e)**
il/elle/on	**est resté(e)**
nous	**sommes resté(e)s**
vous	**êtes resté(e)(s)**
ils/elles	**sont resté(e)s**

PRESENT PARTICIPLE
restant

FUTURE

je	**resterai**
tu	**resteras**
il/elle/on	**restera**
nous	**resterons**
vous	**resterez**
ils/elles	**resteront**

PAST HISTORIC

je	**restai**
tu	**restas**
il/elle/on	**resta**
nous	**restâmes**
vous	**restâtes**
ils/elles	**restèrent**

IMPERATIVE
reste / restons / restez

PRESENT SUBJUNCTIVE

je	**reste**
tu	**restes**
il/elle/on	**reste**
nous	**restions**
vous	**restiez**
ils/elles	**restent**

IMPERFECT

je	**restais**
tu	**restais**
il/elle/on	**restait**
nous	**restions**
vous	**restiez**
ils/elles	**restaient**

PAST PARTICIPLE
resté

CONDITIONAL

je	**resterais**
tu	**resterais**
il/elle/on	**resterait**
nous	**resterions**
vous	**resteriez**
ils/elles	**resteraient**

PLUPERFECT

j'	**étais resté(e)**
tu	**étais resté(e)**
il/elle/on	**était resté(e)**
nous	**étions resté(e)s**
vous	**étiez resté(e)(s)**
ils/elles	**étaient resté(e)s**

EXAMPLE PHRASES

Cet été, je **reste** en Écosse.
I'm staying in Scotland this summer.

Ils ne **sont** pas **restés** très longtemps.
They didn't stay very long.

Elle aimerait que Marianne **reste** dormir ce soir.
She'd like Marianne to stay for a sleepover tonight.

Il leur **restait** encore un peu d'argent.
They still had some money left.

Si tu finis les biscuits il n'en **restera** plus pour ce soir.
If you finish the biscuits there won't be any left for tonight.

Il **resta** dans sa chambre toute la soirée.
He stayed in his bedroom all evening.

Si c'était à moi de choisir, je **resterais** à la maison.
If it were my choice, I'd stay home.

Nous **étions restés** à la maison pour regarder le match de football.
We'd stayed home to watch the football match.

Reste ici!
Stay here!

je/j' = I **tu** = you **il** = he/it **elle** = she/it **on** = we/one **nous** = we **vous** = you **ils/elles** = they

retourner (to return; to turn)

PRESENT

je	**retourne**
tu	**retournes**
il/elle/on	**retourne**
nous	**retournons**
vous	**retournez**
ils/elles	**retournent**

PRESENT SUBJUNCTIVE

je	**retourne**
tu	**retournes**
il/elle/on	**retourne**
nous	**retournions**
vous	**retourniez**
ils/elles	**retournent**

PERFECT

je	**suis retourné(e)**
tu	**es retourné(e)**
il/elle/on	**est retourné(e)**
nous	**sommes retourné(e)s**
vous	**êtes retourné(e)(s)**
ils/elles	**sont retourné(e)s**

IMPERFECT

je	**retournais**
tu	**retournais**
il/elle/on	**retournait**
nous	**retournions**
vous	**retourniez**
ils/elles	**retournaient**

PRESENT PARTICIPLE
retournant

PAST PARTICIPLE
retourné

In the perfect and the pluperfect, use the auxiliary **avoir** when there is a direct object.

FUTURE

je	**retournerai**
tu	**retourneras**
il/elle/on	**retournera**
nous	**retournerons**
vous	**retournerez**
ils/elles	**retourneront**

CONDITIONAL

je	**retournerais**
tu	**retournerais**
il/elle/on	**retournerait**
nous	**retournerions**
vous	**retourneriez**
ils/elles	**retourneraient**

PAST HISTORIC

je	**retournai**
tu	**retournas**
il/elle/on	**retourna**
nous	**retournâmes**
vous	**retournâtes**
ils/elles	**retournèrent**

PLUPERFECT

j'	**étais retourné(e)**
tu	**étais retourné(e)**
il/elle/on	**était retourné(e)**
nous	**étions retourné(e)s**
vous	**étiez retourné(e)(s)**
ils/elles	**étaient retourné(e)s**

IMPERATIVE
retourne / retournons / retournez

EXAMPLE PHRASES

J'aimerais bien **retourner** en Italie un jour.
I'd like to go back to Italy one day.

Cet été, nous **retournons** en Grèce.
We're going back to Greece this summer.

Est-ce que tu **es retournée** à Londres?
Have you ever been back to London?

Il va falloir que je **retourne** voir le film.
I'll have to go back to see the film.

Elle **retournait** rarement dans son pays natal.
She rarely went back to her native country.

Je ne **retournerai** jamais les voir.
I'll never go back to see them.

Elle déjeuna rapidement et **retourna** travailler.
She had a quick lunch and went back to work.

Il disait qu'il ne **retournerait** jamais vivre avec elle.
He said that he would never go back to live with her.

Elle **avait retourné** la carte pour vérifier.
She had turned the card over to check.

Zoë, **retourne**-toi!
Turn around, Zoë!

je/j' = I   **tu** = you   **il** = he/it   **elle** = she/it   **on** = we/one   **nous** = we   **vous** = you   **ils/elles** = they

réussir (to be successful)

PRESENT

je	**réussis**
tu	**réussis**
il/elle/on	**réussit**
nous	**réussissons**
vous	**réussissez**
ils/elles	**réussissent**

PRESENT SUBJUNCTIVE

je	**réussisse**
tu	**réussisses**
il/elle/on	**réussisse**
nous	**réussissions**
vous	**réussissiez**
ils/elles	**réussissent**

PERFECT

j'	**ai réussi**
tu	**as réussi**
il/elle/on	**a réussi**
nous	**avons réussi**
vous	**avez réussi**
ils/elles	**ont réussi**

IMPERFECT

je	**réussissais**
tu	**réussissais**
il/elle/on	**réussissait**
nous	**réussissions**
vous	**réussissiez**
ils/elles	**réussissaient**

PRESENT PARTICIPLE

réussissant

PAST PARTICIPLE

réussi

FUTURE

je	**réussirai**
tu	**réussiras**
il/elle/on	**réussira**
nous	**réussirons**
vous	**réussirez**
ils/elles	**réussiront**

CONDITIONAL

je	**réussirais**
tu	**réussirais**
il/elle/on	**réussirait**
nous	**réussirions**
vous	**réussiriez**
ils/elles	**réussiraient**

PAST HISTORIC

je	**réussis**
tu	**réussis**
il/elle/on	**réussit**
nous	**réussîmes**
vous	**réussîtes**
ils/elles	**réussirent**

PLUPERFECT

j'	**avais réussi**
tu	**avais réussi**
il/elle/on	**avait réussi**
nous	**avions réussi**
vous	**aviez réussi**
ils/elles	**avaient réussi**

IMPERATIVE

réussis / réussissons / réussissez

EXAMPLE PHRASES

Il faut se battre pour **réussir** dans la vie.
You have to fight to be successful
in life.

Tous ses enfants **ont** très bien **réussi**.
All her children are very successful.

J'aimerais qu'il **réussisse** à son permis
de conduire.
I'd like him to pass his driving test.

Elle **réussissait** toujours à me faire rire
quand j'étais triste.
She always managed to make me laugh
when I was sad.

Je suis sûr que tu **réussiras** à ton
examen.
I'm sure you'll pass your exam.

Finalement, elle **réussit** à le convaincre.
She eventually managed to convince
him.

Je **réussirais** peut-être mes gâteaux si
j'avais un four qui marchait.
My cakes might turn out fine if I had an
oven that worked.

Elle **avait réussi** à battre le record du
monde.
She had succeeded in beating the world
record.

je/j' = I **tu** = you **il** = he/it **elle** = she/it **on** = we/one **nous** = we **vous** = you **ils/elles** = they

se réveiller (to wake up)

PRESENT

je	**me réveille**
tu	**te réveilles**
il/elle/on	**se réveille**
nous	**nous réveillons**
vous	**vous réveillez**
ils/elles	**se réveillent**

PRESENT SUBJUNCTIVE

je	**me réveille**
tu	**te réveilles**
il/elle/on	**se réveille**
nous	**nous réveillions**
vous	**vous réveilliez**
ils/elles	**se réveillent**

PERFECT

je	**me suis réveillé(e)**
tu	**t'es réveillé(e)**
il/elle/on	**s'est réveillé(e)**
nous	**nous sommes réveillé(e)s**
vous	**vous êtes réveillé(e)(s)**
ils/elles	**se sont réveillé(e)s**

IMPERFECT

je	**me réveillais**
tu	**te réveillais**
il/elle/on	**se réveillait**
nous	**nous réveillions**
vous	**vous réveilliez**
ils/elles	**se réveillaient**

PRESENT PARTICIPLE

se réveillant

PAST PARTICIPLE

réveillé

FUTURE

je	**me réveillerai**
tu	**te réveilleras**
il/elle/on	**se réveillera**
nous	**nous réveillerons**
vous	**vous réveillerez**
ils/elles	**se réveilleront**

CONDITIONAL

je	**me réveillerais**
tu	**te réveillerais**
il/elle/on	**se réveillerait**
nous	**nous réveillerions**
vous	**vous réveilleriez**
ils/elles	**se réveilleraient**

PAST HISTORIC

je	**me réveillai**
tu	**te réveillas**
il/elle/on	**se réveilla**
nous	**nous reveillâmes**
vous	**vous réveillâtes**
ils/elles	**se réveillèrent**

PLUPERFECT

je	**m'étais réveillé(e)**
tu	**t'étais réveillé(e)**
il/elle/on	**s'était réveillé(e)**
nous	**nous étions réveillé(e)s**
vous	**vous étiez réveillé(e)(s)**
ils/elles	**s'étaient réveillé(e)s**

IMPERATIVE

réveille-toi / réveillons-nous / réveillez-vous

EXAMPLE PHRASES

Je **me réveille** à sept heures tous les matins.
I wake up at seven every morning.

Il **s'est réveillé** en retard.
He overslept.

Il faut que je **me réveille** à cinq heures demain matin.
I have to get up at five tomorrow morning.

Elle **se réveillait** toujours avant moi.
She always woke up before me.

Louise ne **se réveillera** probablement pas avant neuf heures.
Louise probably won't wake up before nine.

Elle **se réveilla** en sursaut.
She woke up with a start.

Je ne **me réveillerais** pas sans mon réveil.
I wouldn't wake up without my alarm clock.

Elle ne **s'était** pas **réveillée** quand je l'avais appelée.
She hadn't woken up when I had called her.

Réveille-toi: il est huit heures!
Wake up - it's eight!

je/j' = I **tu** = you **il** = he/it **elle** = she/it **on** = we/one **nous** = we **vous** = you **ils/elles** = they

revenir (to come back)

PRESENT

je	**reviens**
tu	**reviens**
il/elle/on	**revient**
nous	**revenons**
vous	**revenez**
ils/elles	**reviennent**

PRESENT SUBJUNCTIVE

je	**revienne**
tu	**reviennes**
il/elle/on	**revienne**
nous	**revenions**
vous	**reveniez**
ils/elles	**reviennent**

PERFECT

je	**suis revenu(e)**
tu	**es revenu(e)**
il/elle/on	**est revenu(e)**
nous	**sommes revenu(e)s**
vous	**êtes revenu(e)(s)**
ils/elles	**sont revenu(e)s**

IMPERFECT

je	**revenais**
tu	**revenais**
il/elle/on	**revenait**
nous	**revenions**
vous	**reveniez**
ils/elles	**revenaient**

PRESENT PARTICIPLE

revenant

PAST PARTICIPLE

revenu

FUTURE

je	**reviendrai**
tu	**reviendras**
il/elle/on	**reviendra**
nous	**reviendrons**
vous	**reviendrez**
ils/elles	**reviendront**

CONDITIONAL

je	**reviendrais**
tu	**reviendrais**
il/elle/on	**reviendrait**
nous	**reviendrions**
vous	**reviendriez**
ils/elles	**reviendraient**

PAST HISTORIC

je	**revins**
tu	**revins**
il/elle/on	**revint**
nous	**revînmes**
vous	**revîntes**
ils/elles	**revinrent**

PLUPERFECT

j'	**étais revenu(e)**
tu	**étais revenu(e)**
il/elle/on	**était revenu(e)**
nous	**étions revenu(e)s**
vous	**étiez revenu(e)(s)**
ils/elles	**étaient revenu(e)s**

IMPERATIVE

reviens / revenons / revenez

EXAMPLE PHRASES

Je **reviens** dans cinq minutes!
I'll be back in five minutes!

Ça me **revient**!
It's coming back to me now!

Mon chat n'**est** toujours pas **revenu**.
My cat still hasn't come back.

J'aimerais qu'il **revienne** me voir.
I'd like him to come back to see me.

Son chien se promenait souvent loin de chez lui mais il **revenait** toujours.
His dog often wandered far away from his house, but he'd always come back.

Je ne **reviendrai** jamais ici.
I'll never come back here.

Il **revint** nous voir le lendemain.
He came back to see us the next day.

Elle ne **reviendrait** pas si elle avait le choix.
She wouldn't come back if she had the choice.

Ils **étaient revenus** le soir même avec leur fille.
They had come back that same evening with their daughter.

Philippe! **Reviens** immédiatement!
Philippe! Come back immediately!

je/j' = I   **tu** = you   **il** = he/it   **elle** = she/it   **on** = we/one   **nous** = we   **vous** = you   **ils/elles** = they

rire (to laugh)

PRESENT

je	**ris**
tu	**ris**
il/elle/on	**rit**
nous	**rions**
vous	**riez**
ils/elles	**rient**

PRESENT SUBJUNCTIVE

je	**rie**
tu	**ries**
il/elle/on	**rie**
nous	**riions**
vous	**riiez**
ils/elles	**rient**

PERFECT

j'	**ai ri**
tu	**as ri**
il/elle/on	**a ri**
nous	**avons ri**
vous	**avez ri**
ils/elles	**ont ri**

IMPERFECT

je	**riais**
tu	**riais**
il/elle/on	**riait**
nous	**riions**
vous	**riiez**
ils/elles	**riaient**

PRESENT PARTICIPLE

riant

PAST PARTICIPLE

ri

FUTURE

je	**rirai**
tu	**riras**
il/elle/on	**rira**
nous	**rirons**
vous	**rirez**
ils/elles	**riront**

CONDITIONAL

je	**rirais**
tu	**rirais**
il/elle/on	**rirait**
nous	**ririons**
vous	**ririez**
ils/elles	**riraient**

PAST HISTORIC

je	**ris**
tu	**ris**
il/elle/on	**rit**
nous	**rîmes**
vous	**rîtes**
ils/elles	**rirent**

PLUPERFECT

j'	**avais ri**
tu	**avais ri**
il/elle/on	**avait ri**
nous	**avions ri**
vous	**aviez ri**
ils/elles	**avaient ri**

IMPERATIVE

ris / rions / riez

EXAMPLE PHRASES

C'était juste pour **rire**.
It was only for a laugh.

Elle **rit** toujours de mes plaisanteries.
She always laughs at my jokes.

On **a** bien **ri**.
We had a good laugh.

Je n'aime pas qu'on **rie** derrière mon dos.
I don't like it when people laugh behind my back.

Tu ne **riras** pas tant quand ce sera ton tour.
You won't be laughing so much when it's your turn.

Elle **rit** quand il lui raconta l'histoire.
She laughed when he told her the story.

Il ne **rirait** pas s'il savait où tu es allé.
He wouldn't be laughing if he knew where you've been.

Ils **avaient ri** quand elle leur avait raconté ce qui s'était passé.
They had laughed when she had told them what had happened.

Ne **ris** pas, ce n'est pas drôle!
Don't laugh, it's not funny!

---

je/j' = I   **tu** = you   **il** = he/it   **elle** = she/it   **on** = we/one   **nous** = we   **vous** = you   **ils/elles** = they

rompre (to break; to split up)

PRESENT

je	**romps**
tu	**romps**
il/elle/on	**rompt**
nous	**rompons**
vous	**rompez**
ils/elles	**rompent**

PRESENT SUBJUNCTIVE

je	**rompe**
tu	**rompes**
il/elle/on	**rompe**
nous	**rompions**
vous	**rompiez**
ils/elles	**rompent**

PERFECT

j'	**ai rompu**
tu	**as rompu**
il/elle/on	**a rompu**
nous	**avons rompu**
vous	**avez rompu**
ils/elles	**ont rompu**

IMPERFECT

je	**rompais**
tu	**rompais**
il/elle/on	**rompait**
nous	**rompions**
vous	**rompiez**
ils/elles	**rompaient**

PRESENT PARTICIPLE
rompant

PAST PARTICIPLE
rompu

FUTURE

je	**romprai**
tu	**rompras**
il/elle/on	**rompra**
nous	**romprons**
vous	**romprez**
ils/elles	**rompront**

CONDITIONAL

je	**romprais**
tu	**romprais**
il/elle/on	**romprait**
nous	**romprions**
vous	**rompriez**
ils/elles	**rompraient**

PAST HISTORIC

je	**rompis**
tu	**rompis**
il/elle/on	**rompit**
nous	**rompîmes**
vous	**rompîtes**
ils/elles	**rompirent**

PLUPERFECT

j'	**avais rompu**
tu	**avais rompu**
il/elle/on	**avait rompu**
nous	**avions rompu**
vous	**aviez rompu**
ils/elles	**avaient rompu**

IMPERATIVE
romps / rompons / rompez

EXAMPLE PHRASES

Elle **a rompu** le silence.
She broke the silence.

Paul et Jo **ont rompu**.
Paul and Jo have split up.

Ils ont tiré sur la corde jusqu'à ce qu'elle **rompe**.
They pulled on the rope until it broke.

Il **rompit** le silence en entrant.
He broke the silence when he came in.

Le charme **était rompu**.
The spell was broken.

Il **avait** déjà **rompu** avec Alice quand il a rencontré Christine.
He'd already split up with Alice when he met Christine.

je/j' = I **tu** = you **il** = he/it **elle** = she/it **on** = we/one **nous** = we **vous** = you **ils/elles** = they

savoir (to know)

PRESENT

je	**sais**
tu	**sais**
il/elle/on	**sait**
nous	**savons**
vous	**savez**
ils/elles	**savent**

PRESENT SUBJUNCTIVE

je	**sache**
tu	**saches**
il/elle/on	**sache**
nous	**sachions**
vous	**sachiez**
ils/elles	**sachent**

PERFECT

j'	**ai su**
tu	**as su**
il/elle/on	**a su**
nous	**avons su**
vous	**avez su**
ils/elles	**ont su**

IMPERFECT

je	**savais**
tu	**savais**
il/elle/on	**savait**
nous	**savions**
vous	**saviez**
ils/elles	**savaient**

PRESENT PARTICIPLE

sachant

PAST PARTICIPLE

su

FUTURE

je	**saurai**
tu	**sauras**
il/elle/on	**saura**
nous	**saurons**
vous	**saurez**
ils/elles	**sauront**

CONDITIONAL

je	**saurais**
tu	**saurais**
il/elle/on	**saurait**
nous	**saurions**
vous	**sauriez**
ils/elles	**sauraient**

PAST HISTORIC

je	**sus**
tu	**sus**
il/elle/on	**sut**
nous	**sûmes**
vous	**sûtes**
ils/elles	**surent**

PLUPERFECT

j'	**avais su**
tu	**avais su**
il/elle/on	**avait su**
nous	**avions su**
vous	**aviez su**
ils/elles	**avaient su**

IMPERATIVE

sache / sachons / sachez

EXAMPLE PHRASES

Tu **sais** ce que tu vas faire l'année prochaine?
Do you know what you're going to do next year?

Je ne **sais** pas.
I don't know.

Elle ne **sait** pas nager.
She can't swim.

Je voulais qu'il le **sache**.
I wanted him to know about it.

Tu **savais** que son père était enseignant?
Did you know that her father was a teacher?

Elle ne **saura** pas où on est.
She won't know where we are.

Il ne le **sut** que beaucoup plus tard.
He only knew about it a lot later.

Tous ces enfants **sauraient** lire si on leur apprenait.
All these children would be able to read if they were taught.

Ils ne l'**avaient su** que beaucoup plus tard.
They hadn't known about it until a lot later.

je/j' = I   **tu** = you   **il** = he/it   **elle** = she/it   **on** = we/one   **nous** = we   **vous** = you   **ils/elles** = they

sentir (to smell; to feel)

PRESENT

je	**sens**
tu	**sens**
il/elle/on	**sent**
nous	**sentons**
vous	**sentez**
ils/elles	**sentent**

PRESENT SUBJUNCTIVE

je	**sente**
tu	**sentes**
il/elle/on	**sente**
nous	**sentions**
vous	**sentiez**
ils/elles	**sentent**

PERFECT

j'	**ai senti**
tu	**as senti**
il/elle/on	**a senti**
nous	**avons senti**
vous	**avez senti**
ils/elles	**ont senti**

IMPERFECT

je	**sentais**
tu	**sentais**
il/elle/on	**sentait**
nous	**sentions**
vous	**sentiez**
ils/elles	**sentaient**

PRESENT PARTICIPLE
sentant

PAST PARTICIPLE
senti

FUTURE

je	**sentirai**
tu	**sentiras**
il/elle/on	**sentira**
nous	**sentirons**
vous	**sentirez**
ils/elles	**sentiront**

CONDITIONAL

je	**sentirais**
tu	**sentirais**
il/elle/on	**sentirait**
nous	**sentirions**
vous	**sentiriez**
ils/elles	**sentiraient**

PAST HISTORIC

je	**sentis**
tu	**sentis**
il/elle/on	**sentit**
nous	**sentîmes**
vous	**sentîtes**
ils/elles	**sentirent**

PLUPERFECT

j'	**avais senti**
tu	**avais senti**
il/elle/on	**avait senti**
nous	**avions senti**
vous	**aviez senti**
ils/elles	**avaient senti**

IMPERATIVE
sens / sentons / sentez

EXAMPLE PHRASES

Ça **sent** bon ici.
It smells nice here.

Elle ne se **sent** pas bien.
She's not feeling well.

Je n'**ai** rien **senti**.
I didn't feel a thing.

Ça **sentait** mauvais.
It smelt bad.

Ne vous inquiétez pas: vous ne **sentirez** rien.
Don't worry – you won't feel a thing.

Il **sentit** que ce n'était pas le bon moment.
He felt that it wasn't the right time.

Elle se **sentirait** mieux si elle se reposait.
She'd feel better if she rested.

Il n'**avait** rien **senti** pendant l'opération.
He hadn't felt a thing during the operation.

Sens ces fleurs.
Smell these flowers.

je/j' = I   **tu** = you   **il** = he/it   **elle** = she/it   **on** = we/one   **nous** = we   **vous** = you   **ils/elles** = they

servir (to serve; to be of use to)

PRESENT

je	**sers**
tu	**sers**
il/elle/on	**sert**
nous	**servons**
vous	**servez**
ils/elles	**servent**

PRESENT SUBJUNCTIVE

je	**serve**
tu	**serves**
il/elle/on	**serve**
nous	**servions**
vous	**serviez**
ils/elles	**servent**

PERFECT

j'	**ai servi**
tu	**as servi**
il/elle/on	**a servi**
nous	**avons servi**
vous	**avez servi**
ils/elles	**ont servi**

IMPERFECT

je	**servais**
tu	**servais**
il/elle/on	**servait**
nous	**servions**
vous	**serviez**
ils/elles	**servaient**

PRESENT PARTICIPLE
servant

PAST PARTICIPLE
servi

FUTURE

je	**servirai**
tu	**serviras**
il/elle/on	**servira**
nous	**servirons**
vous	**servirez**
ils/elles	**serviront**

CONDITIONAL

je	**servirais**
tu	**servirais**
il/elle/on	**servirait**
nous	**servirions**
vous	**serviriez**
ils/elles	**serviraient**

PAST HISTORIC

je	**servis**
tu	**servis**
il/elle/on	**servit**
nous	**servîmes**
vous	**servîtes**
ils/elles	**servirent**

PLUPERFECT

j'	**avais servi**
tu	**avais servi**
il/elle/on	**avait servi**
nous	**avions servi**
vous	**aviez servi**
ils/elles	**avaient servi**

IMPERATIVE
sers / servons / servez

EXAMPLE PHRASES

On vous **sert**?
Are you being served?

Ça **sert** à quoi ce bouton?
What is this button for?

Servez-vous.
Help yourself.

Il faut que je **serve** la soupe.
I have to serve the soup.

Ça ne **servait** à rien de le supplier.
It was no use begging him.

Ces boîtes te **serviront** quand tu déménageras.
You'll find these boxes useful when you move house.

Elle leur **servit** des profiteroles en dessert.
She served them profiteroles for dessert.

Ça ne **servirait** à rien d'y aller maintenant.
It would serve no purpose to go there now.

Cette valise n'**avait** pas **servi** depuis dix ans.
This suitcase hadn't been used for ten years.

je/j' = I **tu** = you **il** = he/it **elle** = she/it **on** = we/one **nous** = we **vous** = you **ils/elles** = they

sortir (to go out; to take out)

PRESENT

je	**sors**
tu	**sors**
il/elle/on	**sort**
nous	**sortons**
vous	**sortez**
ils/elles	**sortent**

PRESENT SUBJUNCTIVE

je	**sorte**
tu	**sortes**
il/elle/on	**sorte**
nous	**sortions**
vous	**sortiez**
ils/elles	**sortent**

PERFECT

je	**suis sorti(e)**
tu	**es sorti(e)**
il/elle/on	**est sorti(e)**
nous	**sommes sorti(e)s**
vous	**êtes sorti(e)(s)**
ils/elles	**sont sorti(e)s**

IMPERFECT

je	**sortais**
tu	**sortais**
il/elle/on	**sortait**
nous	**sortions**
vous	**sortiez**
ils/elles	**sortaient**

PRESENT PARTICIPLE

sortant

PAST PARTICIPLE

sorti

FUTURE

je	**sortirai**
tu	**sortiras**
il/elle/on	**sortira**
nous	**sortirons**
vous	**sortirez**
ils/elles	**sortiront**

CONDITIONAL

je	**sortirais**
tu	**sortirais**
il/elle/on	**sortirait**
nous	**sortirions**
vous	**sortiriez**
ils/elles	**sortiraient**

PAST HISTORIC

je	**sortis**
tu	**sortis**
il/elle/on	**sortit**
nous	**sortîmes**
vous	**sortîtes**
ils/elles	**sortirent**

PLUPERFECT

j'	**étais sorti(e)**
tu	**étais sorti(e)**
il/elle/on	**était sorti(e)**
nous	**étions sorti(e)s**
vous	**étiez sorti(e)(s)**
ils/elles	**étaient sorti(e)s**

IMPERATIVE

sors / sortons / sortez

EXAMPLE PHRASES

Aurélie **sort** avec Bruno.
Aurélie is going out with Bruno.

Je ne **suis** pas **sortie** ce week-end.
I didn't go out this weekend.

Je n'**ai** pas **sorti** le chien parce qu'il pleuvait.
I didn't take the dog out for a walk because it was raining.

Je ne veux pas que tu **sortes** habillée comme ça.
I don't want you to go out dressed like that.

Il **sortait** quand c'est arrivé.
He was going out when it happened.

Je **sortirai** la poubelle en partant.
I'll take out the bin on my way out.

Il **sortit** une photo de sa poche.
He took a photo out of his pocket.

Elle ne **sortirait** jamais de chez elle si son mari ne l'y obligeait pas.
She'd never leave her house if her husband didn't force her.

Elle **était sortie** de l'hôpital la veille.
She had come out of hospital the day before.

Sortez en silence.
Go out quietly.

In the perfect and the imperfect, use the auxiliary **avoir** when there is a direct object.

je/j' = I **tu** = you **il** = he/it **elle** = she/it **on** = we/one **nous** = we **vous** = you **ils/elles** = they

souffrir (to be in pain)

PRESENT

je	**souffre**
tu	**souffres**
il/elle/on	**souffre**
nous	**souffrons**
vous	**souffrez**
ils/elles	**souffrent**

PRESENT SUBJUNCTIVE

je	**souffre**
tu	**souffres**
il/elle/on	**souffre**
nous	**souffrions**
vous	**souffriez**
ils/elles	**souffrent**

PERFECT

j'	**ai souffert**
tu	**as souffert**
il/elle/on	**a souffert**
nous	**avons souffert**
vous	**avez souffert**
ils/elles	**ont souffert**

IMPERFECT

je	**souffrais**
tu	**souffrais**
il/elle/on	**souffrait**
nous	**souffrions**
vous	**souffriez**
ils/elles	**souffraient**

PRESENT PARTICIPLE
souffrant

PAST PARTICIPLE
souffert

FUTURE

je	**souffrirai**
tu	**souffriras**
il/elle/on	**souffrira**
nous	**souffrirons**
vous	**souffrirez**
ils/elles	**souffriront**

CONDITIONAL

je	**souffrirais**
tu	**souffrirais**
il/elle/on	**souffrirait**
nous	**souffririons**
vous	**souffririez**
ils/elles	**souffriraient**

PAST HISTORIC

je	**souffris**
tu	**souffris**
il/elle/on	**souffrit**
nous	**souffrîmes**
vous	**souffrîtes**
ils/elles	**souffrirent**

PLUPERFECT

j'	**avais souffert**
tu	**avais souffert**
il/elle/on	**avait souffert**
nous	**avions souffert**
vous	**aviez souffert**
ils/elles	**avaient souffert**

IMPERATIVE
souffre / souffrons / souffrez

EXAMPLE PHRASES

Il **souffre** beaucoup.
He's in a lot of pain.

Elle **a** beaucoup **souffert** quand il l'a quittée.
She suffered a lot when he left her.

J'ai peur qu'il ne **souffre**.
I'm scared he might be suffering.

Il **souffrait** de ne plus la voir.
It pained him not to see her any more.

Je te promets que tu ne **souffriras** pas trop.
I promise that you won't be in too much pain.

Ils **souffrirent** en silence.
They suffered in silence.

Elle ne **souffrirait** pas tant si elle prenait son médicament.
She wouldn't suffer so much if she took her medicine.

Elle **avait** beaucoup **souffert** durant son enfance.
She had suffered a lot during her childhood.

Souffre en silence.
Suffer in silence.

---

je/j' = I   **tu** = you   **il** = he/it   **elle** = she/it   **on** = we/one   **nous** = we   **vous** = you   **ils/elles** = they

se souvenir (to remember)

PRESENT

je	**me souviens**
tu	**te souviens**
il/elle/on	**se souvient**
nous	**nous souvenons**
vous	**vous souvenez**
ils/elles	**se souviennent**

PRESENT SUBJUNCTIVE

je	**me souvienne**
tu	**te souviennes**
il/elle/on	**se souvienne**
nous	**nous souvenions**
vous	**vous souveniez**
ils/elles	**se souviennent**

PERFECT

je	**me suis souvenu(e)**
tu	**t'es souvenu(e)**
il/elle/on	**s'est souvenu(e)**
nous	**nous sommes souvenu(e)s**
vous	**vous êtes souvenu(e)(s)**
ils/elles	**se sont souvenu(e)s**

IMPERFECT

je	**me souvenais**
tu	**te souvenais**
il/elle/on	**se souvenait**
nous	**nous souvenions**
vous	**vous souveniez**
ils/elles	**se souvenaient**

PRESENT PARTICIPLE

se souvenant

PAST PARTICIPLE

souvenu

FUTURE

je	**me souviendrai**
tu	**te souviendras**
il/elle/on	**se souviendra**
nous	**nous souviendrons**
vous	**vous souviendrez**
ils/elles	**se souviendront**

CONDITIONAL

je	**me souviendrais**
tu	**te souviendrais**
il/elle/on	**se souviendrait**
nous	**nous souviendrions**
vous	**vous souviendriez**
ils/elles	**se souviendraient**

PAST HISTORIC

je	**me souvins**
tu	**te souvins**
il/elle/on	**se souvint**
nous	**nous souvînmes**
vous	**vous souvîntes**
ils/elles	**se souvinrent**

PLUPERFECT

je	**m'étais souvenu(e)**
tu	**t'étais souvenu(e)**
il/elle/on	**s'était souvenu(e)**
nous	**nous étions souvenu(e)s**
vous	**vous étiez souvenu(e)(s)**
ils/elles	**s'étaient souvenu(e)s**

IMPERATIVE

souviens-toi / souvenons-nous / souvenez-vous

EXAMPLE PHRASES

Je ne **me souviens** pas de son adresse.
I can't remember his address.

Te souviens-tu du jour où Pierre s'est cassé le bras?
Do you remember the day when Pierre broke his arm?

Souviens-toi: il neigeait ce jour-là.
Remember – it was snowing that day.

Je ne crois pas qu'elle **s'en souvienne**.
I don't think that she remembers it.

Il ne **se souvenait** pas où il avait mis ses clés.
He couldn't remember where he'd put his keys.

Fais-lui une liste, sinon il ne **se souviendra** pas de ce qu'il doit acheter.
Make him a list, otherwise he won't remember what he has to buy.

Elle **se souvint** qu'elle leur avait promis une surprise.
She remembered that she'd promised them a surprise.

Si je ne prenais pas de notes, je ne **me souviendrais** pas de mes cours.
If I didn't take notes, I wouldn't remember my lessons.

Il **s'était souvenu** un peu tard de son anniversaire.
He had remembered her birthday a little late.

---

je/j' = I   **tu** = you   **il** = he/it   **elle** = she/it   **on** = we/one   **nous** = we   **vous** = you   **ils/elles** = they

suffire (to be enough)

PRESENT

je	**suffis**
tu	**suffis**
il/elle/on	**suffit**
nous	**suffisons**
vous	**suffisez**
ils/elles	**suffisent**

PRESENT SUBJUNCTIVE

je	**suffise**
tu	**suffises**
il/elle/on	**suffise**
nous	**suffisions**
vous	**suffisiez**
ils/elles	**suffisent**

PERFECT

j'	**ai suffi**
tu	**as suffi**
il/elle/on	**a suffi**
nous	**avons suffi**
vous	**avez suffi**
ils/elles	**ont suffi**

IMPERFECT

je	**suffisais**
tu	**suffisais**
il/elle/on	**suffisait**
nous	**suffisions**
vous	**suffisiez**
ils/elles	**suffisaient**

PRESENT PARTICIPLE

suffisant

PAST PARTICIPLE

suffi

FUTURE

je	**suffirai**
tu	**suffiras**
il/elle/on	**suffira**
nous	**suffirons**
vous	**suffirez**
ils/elles	**suffiront**

CONDITIONAL

je	**suffirais**
tu	**suffirais**
il/elle/on	**suffirait**
nous	**suffirions**
vous	**suffiriez**
ils/elles	**suffiraient**

PAST HISTORIC

je	**suffis**
tu	**suffis**
il/elle/on	**suffit**
nous	**suffîmes**
vous	**suffîtes**
ils/elles	**suffirent**

PLUPERFECT

j'	**avais suffi**
tu	**avais suffi**
il/elle/on	**avait suffi**
nous	**avions suffi**
vous	**aviez suffi**
ils/elles	**avaient suffi**

IMPERATIVE

suffis / suffisons / suffisez

EXAMPLE PHRASES

Ça **suffit**!
That's enough!

Ses jouets lui **suffisent**.
His toys are enough for him.

Une séance avec l'ostéopathe **a suffi**
  pour me soulager.
One session with the osteopath was
  enough to ease the pain.

Il **suffisait** de me le demander.
You only had to ask.

Ça te **suffira**, dix euros?
Will ten euros be enough?

Sa promesse lui **suffit**: il lui faisait
  confiance.
Her promise was enough for him –
  he trusted her.

Il **suffirait** de se dépêcher un peu pour
  le rattraper.
We'd only have to hurry a little to catch
  up with him.

Il nous **avait suffi** d'aller à la
  bibliothèque municipale pour trouver
  le livre.
We only had to go to the community
  library to find the book.

---

je/j' = I   **tu** = you   **il** = he/it   **elle** = she/it   **on** = we/one   **nous** = we   **vous** = you   **ils/elles** = they

suivre (to follow)

PRESENT
je	**suis**
tu	**suis**
il/elle/on	**suit**
nous	**suivons**
vous	**suivez**
ils/elles	**suivent**

PRESENT SUBJUNCTIVE
je	**suive**
tu	**suives**
il/elle/on	**suive**
nous	**suivions**
vous	**suiviez**
ils/elles	**suivent**

PERFECT
j'	**ai suivi**
tu	**as suivi**
il/elle/on	**a suivi**
nous	**avons suivi**
vous	**avez suivi**
ils/elles	**ont suivi**

IMPERFECT
je	**suivais**
tu	**suivais**
il/elle/on	**suivait**
nous	**suivions**
vous	**suiviez**
ils/elles	**suivaient**

PRESENT PARTICIPLE
suivant

PAST PARTICIPLE
suivi

FUTURE
je	**suivrai**
tu	**suivras**
il/elle/on	**suivra**
nous	**suivrons**
vous	**suivrez**
ils/elles	**suivront**

CONDITIONAL
je	**suivrais**
tu	**suivrais**
il/elle/on	**suivrait**
nous	**suivrions**
vous	**suivriez**
ils/elles	**suivraient**

PAST HISTORIC
je	**suivis**
tu	**suivis**
il/elle/on	**suivit**
nous	**suivîmes**
vous	**suivîtes**
ils/elles	**suivirent**

PLUPERFECT
j'	**avais suivi**
tu	**avais suivi**
il/elle/on	**avait suivi**
nous	**avions suivi**
vous	**aviez suivi**
ils/elles	**avaient suivi**

IMPERATIVE
suis / suivons / suivez

EXAMPLE PHRASES

Elle n'arrive pas à **suivre** en maths.
She can't keep up in maths.

Mon chat me **suit** partout dans la maison.
My cat follows me all around the house.

Il **a suivi** un cours d'allemand pendant six mois.
He did a German course for six months.

Je n'aime pas qu'il me **suive** partout comme un petit chien.
I don't like him following me everywhere like a dog.

Ils nous **suivaient** à vélo.
They were cycling behind us.

Je vous **suivrai** de loin.
I'll follow you at a distance.

Elle le **suivit** dans son bureau.
She followed him into his office.

Il lui dit qu'il la **suivrait** en voiture.
He told her that he would follow her in his car.

Je n'**avais** pas bien **suivi** les derniers événements.
I hadn't really been following the latest events.

Suivez-moi.
Follow me.

je/j' = I **tu** = you **il** = he/it **elle** = she/it **on** = we/one **nous** = we **vous** = you **ils/elles** = they

se taire (to stop talking)

PRESENT

je	**me tais**
tu	**te tais**
il/elle/on	**se tait**
nous	**nous taisons**
vous	**vous taisez**
ils/elles	**se taisent**

PRESENT SUBJUNCTIVE

je	**me taise**
tu	**te taises**
il/elle/on	**se taise**
nous	**nous taisions**
vous	**vous taisiez**
ils/elles	**se taisent**

PERFECT

je	**me suis tu(e)**
tu	**t'es tu(e)**
il/elle/on	**s'est tu(e)**
nous	**nous sommes tu(e)s**
vous	**vous êtes tu(e)(s)**
ils/elles	**se sont tu(e)s**

IMPERFECT

je	**me taisais**
tu	**te taisais**
il/elle/on	**se taisait**
nous	**nous taisions**
vous	**vous taisiez**
ils/elles	**se taisaient**

PRESENT PARTICIPLE
se taisant

PAST PARTICIPLE
tu

FUTURE

je	**me tairai**
tu	**te tairas**
il/elle/on	**se taira**
nous	**nous tairons**
vous	**vous tairez**
ils/elles	**se tairont**

CONDITIONAL

je	**me tairais**
tu	**te tairais**
il/elle/on	**se tairait**
nous	**nous tairions**
vous	**vous tairiez**
ils/elles	**se tairaient**

PAST HISTORIC

je	**me tus**
tu	**te tus**
il/elle/on	**se tut**
nous	**nous tûmes**
vous	**vous tûtes**
ils/elles	**se turent**

PLUPERFECT

je	**m'étais tu(e)**
tu	**t'étais tu(e)**
il/elle/on	**s'était tu(e)**
nous	**nous étions tu(e)s**
vous	**vous étiez tu(e)(s)**
ils/elles	**s'étaient tu(e)s**

IMPERATIVE
tais-toi / taisons-nous / taisez-vous

EXAMPLE PHRASES

Je préfère **me taire** quand ils se disputent.
I prefer to keep quiet when they argue.

Il **s'est tu**.
He stopped talking.

Sophie, **tais-toi**!
Be quiet, Sophie!

Taisez-vous!
Be quiet!

Je **me tairai** si tu me laisses finir ma phrase.
I'll stop talking if you let me finish my sentence.

Elle **se tut**.
She stopped talking.

Je me **tairais** si j'étais sûr que tu n'allais pas inventer un mensonge.
I'd stop talking if I were sure that you wouldn't invent some lie.

Il **s'était tu** et tout resta silencieux pendant quelques minutes.
He had stopped talking and for a few minutes all was silent.

je/j' = I **tu** = you **il** = he/it **elle** = she/it **on** = we/one **nous** = we **vous** = you **ils/elles** = they

tenir (to hold)

PRESENT

je	**tiens**
tu	**tiens**
il/elle/on	**tient**
nous	**tenons**
vous	**tenez**
ils/elles	**tiennent**

PERFECT

j'	**ai tenu**
tu	**as tenu**
il/elle/on	**a tenu**
nous	**avons tenu**
vous	**avez tenu**
ils/elles	**ont tenu**

PRESENT PARTICIPLE
tenant

FUTURE

je	**tiendrai**
tu	**tiendras**
il/elle/on	**tiendra**
nous	**tiendrons**
vous	**tiendrez**
ils/elles	**tiendront**

PAST HISTORIC

je	**tins**
tu	**tins**
il/elle/on	**tint**
nous	**tînmes**
vous	**tîntes**
ils/elles	**tinrent**

IMPERATIVE
tiens / tenons / tenez

PRESENT SUBJUNCTIVE

je	**tienne**
tu	**tiennes**
il/elle/on	**tienne**
nous	**tenions**
vous	**teniez**
ils/elles	**tiennent**

IMPERFECT

je	**tenais**
tu	**tenais**
il/elle/on	**tenait**
nous	**tenions**
vous	**teniez**
ils/elles	**tenaient**

PAST PARTICIPLE
tenu

CONDITIONAL

je	**tiendrais**
tu	**tiendrais**
il/elle/on	**tiendrait**
nous	**tiendrions**
vous	**tiendriez**
ils/elles	**tiendraient**

PLUPERFECT

j'	**avais tenu**
tu	**avais tenu**
il/elle/on	**avait tenu**
nous	**avions tenu**
vous	**aviez tenu**
ils/elles	**avaient tenu**

EXAMPLE PHRASES

Il **tient** de son père.
He takes after his father.

Tiens-moi la main.
Hold my hand.

Tiens, prends mon stylo.
Here, have my pen.

Tiens-toi droit!
Sit up straight!

Elle **tenait** beaucoup à son chat.
She was really attached to her cat.

Vous ne pourrez pas tomber car je vous
tiendrai le bras.
There's no chance of you falling as I'll be
holding your arm.

Il **tint** sa promesse.
He kept his promise.

Il ne me **tiendrait** pas la main s'il voyait
un de ses copains.
He wouldn't hold my hand if he saw one
of his friends.

Elle **avait tenu** à y aller.
She insisted on going.

je/j' = I   **tu** = you   **il** = he/it   **elle** = she/it   **on** = we/one   **nous** = we   **vous** = you   **ils/elles** = they

tomber (to fall)

PRESENT

je	**tombe**
tu	**tombes**
il/elle/on	**tombe**
nous	**tombons**
vous	**tombez**
ils/elles	**tombent**

PERFECT

je	**suis tombé(e)**
tu	**es tombé(e)**
il/elle/on	**est tombé(e)**
nous	**sommes tombé(e)s**
vous	**êtes tombé(e)(s)**
ils/elles	**sont tombé(e)s**

PRESENT PARTICIPLE
tombant

FUTURE

je	**tomberai**
tu	**tomberas**
il/elle/on	**tombera**
nous	**tomberons**
vous	**tomberez**
ils/elles	**tomberont**

PAST HISTORIC

je	**tombai**
tu	**tombas**
il/elle/on	**tomba**
nous	**tombâmes**
vous	**tombâtes**
ils/elles	**tombèrent**

IMPERATIVE
tombe / tombons / tombez

PRESENT SUBJUNCTIVE

je	**tombe**
tu	**tombes**
il/elle/on	**tombe**
nous	**tombions**
vous	**tombiez**
ils/elles	**tombent**

IMPERFECT

je	**tombais**
tu	**tombais**
il/elle/on	**tombait**
nous	**tombions**
vous	**tombiez**
ils/elles	**tombaient**

PAST PARTICIPLE
tombé

CONDITIONAL

je	**tomberais**
tu	**tomberais**
il/elle/on	**tomberait**
nous	**tomberions**
vous	**tomberiez**
ils/elles	**tomberaient**

PLUPERFECT

j'	**étais tombé(e)**
tu	**étais tombé(e)**
il/elle/on	**était tombé(e)**
nous	**étions tombé(e)s**
vous	**étiez tombé(e)(s)**
ils/elles	**étaient tombé(e)s**

EXAMPLE PHRASES

Attention, tu vas **tomber**!
Be careful, you'll fall!

Ça **tombe** bien.
That's lucky.

Nicole **est tombée** de son cheval.
Nicole fell off her horse.

Il **tombait** de sommeil.
He was asleep on his feet.

Elle s'est fait mal en **tombant** dans l'escalier.
She hurt herself falling down the stairs.

J'espère qu'il ne **tombera** pas de son cheval.
I hope he won't fall off his horse.

La tasse **tomba** par terre et se cassa.
The cup fell on the floor and broke.

Tu ne **tomberais** pas si souvent si tu regardais où tu marches.
You wouldn't fall so often if you watched where you were going.

Il **était** mal **tombé** et s'était cassé le bras.
He'd fallen awkwardly and had broken his arm.

je/j' = I **tu** = you **il** = he/it **elle** = she/it **on** = we/one **nous** = we **vous** = you **ils/elles** = they

traire (to milk)

PRESENT

je	**trais**
tu	**trais**
il/elle/on	**trait**
nous	**trayons**
vous	**trayez**
ils/elles	**traient**

PRESENT SUBJUNCTIVE

je	**traie**
tu	**traies**
il/elle/on	**traie**
nous	**trayions**
vous	**trayiez**
ils/elles	**traient**

PERFECT

j'	**ai trait**
tu	**as trait**
il/elle/on	**a trait**
nous	**avons trait**
vous	**avez trait**
ils/elles	**ont trait**

IMPERFECT

je	**trayais**
tu	**trayais**
il/elle/on	**trayait**
nous	**trayions**
vous	**trayiez**
ils/elles	**trayaient**

PRESENT PARTICIPLE
trayant

PAST PARTICIPLE
trait

FUTURE

je	**trairai**
tu	**trairas**
il/elle/on	**traira**
nous	**trairons**
vous	**trairez**
ils/elles	**trairont**

CONDITIONAL

je	**trairais**
tu	**trairais**
il/elle/on	**trairait**
nous	**trairions**
vous	**trairiez**
ils/elles	**trairaient**

PAST HISTORIC
not used

PLUPERFECT

j'	**avais trait**
tu	**avais trait**
il/elle/on	**avait trait**
nous	**avions trait**
vous	**aviez trait**
ils/elles	**avaient trait**

IMPERATIVE
trais / trayons / trayez

EXAMPLE PHRASES·

À la ferme, on a appris à **traire** les vaches.
We learnt to milk cows on the farm.

Elle **trait** les vaches à six heures du matin.
She milks the cows at six am.

Nous **avons trait** les vaches.
We milked the cows.

Il faut qu'elle **traie** les vaches de bonne heure tous les matins.
She has to milk the cows early every morning.

On **trayait** les vaches avant d'aller à l'école.
We milked the cows before going to school.

Je **trairai** les vaches pour toi quand tu seras parti.
I'll milk the cows for you when you're away.

Je **trairais** les brebis si je savais comment faire.
I'd milk the ewes if I knew what to do.

Cela faisait longtemps qu'elle n'**avait** pas **trait** une vache.
She hadn't milked a cow for a long time.

je/j' = I **tu** = you **il** = he/it **elle** = she/it **on** = we/one **nous** = we **vous** = you **ils/elles** = they

vaincre (to defeat)

PRESENT

je	**vaincs**
tu	**vaincs**
il/elle/on	**vainc**
nous	**vainquons**
vous	**vainquez**
ils/elles	**vainquent**

PRESENT SUBJUNCTIVE

je	**vainque**
tu	**vainques**
il/elle/on	**vainque**
nous	**vainquions**
vous	**vainquiez**
ils/elles	**vainquent**

PERFECT

j'	**ai vaincu**
tu	**as vaincu**
il/elle/on	**a vaincu**
nous	**avons vaincu**
vous	**avez vaincu**
ils/elles	**ont vaincu**

IMPERFECT

je	**vainquais**
tu	**vainquais**
il/elle/on	**vainquait**
nous	**vainquions**
vous	**vainquiez**
ils/elles	**vainquaient**

PRESENT PARTICIPLE
vainquant

PAST PARTICIPLE
vaincu

FUTURE

je	**vaincrai**
tu	**vaincras**
il/elle/on	**vaincra**
nous	**vaincrons**
vous	**vaincrez**
ils/elles	**vaincront**

CONDITIONAL

je	**vaincrais**
tu	**vaincrais**
il/elle/on	**vaincrait**
nous	**vaincrions**
vous	**vaincriez**
ils/elles	**vaincraient**

PAST HISTORIC

je	**vainquis**
tu	**vainquis**
il/elle/on	**vainquit**
nous	**vainquîmes**
vous	**vainquîtes**
ils/elles	**vainquirent**

PLUPERFECT

j'	**avais vaincu**
tu	**avais vaincu**
il/elle/on	**avait vaincu**
nous	**avions vaincu**
vous	**aviez vaincu**
ils/elles	**avaient vaincu**

IMPERATIVE
vaincs / vainquons / vainquez

EXAMPLE PHRASES

Il a réussi à **vaincre** sa timidité.
He managed to overcome his shyness.

L'armée **a été vaincue**.
The army was defeated.

La France **a vaincu** la Corée trois buts
à deux.
France beat Korea three goals to two.

Tu ne **vaincras** pas ta peur en restant
dans ta chambre.
You won't overcome your fear if you
stay in your bedroom.

Ils **vainquirent** l'armée ennemie après
une bataille acharnée.
They defeated the enemy army after
a fierce battle.

Elle **avait** déjà **vaincu** cette adversaire.
She'd already beaten this opponent.

je/j' = I   **tu** = you   **il** = he/it   **elle** = she/it   **on** = we/one   **nous** = we   **vous** = you   **ils/elles** = they

valoir (to be worth)

PRESENT

je	**vaux**
tu	**vaux**
il/elle/on	**vaut**
nous	**valons**
vous	**valez**
ils/elles	**valent**

PRESENT SUBJUNCTIVE

je	**vaille**
tu	**vailles**
il/elle/on	**vaille**
nous	**valions**
vous	**valiez**
ils/elles	**vaillent**

PERFECT

j'	**ai valu**
tu	**as valu**
il/elle/on	**a valu**
nous	**avons valu**
vous	**avez valu**
ils/elles	**ont valu**

IMPERFECT

je	**valais**
tu	**valais**
il/elle/on	**valait**
nous	**valions**
vous	**valiez**
ils/elles	**valaient**

PRESENT PARTICIPLE
valant

PAST PARTICIPLE
valu

FUTURE

je	**vaudrai**
tu	**vaudras**
il/elle/on	**vaudra**
nous	**vaudrons**
vous	**vaudrez**
ils/elles	**vaudront**

CONDITIONAL

je	**vaudrais**
tu	**vaudrais**
il/elle/on	**vaudrait**
nous	**vaudrions**
vous	**vaudriez**
ils/elles	**vaudraient**

PAST HISTORIC

je	**valus**
tu	**valus**
il/elle/on	**valut**
nous	**valûmes**
vous	**valûtes**
ils/elles	**valurent**

PLUPERFECT

j'	**avais valu**
tu	**avais valu**
il/elle/on	**avait valu**
nous	**avions valu**
vous	**aviez valu**
ils/elles	**avaient valu**

IMPERATIVE
vaux / valons / valez

EXAMPLE PHRASES

Ça **vaut** combien?
How much is it worth?

Ça ne **vaut** pas la peine de s'inquiéter.
It's not worth worrying about.

Cette voiture **vaut** très cher.
That car's worth a lot of money.

Il **valait** mieux ne pas y penser.
It was best not to think about it.

Ça **vaudra** sûrement la peine d'y aller.
It will probably be worth going.

Ça **vaudrait** la peine d'essayer.
It would be worth a try.

Il **vaudrait** mieux que tu demandes la permission.
You'd be best to ask for permission.

Son insolence lui **avait valu** une punition.
His cheek had earned him a punishment.

---

je/j' = I   **tu** = you   **il** = he/it   **elle** = she/it   **on** = we/one   **nous** = we   **vous** = you   **ils/elles** = they

vendre (to sell)

PRESENT

je	**vends**
tu	**vends**
il/elle/on	**vend**
nous	**vendons**
vous	**vendez**
ils/elles	**vendent**

PRESENT SUBJUNCTIVE

je	**vende**
tu	**vendes**
il/elle/on	**vende**
nous	**vendions**
vous	**vendiez**
ils/elles	**vendent**

PERFECT

j'	**ai vendu**
tu	**as vendu**
il/elle/on	**a vendu**
nous	**avons vendu**
vous	**avez vendu**
ils/elles	**ont vendu**

IMPERFECT

je	**vendais**
tu	**vendais**
il/elle/on	**vendait**
nous	**vendions**
vous	**vendiez**
ils/elles	**vendaient**

PRESENT PARTICIPLE

vendant

PAST PARTICIPLE

vendu

FUTURE

je	**vendrai**
tu	**vendras**
il/elle/on	**vendra**
nous	**vendrons**
vous	**vendrez**
ils/elles	**vendront**

CONDITIONAL

je	**vendrais**
tu	**vendrais**
il/elle/on	**vendrait**
nous	**vendrions**
vous	**vendriez**
ils/elles	**vendraient**

PAST HISTORIC

je	**vendis**
tu	**vendis**
il/elle/on	**vendit**
nous	**vendîmes**
vous	**vendîtes**
ils/elles	**vendirent**

PLUPERFECT

j'	**avais vendu**
tu	**avais vendu**
il/elle/on	**avait vendu**
nous	**avions vendu**
vous	**aviez vendu**
ils/elles	**avaient vendu**

IMPERATIVE

vends / vendons / vendez

EXAMPLE PHRASES

Elle voudrait **vendre** sa voiture.
She would like to sell her car.

Est-ce que vous **vendez** des piles?
Do you sell batteries?

Il m'**a vendu** son vélo pour cinquante euros.
He sold me his bike for fifty euros.

Il **vendait** des glaces sur la plage.
He sold ice creams on the beach.

Tu ne **vendras** rien à ce prix-là.
You'll never sell anything at that price.

Elle **vendit** son appartement et partit vivre en Provence.
She sold her flat and went to live in Provence.

Je ne **vendrais** pas ce piano pour tout l'or du monde.
I wouldn't sell this piano for all the gold in the world.

Il **avait** déjà **vendu** sa maison.
He'd already sold his house.

je/j' = I **tu** = you **il** = he/it **elle** = she/it **on** = we/one **nous** = we **vous** = you **ils/elles** = they

venir (to come)

PRESENT
je	**viens**
tu	**viens**
il/elle/on	**vient**
nous	**venons**
vous	**venez**
ils/elles	**viennent**

PRESENT SUBJUNCTIVE
je	**vienne**
tu	**viennes**
il/elle/on	**vienne**
nous	**venions**
vous	**veniez**
ils/elles	**viennent**

PERFECT
je	**suis venu(e)**
tu	**es venu(e)**
il/elle/on	**est venu(e)**
nous	**sommes venu(e)s**
vous	**êtes venu(e)(s)**
ils/elles	**sont venu(e)s**

IMPERFECT
je	**venais**
tu	**venais**
il/elle/on	**venait**
nous	**venions**
vous	**veniez**
ils/elles	**venaient**

PRESENT PARTICIPLE
venant

PAST PARTICIPLE
venu

FUTURE
je	**viendrai**
tu	**viendras**
il/elle/on	**viendra**
nous	**viendrons**
vous	**viendrez**
ils/elles	**viendront**

CONDITIONAL
je	**viendrais**
tu	**viendrais**
il/elle/on	**viendrait**
nous	**viendrions**
vous	**viendriez**
ils/elles	**viendraient**

PAST HISTORIC
je	**vins**
tu	**vins**
il/elle/on	**vint**
nous	**vînmes**
vous	**vîntes**
ils/elles	**vinrent**

PLUPERFECT
j'	**étais venu(e)**
tu	**étais venu(e)**
il/elle/on	**était venu(e)**
nous	**étions venu(e)s**
vous	**étiez venu(e)(s)**
ils/elles	**étaient venu(e)s**

IMPERATIVE
viens / venons / venez

EXAMPLE PHRASES

Fatou et Malik **viennent** du Sénégal.
Fatou and Malik come from Senegal.

Ils **sont venus** la voir ce matin.
They came to see her this morning.

Elle aimerait que tu **viennes** à son mariage.
She'd like you to come to her wedding.

Je **venais** de finir mes devoirs quand ils sont arrivés.
I'd just finished my homework when they arrived.

Elle ne **viendra** pas cette année.
She won't be coming this year.

Il **vint** nous voir après la messe.
He came to see us after mass.

Elle **viendrait** avec nous si elle n'avait pas tant de travail.
She'd come with us if she didn't have so much work.

Ils **étaient venus** nous annoncer leurs fiançailles.
They had come to tell us that they had got engaged.

Viens avec moi!
Come with me!

je/j' = I **tu** = you **il** = he/it **elle** = she/it **on** = we/one **nous** = we **vous** = you **ils/elles** = they

vêtir (to dress)

PRESENT

je	**vêts**
tu	**vêts**
il/elle/on	**vêt**
nous	**vêtons**
vous	**vêtez**
ils/elles	**vêtent**

PRESENT SUBJUNCTIVE

je	**vête**
tu	**vêtes**
il/elle/on	**vête**
nous	**vêtions**
vous	**vêtiez**
ils/elles	**vêtent**

PERFECT

j'	**ai vêtu**
tu	**as vêtu**
il/elle/on	**a vêtu**
nous	**avons vêtu**
vous	**avez vêtu**
ils/elles	**ont vêtu**

IMPERFECT

je	**vêtais**
tu	**vêtais**
il/elle/on	**vêtait**
nous	**vêtions**
vous	**vêtiez**
ils/elles	**vêtaient**

PRESENT PARTICIPLE
vêtant

PAST PARTICIPLE
vêtu

FUTURE

je	**vêtirai**
tu	**vêtiras**
il/elle/on	**vêtira**
nous	**vêtirons**
vous	**vêtirez**
ils/elles	**vêtiront**

CONDITIONAL

je	**vêtirais**
tu	**vêtirais**
il/elle/on	**vêtirait**
nous	**vêtirions**
vous	**vêtiriez**
ils/elles	**vêtiraient**

PAST HISTORIC

je	**vêtis**
tu	**vêtis**
il/elle/on	**vêtit**
nous	**vêtîmes**
vous	**vêtîtes**
ils/elles	**vêtirent**

PLUPERFECT

j'	**avais vêtu**
tu	**avais vêtu**
il/elle/on	**avait vêtu**
nous	**avions vêtu**
vous	**aviez vêtu**
ils/elles	**avaient vêtu**

IMPERATIVE
vêts / vêtons / vêtez

EXAMPLE PHRASES

Il faut se lever, se laver et se **vêtir** en dix minutes.
You have to get up, get washed and get dressed in ten minutes.

Vous n'**êtes** pas **vêtus** suffisamment chaudement pour aller jouer dehors.
You're not dressed warmly enough to go and play outside.

Tu **es** bizarrement **vêtu** aujourd'hui!
You are strangely dressed today!

Nous vîmes une mariée tout de blanc **vêtue**.
We saw a bride dressed all in white.

Il **était vêtu** d'un pantalon et d'un pull.
He was wearing trousers and a jumper.

Nous **étions** chaudement **vêtus**.
We were warmly dressed.

Il **était** toujours bien **vêtu**.
He was always well dressed.

Ils n'**étaient** pas **vêtus** de façon adéquate pour aller marcher dans les montagnes.
They weren't properly dressed to go hill-walking.

je/j' = I **tu** = you **il** = he/it **elle** = she/it **on** = we/one **nous** = we **vous** = you **ils/elles** = they

vivre (to live)

PRESENT	
je	**vis**
tu	**vis**
il/elle/on	**vit**
nous	**vivons**
vous	**vivez**
ils/elles	**vivent**

PRESENT SUBJUNCTIVE	
je	**vive**
tu	**vives**
il/elle/on	**vive**
nous	**vivions**
vous	**viviez**
ils/elles	**vivent**

PERFECT	
j'	**ai vécu**
tu	**as vécu**
il/elle/on	**a vécu**
nous	**avons vécu**
vous	**avez vécu**
ils/elles	**ont vécu**

IMPERFECT	
je	**vivais**
tu	**vivais**
il/elle/on	**vivait**
nous	**vivions**
vous	**viviez**
ils/elles	**vivaient**

PRESENT PARTICIPLE
vivant

PAST PARTICIPLE
vécu

FUTURE	
je	**vivrai**
tu	**vivras**
il/elle/on	**vivra**
nous	**vivrons**
vous	**vivrez**
ils/elles	**vivront**

CONDITIONAL	
je	**vivrais**
tu	**vivrais**
il/elle/on	**vivrait**
nous	**vivrions**
vous	**vivriez**
ils/elles	**vivraient**

PAST HISTORIC	
je	**vécus**
tu	**vécus**
il/elle/on	**vécut**
nous	**vécûmes**
vous	**vécûtes**
ils/elles	**vécurent**

PLUPERFECT	
j'	**avais vécu**
tu	**avais vécu**
il/elle/on	**avait vécu**
nous	**avions vécu**
vous	**aviez vécu**
ils/elles	**avaient vécu**

IMPERATIVE
vis / vivons / vivez

EXAMPLE PHRASES

Et ton grand-père? Il **vit** encore?
What about your grandfather? Is he still alive?

Les gorilles **vivent** surtout dans la forêt.
Gorillas mostly live in the forest.

Il **a vécu** dix ans à Lyon.
He lived in Lyons for ten years.

Cela ne faisait pas longtemps qu'ils **vivaient** ensemble.
They hadn't lived together for long.

Vivras-tu avec ta sœur quand tu feras tes études à Paris?
Will you live with your sister when you're studying in Paris?

Elle **vécut** d'abord en Espagne, puis en Italie.
She lived in Spain first and then in Italy.

S'ils n'avaient pas d'enfants, ils ne **vivraient** plus ensemble depuis longtemps.
If they didn't have children they would have stopped living together long ago.

Ils n'**avaient** jamais **vécu** à la campagne.
They'd never lived in the countryside.

je/j' = I   **tu** = you   **il** = he/it   **elle** = she/it   **on** = we/one   **nous** = we   **vous** = you   **ils/elles** = they

voir (to see)

PRESENT
je	**vois**
tu	**vois**
il/elle/on	**voit**
nous	**voyons**
vous	**voyez**
ils/elles	**voient**

PRESENT SUBJUNCTIVE
je	**voie**
tu	**voies**
il/elle/on	**voie**
nous	**voyions**
vous	**voyiez**
ils/elles	**voient**

PERFECT
j'	**ai vu**
tu	**as vu**
il/elle/on	**a vu**
nous	**avons vu**
vous	**avez vu**
ils/elles	**ont vu**

IMPERFECT
je	**voyais**
tu	**voyais**
il/elle/on	**voyait**
nous	**voyions**
vous	**voyiez**
ils/elles	**voyaient**

PRESENT PARTICIPLE
voyant

PAST PARTICIPLE
vu

FUTURE
je	**verrai**
tu	**verras**
il/elle/on	**verra**
nous	**verrons**
vous	**verrez**
ils/elles	**verront**

CONDITIONAL
je	**verrais**
tu	**verrais**
il/elle/on	**verrait**
nous	**verrions**
vous	**verriez**
ils/elles	**verraient**

PAST HISTORIC
je	**vis**
tu	**vis**
il/elle/on	**vit**
nous	**vîmes**
vous	**vîtes**
ils/elles	**virent**

PLUPERFECT
j'	**avais vu**
tu	**avais vu**
il/elle/on	**avait vu**
nous	**avions vu**
vous	**aviez vu**
ils/elles	**avaient vu**

IMPERATIVE
vois / voyons / voyez

EXAMPLE PHRASES

Venez me **voir** quand vous serez à Paris.
Come and see me when you're in Paris.

Est-ce que cette tache se **voit**?
Does that stain show?

Est-ce que tu l'**as vu**?
Have you seen him?

Il ne **voyait** rien sans ses lunettes.
He couldn't see anything without his glasses.

Tu **verras** que je ne t'ai pas menti.
You'll see that I didn't lie to you.

Il la **vit** arriver de loin.
He saw her arrive from a long way off.

Il savait qu'il ne la **verrait** pas avant le lendemain.
He knew that he wouldn't see her until the next day.

Ils ne l'**avaient** pas **vue** depuis son accident.
They hadn't seen her since her accident.

je/j' = I **tu** = you **il** = he/it **elle** = she/it **on** = we/one **nous** = we **vous** = you **ils/elles** = they

vouloir (to want)

PRESENT

je	**veux**
tu	**veux**
il/elle/on	**veut**
nous	**voulons**
vous	**voulez**
ils/elles	**veulent**

PRESENT SUBJUNCTIVE

je	**veuille**
tu	**veuilles**
il/elle/on	**veuille**
nous	**voulions**
vous	**vouliez**
ils/elles	**veuillent**

PERFECT

j'	**ai voulu**
tu	**as voulu**
il/elle/on	**a voulu**
nous	**avons voulu**
vous	**avez voulu**
ils/elles	**ont voulu**

IMPERFECT

je	**voulais**
tu	**voulais**
il/elle/on	**voulait**
nous	**voulions**
vous	**vouliez**
ils/elles	**voulaient**

PRESENT PARTICIPLE
voulant

PAST PARTICIPLE
voulu

FUTURE

je	**voudrai**
tu	**voudras**
il/elle/on	**voudra**
nous	**voudrons**
vous	**voudrez**
ils/elles	**voudront**

CONDITIONAL

je	**voudrais**
tu	**voudrais**
il/elle/on	**voudrait**
nous	**voudrions**
vous	**voudriez**
ils/elles	**voudraient**

PAST HISTORIC

je	**voulus**
tu	**voulus**
il/elle/on	**voulut**
nous	**voulûmes**
vous	**voulûtes**
ils/elles	**voulurent**

PLUPERFECT

j'	**avais voulu**
tu	**avais voulu**
il/elle/on	**avait voulu**
nous	**avions voulu**
vous	**aviez voulu**
ils/elles	**avaient voulu**

IMPERATIVE
veuille / veuillons / veuillez

EXAMPLE PHRASES

Elle **veut** un vélo pour Noël.
She wants a bike for Christmas.

Veux-tu que je t'aide?
Do you want me to help you?

Il n'**a** pas **voulu** te déranger.
He didn't want to disturb you.

Ils **voulaient** aller au cinéma.
They wanted to go to the cinema.

Ils ne **voudront** pas partir trop tard.
They won't want to leave too late.

Elle ne **voulut** pas les inquiéter.
She didn't want to worry them.

Tu **voudrais** une tasse de thé?
Would you like a cup of tea?

Il n'**avait** pas **voulu** partir sans lui dire
  au revoir.
He hadn't wanted to leave without
  saying goodbye to her.

je/j' = I **tu** = you **il** = he/it **elle** = she/it **on** = we/one **nous** = we **vous** = you **ils/elles** = they

se vouvoyer (to address each other as "vous")

PRESENT

on	**se vouvoie**
nous	**nous vouvoyons**
vous	**vous vouvoyez**
ils/elles	**se vouvoient**

PRESENT SUBJUNCTIVE

on	**se vouvoie**
nous	**nous vouvoyions**
vous	**vous vouvoyiez**
ils/elles	**se vouvoient**

PERFECT

on	**s'est vouvoyé**
nous	**nous sommes vouvoyé(e)s**
vous	**vous êtes vouvoyé(e)s**
ils/elles	**se sont vouvoyé(e)s**

IMPERFECT

on	**se vouvoyait**
nous	**nous vouvoyions**
vous	**vous vouvoyiez**
ils/elles	**se vouvoyaient**

PRESENT PARTICIPLE
se vouvoyant

PAST PARTICIPLE
vouvoyé

FUTURE

on	**se vouvoiera**
nous	**nous vouvoierons**
vous	**vous vouvoierez**
ils/elles	**se vouvoieront**

CONDITIONAL

on	**se vouvoierait**
nous	**nous vouvoierions**
vous	**vous vouvoieriez**
ils/elles	**se vouvoieraient**

PAST HISTORIC

on	**se vouvoya**
nous	**nous vouvoyâmes**
vous	**vous vouvoyâtes**
ils/elles	**se vouvoyèrent**

PLUPERFECT

on	**s'était vouvoyé**
nous	**nous étions vouvoyé(e)s**
vous	**vous étiez vouvoyé(e)s**
ils/elles	**s'étaient vouvoyé(e)s**

IMPERATIVE
not used

EXAMPLE PHRASES

Avec Hélène, on **se vouvoie** encore.
Hélène and I are still addressing each other as "vous".

Vous **vous êtes** toujours **vouvoyés** avec Michel?
Have you and Michel always addressed each other as "vous"?

Je préférerais qu'on **se vouvoie**.
I'd rather we addressed each other as "vous".

Ils ne **se vouvoyaient** plus.
They weren't addressing each other as "vous" any more.

Je te parie qu'ils **se vouvoieront**.
I bet they'll address each other as "vous".

Ils **se vouvoyèrent** les premiers jours.
They addressed each other as "vous" for the first few days.

On **se vouvoierait** encore si je n'avais rien dit.
We'd still be addressing each other as "vous" if I hadn't said anything.

Nous **nous étions vouvoyés** au début.
We'd addressed each other as "vous" at the beginning.

je/j' = I **tu** = you **il** = he/it **elle** = she/it **on** = we/one **nous** = we **vous** = you **ils/elles** = they

verb index

How to use the Verb Index

The verbs in bold are the model verbs which you will find in the Verb Tables. All the other verbs follow one of these patterns, so the number next to each verb indicates which pattern fits this particular verb. For example, **aider** (to help) follows the same pattern as **donner** (number 70 in the Verb Tables). All the verbs are in alphabetical order. For reflexive verbs like **s'asseoir** (to sit down) or **se taire** (to stop talking), look under **asseoir** or **taire**, not under **s'** or **se**.

Superior numbers ([1], [2] etc) refer you to notes on page 230. These notes explain any differences between the verbs and their model.

With the exception of reflexive verbs which always take **être**, all verbs have the same auxiliary (**être** or **avoir**) as their model verb. There are a few exceptions which are indicated by a superior number [1] or [2]. An asterisk (*) means that the verb takes **avoir** when it is used with a direct object, and **être** when it isn't. For more information on verbs that take either **avoir** or **être**, see pages 88–89.